Lilacs by the Kitchen Door

Prairie life on the family farm.

Sheri Hathaway

Lilacs by the Kitchen Door

Copyright © Sheri Hathaway

All rights reserved in all media. No part of this book may be used, reproduced, stored in a retrieval system or transmitted in any form or by any means without prior written permission of the publisher, except in the case of brief quotations used in critical articles and reviews.

This book is based on the lives of the dear people who once lived in Marwayne, Alberta, Canada. In some situations where no record exists and no living person has a memory of it, I have imagined how an event may take place. I have kept all events as close as possible to actual fact.

Cover design by Cindy Buckshon
Cover images from Adobe Stock Photography and Vecteezy
Family tree by Sheri Hathaway
Interior design by Cindy Buckshon

ISBN (e-book): 978-1-7388223-0-0
ISBN (softcover): 978-1-7388223-1-7
ISBN (hardcover): 978-1-7388223-2-4

For all people of the Prairie.
Stay strong. Love your land. Grow beauty.

Table of Contents

Table of Contents	4
Acknowledgements	7
Introduction	8
1. Harold's First Love	10
2. Louise	18
3. Tumbleweed on Barbed Wire	28
4. Reserved in War	38
5. Louise's War	46
6. On Holiday from War	52
7. Married Bliss	58
8. Walking the Clear Range Farm	64
9. Hailed Out and Knocked Down	72
10. Richard	78
11. A Big Change in Harvesting	86
12. Connecting Neighbours	90
13. Throwing Rocks t the House	98
14. Choosing to Laugh	102
15. Empowered by Electricity	108
16. Milton	112
17. Getting There	118
18. Finding Childcare in 1956	126

19. Aunt Mattie	132
20. Working with Neighbours	138
21. How We Spent Our Summer Holidays	142
22. Janet and Andy	148
23 Ten-year-old's Letter	154
24. Kids and Cows	156
25. It's A Farm Dog's Life	164
26. Gardens for food and more	168
27. A Farm Wife's Prayer	172
28. Our Rodeo in the Bush	174
29. This is Snow Fun	178
30. Our Sojourn for a Christmas Tree	182
31. A Most Successful Holiday	186
32. Apology	192
33. If You Can't Move	196
34. Tragedy	204
35. The Program	218
36. Life with Louise	222
Endnotes	242
Bibliography	244
About the Author	254

FAMILY TREE
of family members mentioned in this book

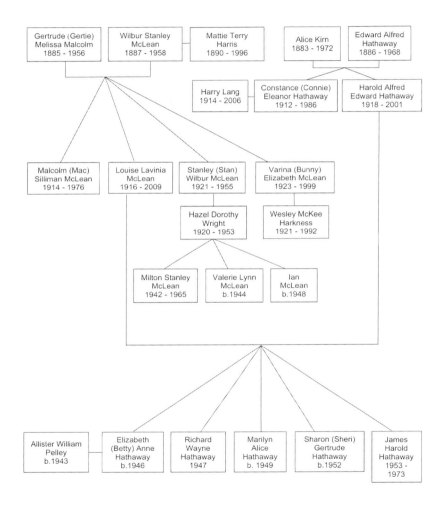

❁ Acknowledgements ❁

Details of these stories came from many sources: my mother's diaries, photo albums, her stories in four community history books, her own book of family history, as well as family letters she saved.

Memories were also shared by my sister, Marilyn Blomquist, my cousin, Ian McLean, and my son, Clayton Henderson. My sister, Betty Anne Pelley shared a copy of James' letter in Chapter 23.

Glen Lorenz granted permission to quote his story, "Bridging the Communication Gap" from *Echoes of Marwayne Area*, the first book of the series. Also, Bernard Weighill and Lewis Young granted permission to have their names published therein, being mentioned in this story.

I also have professionals to thank for their expert help in various ways:

- Ceilidh Auger-Day, History of Medicine, Department of History at the University of Saskatchewan, for her insights on the Eugenics Movement, the treatment for adult mental illness in the forties, occiput posterior birth, and hydrocephalus in infants
- Dr. Jared Prisciak for explaining cauda equina syndrome
- archivists, Gayla McMillan and Corine Price, Lloydminster Regional Archives, for research advice on this and other projects
- Michelle Harvey, County of Vermilion River #24, for searching County records, as well as examining the land titles for the Clear Range farm and confirming my conclusions on its final outcome
- Justin Cuffe, Curator of Transportation Collections, Reynolds-Alberta Museum who identified Wilbur McLean's car
- On behalf of the Saskatchewan Western Development Museum, Joan Champ granted permission to quote her comments on pre-electrical farm life
- Elizabeth McLachlan granted permission to quote excerpts from "Louise's Story" in her book, *With Unshakable Persistence*
- Also, many thanks to my writer friends, Janice Dick and Cindy Buckshon for their encouragement and advice

A heartfelt thank you to all.

❀ Introduction ❀

"Will you take my diaries?" The news that she would not return to her room in the seniors' residence after her hospital stay triggered no small anxiety for my mother. From here on in, she needed long-term care and my sister and I moved her things to her new room in the Dr. Cooke Extended Care Centre in Lloydminster, Alberta. From her hospital bed, she tried to direct the move.

"Yes," I said.

She nodded and laid back. Then a new thought brought her forward again.

"Will you read them?"

"Yes."

She leaned back and closed her eyes. "I always wondered why I bothered," she said. "I thought maybe no one would read them."

She'd said this at least once before in my childhood. "What are you writing at for so long?" I asked as she concentrated on a book at the dining room table.

"I'm getting caught up in my diary. I don't know why I bother. Chances are, no one will read it."

It may seem strange that she hoped someone might read her diaries, and I'll admit I struggle to explain it myself, but my mother struggled to manage an overactive imagination, meshed with a flock of fears and driven by strong ambition and competitive drive. She held back parts of herself while hoping someone saw the person she hoped to become. She kept us all on our toes.

In spite of individual personalities and some devastating tragedies, my parents' story navigates the same events that affected everyone in those days. A change occurred over the years that they didn't notice. The forties' way of thinking differs from our rationale today. Times have changed—we have changed. We can be thankful for some aspects of progress in our lives today, but in other ways, we regret the loss.

This book honors those intrepid souls who lived, loved and laughed through their days, oblivious of an alternative lifestyle crouching on the horizon—the days of cell phones, computers and internet. They lived in a tangible world, where one could see the lines that carried telephone conversations, remembered important dates by writing them on their paper calendar hanging on their kitchen wall, held a package of photographs in their hands ordered from the developers, and learned about current issues from periodicals made of paper.

In this drama, my parents fill the role as main characters, surrounded by a supporting cast of friends and family. They represent most rural prairie dwellers of North America, living their lives through the forties, fifties and sixties. Most chapters can stand alone. Think of it as a fruit basket. Pick the ones you like or settle in for a long buffet.

Some chapters originated in the Western Producer, but in this book, I'm able to expand on them and dig deeper into them. Others haven't seen the light of day. Each one covers its own topic.

The stories in this book took place on Treaty Six Territory, ancestral territory of the Cree and homeland of the Metis Nation.

1.
❀ Harold's First Love ❀

At five foot ten my father, Harold Hathaway, always walked with straight back and shoulders, perhaps from carrying pails of milk, perhaps to look as tall as possible. He never lost or gained a pound over his adult years. His dark hair wasn't thick, but he never went bald and he always kept it neat. A clean-shaven face dictated men's fashion in those days and Harold, along with every other man, shaved every day whether dressed in coveralls or a suit. His wife, Louise, claimed his sky-blue eyes changed to a lighter tint when he felt unwell.

Loyalty reigned supreme in his list of priorities. Once he selected a business, organization or philosophy, he remained fastened to it like a burr in the dog's tail. The Wheat Pool, the Co-op and church became his life service. Once, never darkening the door of a church except for a wedding, it became as habitual as shaving. Every Sunday morning he'd perform his ablutions, dress in a suit, put on his shoes, and lie on the couch to wait for Louise, hat in hand. If he arrived on time at the church doors, he exclaimed about being late. We often arrived in time to unlock the door since he owned a church key. Early arrival became so habitual that, after sixty years of waiting for Louise, one Sunday he left her at home and went to church alone. He wasn't late for church, but he never did that again.

His faithfulness to the Co-op remained just as religious. As president of the Marwayne Co-op board, he maneuvered the store into an amalgamation with the Lloydminster branch. He then served on the Lloydminster Co-op board for eighteen years. All shopping had to be done there. If the Co-op didn't have it, then it wasn't to be had. On trips to Lloydminster for errands, it was the only store we set foot in. My mother, Louise, felt guilty if she went to the mall where other chain stores resided. To shop outside the Co-op had you shot at dawn for treason.

In contrast to his father, he held great respect for authority figures. Once my father and I went together to the doctor since we both had ailments needing attention. I remember Dr. Hemstock leaning against a cupboard, his arms crossed, holding his chin in one hand, one foot crossed over the other while he pondered how to advise my father, having decided he had a stomach ulcer.

"Well," he said, "take a nap every day after lunch."

Harold looked at him, saying nothing while he processed this thunderbolt. Napping in mid-day seemed as foreign to him as buying groceries at Safeway.

Dr. Hemstock understood the look my father gave him. "You don't have to sleep, just lie down and rest for a few minutes, and if you lie on the floor, it'll be good for your back problems, too."

That evening, he sputtered the news to Louise at the supper table, but she encouraged him. So, uncertain and awkward, he began lying on the living room floor after lunch. At night, he liked a pillow over his eyes, so during his mid-day naps, he placed one of Louise's hand crocheted accent pillows, hard and unyielding, leaning against his forehead. Napping became his habit for the simple reason someone of authority told him to do it. We have photos of him napping in unusual places during travel or with a cat curled up on his chest on the living room floor. His ulcer never bothered him again.

Louise, the conscientious teacher, guided her students in the rules of proper grammar and spelling, but Harold, the joker, loved playing with words. He liked to change words for effect, using words like 'guesstimate' for estimate, 'agin' for against, and 'kink' for king when playing cards. Louise didn't always appreciate his humor:

> After graduation, I moved to the city and came home for occasional weekend visits. On one of these visits, only my parents and I were home. We had just finished lunch and lingered at the table to extend our visit. Louise put the milk in the fridge, closed the fridge door and looked at the empty dish on the table. "Where did those four cookies go I just put on the

table?" She looked at me. "Did you eat all those cookies?"

I shook my head but didn't offer an answer.

Harold hesitated but owned up. "I et them," he said.

She frowned at him. "Don't say et. It makes you sound like you never went to school!"

He gave her a look of boyish innocence. "Well, whether I et them or I ate them, those cookies are still gone."

She sat down and took a sip of tea. Their eyes met. He turned sideways in his chair as if to leave but stopped and glanced back at the dish.

"Well, now I need two more cookies on that dish so I can say I ate them."

"Huh!" One laugh. She got his cookies plus one each for herself and me.

Picking up two, he took a bite and chewed. "There," heading for the door, he turned and waggled them. "I ate two cookies. 'Course, I ate a lot more than two but that's what I'm saying." He swung out the door, chewing.

She looked at me, grinned, and rolled her eyes.

He loved the way some words turned off his tongue. "Well, hello there, Mrs. Magillicuddy!" he'd greet a daughter.

Having fun with old expressions, he'd extend their meaning or change their sound. When the chatter of the four kids in the family talking at once filled the house: "You kids quit that racket before you drive me up the wall!"

We'd stop and look at him, waiting for the punch line delivered after the expertly held pause of a professional comedian.

"Across the ceiling and down the other side."

We'd giggle. "Oh, Dad!" His eyes twinkled but he didn't smile, and we were smart enough to stop our clamor.

Over time, he invented new favourites and used them so often they became hinged on our memory of him. We started using them ourselves as an inside family joke. When the grandchildren thronged in the house for a visit and called out, "Hi Grandpa!" He started saying, "Hidey didey! Here comes the thundering herd!" And then added, "The day is shattered!" He loved it, on one particular occasion when a granddaughter, waiting in a restaurant for a coffee visit saw him coming, stood on the bench of the booth and called across the room, "Hidey didey, Grandpa!"

He didn't mind acting the fool for his grandchildren. After a visit, the car, packed with youngsters, headed down the lane, four kids waving to him through the car windows as he stood at the back door. He waved back with two hands and one foot, then changed feet so he could waggle the other. "There's four kids waving and I don't have enough hands for each one. I have to use my feet, but I have to stand on one. Wish I could wave with all hands and feet at the same time. Next time, I guess I'll have to lie on the ground."

To answer an acquaintance's query of "How are you?" he might respond, "I'm standing on my head and dancing on the sky!" or, "Hunky dory!" always enjoying the smile he created. He never swore—he didn't need to. He had enough ammunition in his repertoire to express himself without it. In frustration at a misbehaving child, with twinkling eyes, he'd mock threaten, "I'll nail your ears to the wall, both ears on the same nail."

"Oh, Grandpa."

When exhausted or unwell, "I've been through the wringer,"[1] or "I feel like the Wreck of the Hesperus." We listened to him say he felt like the Wreck of the Hesperus often. Louise found the poem and made a copy for each of us. "Here you go. This is what your father is talking about when he says he feels like the Wreck of the Hesperus." Harold had studied the poem in school, impressing his boyhood imagination with the destruction of the sunken ship. School was short for him, but that poem and other lessons stayed with him all his life.

In contrast to words and reading being natural gifts for him, math endured a continual puzzle. Income tax time always created a flow of interesting outbursts. When the government introduced new policies for farmers, he took his receipts to an accountant, easing his misery somewhat until the bill arrived.

While Louise kept her emotions to herself, Harold wore them on his sleeve. When happy: "Hallelujah," "Hunky dory!" or "Hot diggity!" When frustrated, in particular by a politician, especially Pierre Trudeau: "What the Sam Hill!" Other, milder irritations received something lower in his value scale: "Son of a sea-coat!" or "Son of a gun!"

He never spoke ill of anyone in public, but at home, we heard how he felt about someone who'd been rude. A short person was "a sawed off, driven in little runt", a lazy person was "dead, they just haven't fallen over, yet" and a talkative person, especially given to gossip, was "vaccinated with the gramophone needle." Someone who didn't pay attention—"It goes in one ear and out the other, 'course, there's nothing in between to hold it there."

Whether stranger or friend, if they were very tall—"What's the weather like up there?" The confused looks never phased him. If they didn't smile at first, he'd keep up his brand of comedy until they did, either out of pity or genuine enjoyment.

His pleasure in humor didn't mean he had no interest in serious business of community affairs. Like his father in one aspect at least, he loved being part of business meetings and joined organizational boards for almost all local services, serving terms as chairperson of many: the Bellcamp Rural Telephone committee, the Marwayne Telephone board, the Co-op board, the Marwayne Seed Cleaning Plant board, the Marwayne Cemetery board, the Co-op Implements Ltd (CIL) board, the Marwayne Chamber of Commerce and the Co-op Livestock Association board.

At my wedding supper he made a brief speech. I tensed up when I saw him stand and clear his throat but I saw a side of him I rarely saw. He spoke in an articulate, courteous and confident manner, with no jokes or invented words for humor's sake. I imagined him at a board meeting and the picture widened my perception of him. I felt both proud and relieved.

Having to pay his father's farm debt taught him to hate any liability and to keep meticulous records. He carried a little notebook in his shirt pocket where he documented all purchases. He kept strict records of his farm business in books stored safely in his office desk in the basement.

As a teenager, he hated having to farm with horses—calling them temperamental and labour-intensive—much preferring tractors. "If you take care of your machinery, keep it oiled and repaired, it'll always work for you, and in bad weather you don't have to go outside to feed it. A horse needs feed whether it works or not, and it may decide it doesn't want to work on a particular day. Then you have to convince it."

Harold was born in 1918, went to school in the 1920s and by the Great Depression of the 1930s, he had quit school to farm with his dad, Edward. In the twenties, horses worked only for trips to town, leaving the more arduous field work to tractors. The Depression changed all that for the Hathaways when Edward couldn't afford gas and returned to farming with horses. Horses in the field slowed down the work, affecting Edward's ability to make a living. By 1939, the Depression slowed but poplars had sprung up around the ancient Hart-Parr, parked in the yard.

Confronting the challenge to revive the Hart-Parr after years of neglect, Harold plunged into it. As a novice with machinery, the work frustrated him, but taught him lessons about the inner workings of motors. Each revelation gave him pride and a feeling of accomplishment. Harold found his first true love—tinkering with machinery.

When they moved to the Marwayne farm, he spent winter days repairing his machinery in the old double garage. With a dirt floor and no heat, it offered little more than protection from wind, but that was more than the Clear Range farm offered, having to work in the open prairie. At last, in 1965, he had the money for a proper shop. By installing the concrete floor himself, he could then afford to pay local carpenter Len Espedviedt to build it, with insulation and a chimney hole in the roof for the wood-burning barrel heater he made himself. The new shop gave him every day of winter doing what he loved: adjusting, repairing, and inventing.

"I don't know how he can stay out in that shop all day!" Louise exclaimed. Then she'd allow herself a slow smile and add, "I think he's trying to stay away from me." Rolling her eyes, she'd quip, "That shop is more organized than my kitchen!" He had meticulous habits with his tools. He organized a place for everything.

He would lend you a tool, but you better put it back in place when you were done, or you'd be in trouble, and never—never leave a tool outside! He took the same pride in his machinery, gaining great satisfaction if he improved on an implement's design and function.

He may have had a poor opinion of the old Clear Range farm, calling it "the worst pile of rocks in Alberta" but the new one presented its own igneous challenges as well. Many summer days passed by picking rock in the summer fallowed fields with the stone-boat, recruiting all four kids if they were on holiday from school. I hated trudging through the soft summerfallow, dirt blowing in my eyes, eating sandwiches on the rock pile with grit grinding between my teeth, my hair growing stiff with dust. Once at home, I'd strip off grey clothes, dirt falling out of my waistband, and shower off half an acre of prime farmland. Much to Harold's delight and the children's relief, a more efficient, hydraulic rock picker replaced the old stone-boat and the muscle power of four scrawny kids.

The real contest emerged in the form of the occasional boulder. One memorable behemoth made its debut by breaking a cultivator shoe. Seeming to be about the size of a football at first, Harold thought a hand shovel would suffice to dig it out. Like an iceberg under the sea, the sides sloped out as he dug and continued growing.

He went home for the tractor and his invention he'd called a rock ripper. This was an invention he'd made out of buckets with extended claws out of cultivator shanks and steel that worked better than the commercial bucket for picking up boulders, trees, or anything large. He made a big one for the tractor, a smaller one for the little John Deere, and a third on commission for a neighbour. He could have bought a patent for it and gone into business, but going into manufacturing didn't interest him, not interested in any business other than farming.

Even the rock ripper didn't vanquish the behemoth. The surrounding hole widened as he dug and still hadn't reached its underside. "What the devil!"

He hired the local county man, George Lowrie, with the county-owned Cat to unearth it and push it to the side of the field. It turned out to be as big as a mid-size car.

For other boulders though—say, as big as a horse, the rock ripper worked well and he lifted some pretty big monsters out of the east field with it.

Other devices included a hitch for the front of the pickup so he could tow it as part of his train of implements during transport from one field to another. He also got a couple of blades from somewhere and adjusted them to fit on the tractor, one on the front for plowing snow, the other on the back for dragging the lane in summer to smooth out ruts.

Some smaller projects included patio chairs made of old tractor seats and harrow discs, and a made-to-scale machine shed for a grandson's toy machinery.

In the early 1970s, an addition on the shop, outfitted with a pit in the floor, made changing oil and other maintenance easier. Now he was in seventh heaven and proving it by staying out of the house more than ever, puttering around with machinery until retirement in 1987.

Fifty-three years spent fiddling with machinery must be long enough for anyone, or so Louise thought, but even after moving to Lloydminster, Harold disappeared into the garage to tinker—maintaining the snowblower or lawnmower, sharpening garden equipment, making small repairs on this or that—just playing, ever faithful to his first love.

2.
❈ Louise ❈

Rhubarb Relish

Lilacs and rhubarb have nothing in common except they're both ready for picking at the same time of year. On a sunny day in late spring, I hope you can go out, pull several stalks of rhubarb and cut lots of lilac blooms. You'll need either pruning shears or sturdy scissors for the lilacs, and a paring knife will suffice for the rhubarb, but not yet! Read on.

Rhubarb reigned as a staple in every pioneer garden due to its hardiness in our cold winters. It needs lots of sunshine and water. When picking rhubarb, pull it out from the base to get that pink, shell-like end. If you cut off the stems and leave that funny end on the plant, it won't grow more stalks to replace the ones you took. The poor thing will grow smaller and smaller. So, don't be gentle—just yank them out!

The leaves are poisonous so don't feed them to any bird or animal. They won't hurt plants though, so cut off the leaves and the pink shell-like end and throw them in your compost. Those leaves also make fabulous stepping stones for the crafty person.

I like to take a knife out to the garden with me to do all this cutting outside, spending the most time possible outdoors, but also reducing the chance of bringing insects in the house that may hide in the wrinkles of those big leaves.

Lots of dessert recipes using rhubarb appear in many prairie kitchens in spring, but my family's favourite is my mother's rhubarb relish. Sweet and tangy, I like it best on roast beef but other family members will ask for it on other meats. Experimenting is allowed and encouraged!

I like to store my relish in nice little jars and give it away as Christmas gifts. If you don't seal it in sterilized jars, store it in the fridge. Similar to any other pickle, the vinegar preserves it a long time.

Mother's Rhubarb Relish

> 4 cups chopped rhubarb
> 2 cups chopped onion
> 2 cups vinegar
> 4 cups packed brown sugar
> 2 teaspoons salt
> ½ teaspoon pepper
> 1 teaspoon cinnamon
> ½ teaspoon cloves

> In a large saucepan, mix the rhubarb, onion and vinegar and bring to a boil over medium heat, stirring often. There is a tendency for the solids to sink to the bottom and burn, so it needs lots of stirring throughout all the cooking. Cook uncovered 20 minutes while stirring.
>
> Add all the remaining ingredients, stirring often. Your kitchen will fill with a wonderful spicy aroma. People will ask, "What's cooking?" and you can reply, "Mother's rhubarb relish!" I'm guessing everyone will smile. But keep stirring!
>
> Simmer until thick, about another 30 minutes. Pour into hot, sterilized jars and seal. Makes 2 ½ pints or 5 cups. Enjoy!

⁓

Louise's journey to find her niche in the world jostled like a ride in a Model T on washboard road—that rippling formation on dirt roads named after the old-fashioned hand-held appliance used for laundering clothes. Washboard gave passengers a tooth-jarring ride that also proved dangerous unless the driver slowed down before the car jostled off the road. In a similar way, Louise's life journey forced her to take it slower than she wanted.

She dreamed of nursing like her mother, but Gertie discouraged her, arguing the job demanded such hard work: being on one's feet all day, lifting patients, and working nights. Gertie wanted an easier life for her daughter. Gertie kept her second reason secret for the time being while Louise grew up—the high cost of nurses' training.

The tiny hamlet of Evesham offered Louise a warm and friendly world in which to grow up. She proved to be a bright student from the beginning and, being the only student in her grade in the one room school, her teacher promoted her at the end of grade one to grade three. Many young teachers, most having left school themselves not many years ago, struggled to manage nine grades in one classroom. They developed enterprising strategies to ease their workload, and many skipped a student over a grade if he or she thought the pupil could manage it. This happened a second time for Louise at the end of grade six, sending her out of grade twelve at age sixteen, too young to attend post-academic training, much to her dismay. Her early graduation forced a stay at home for a year.

Promoting her twice during her schooling left her with gaps in her learning. As a teacher herself, she relearned some aspects of, for example, arithmetic from the teachers' manuals and student texts so she could then teach the lessons to her students.

Her year at home of gardening, cooking family meals, feeding chickens, and collecting eggs under her parents' supervision replaced Louise's dream of freedom and independence in the city. Knowing my mother's impatience once she'd made a decision, I can imagine how that year must have played out: a very restless Louise pacing the floor, sighing and arguing with Gertie about taking nurses' training. I think relations with her mother later in life might have been better if circumstances took an alternate route that year.

While Louise waited for life to catch up with her ambition, many a heated argument must have warmed the McLean house until Wilbur intervened to save his sanity.

"I think we better let her take nurse's training."

She began training in September 1933 at Edmonton General Hospital but it only lasted the first three months. Wilbur broke his leg in a farming accident and Gertie wrote to Louise to say she'd have to come home to help on the farm. Universal healthcare wasn't in effect yet, and the Great Depression weighed on everyone. Most patients couldn't afford to pay their medical bills and hospitals struggled to keep going. Even many doctors found themselves on Relief alongside most of their patients.

I believe the real reason Gertie asked her to come home was to open a way to request a refund of Louise's tuition. Louise was no farmer, afraid of livestock and machinery although she milked cows alongside Gertie that year at home.

Her father's injury cancelled any prospect of nurse's training. Gertie and Wilbur existed on the brink of poverty even in good years. Louise once again stayed home until the next fall but Gertie told her that with their now diminished savings, they couldn't afford nurse's training. They borrowed one hundred dollars from Gertie's friend, Janet Loury, for one year of Normal School (teacher's training) in Saskatoon. Adding insult to injury, her parents made the promise to Janet that Louise would repay the loan out of her first year's teaching income.

She never forgave her mother for hindering her dreams of nursing, but I believe Gertie had no other option. For the rest of her life, Louise told anyone who listened that she "really wanted to be a nurse but Mother prevented it."

After the two years of waiting at home, she welcomed independence in the city, enjoying her freedom with friends in Saskatoon. In a big, old house on Avenue B converted into small suites, she shared a tiny apartment with Betty Chisholm, a friend from Evesham schooldays. The house offered temporary lodgings to girls only, and they all attended Normal School.

A landlady by the name of Mrs. Eagle filled a supervisory role. These were the days when young women stayed home until they married so a mother figure in the house oversaw the girls' livelihoods while they lived away from home. Unlike their true mother however, Mrs. Eagle didn't cook for them or supervise their homework or housekeeping chores. For that, the girls took sole responsibility, thus easing their transition into adult life. Mrs. Eagle's presence ensured no inappropriate behavior took place, such as a male visitor in the suites, and she chatted with the girls occasionally to serve as a friend and answer questions about city life.

Enrolling over two hundred students, Normal School divided its roster into groups by classroom, assigning Louise and Betty to Room C. She kept a brief diary of Normal School days, written in a simple notepad of the type used to jot down a grocery list or a telephone message.

Sometime that winter, Louise's parents moved from Macklin, Saskatchewan to Streamstown, Alberta. She was the second of four children and all of her three siblings lived at home: Mac, the oldest, helped Wilbur on the farm, Stanley and Varina (Bunny) were in grades seven and eight. Louise thrived in her independent life, but her mind often turned to the family at home and their upcoming move. "Not moved as yet," she often commented in her diary after receiving a letter from home.

Her notes begin in March 1935. If she ever felt homesick, she had recovered by then, revealing a young woman who felt very comfortable in her single city life.

"A fine day," she wrote. "Went downtown—Bank, Dell's, Bay, Eaton's, Kresge's, Woolworth's. Bessie and Mildred were here to lunch."

On another day: "Party last night—good time—25 present (about), scarcity of boys. Washed, ironed & cleaned before noon. Had dinner & went downtown to library & stores. Phoned Mat today."

Along with the good times though, she recorded the not so good. "Punk today. Mrs. Sherry observing—lots of criticism. Good day to look forward to tomorrow." On May 8th, approaching the end of classes, she commented, "Boy oh boy—the work!"

Even while attending classes and enjoying an active social life, she found time for her faith. Not unusual for those times, faith formed a natural part of almost everyone's life, not an individual's choice as it is today. She often attended church with friends in the same way she went shopping with them or to a party: "Went to Helen, Emily & Guinevere's for a lovely dinner today. An excellent, uplifting sermon at 3rd Avenue (United Church) tonight."

A poignant diary entry relates the day she and some friends went to the Florence Nightingale Service at Knox United Church, held on May 12 to celebrate that famous nurse's birthday and honour the nursing graduates from the three hospitals in the city.

"There were 150 graduate nurses from all the hospitals there," she wrote. "The text was based on Mary & Martha. 'And Mary hath chosen that better part which shall not be taken away from her.'" This text must have pricked her heart, a reminder of her own recent denial of a chance at nursing just the year before. I wonder if she told her friends her thoughts during the walk back to their apartment house. When the three girls from the main floor suite invited them in for ice cream, it must have cheered her up a little. Ice cream was her favourite dessert.

She recorded a couple of events, now in Saskatoon's history, revealing a blossoming interest in public events that coloured the rest of her life although such an interest seems unusual for any nineteen-year-old: "Bessborough[2] and Lady B to arrive tomorrow on CN," she wrote on March 20th, noting the visit by Canada's 14th Governor-General to attend the opening of the CN hotel named after him. Later on May 6th she wrote, "The Jubilee 25th Anniversary of our Majesty King George V and Queen Mary," adding, with disappointment, that she and her friends decided not to attend the sports day celebrations.

Louise finished Normal School in June 1935 and again stayed home while she searched for a teaching position. The Great Depression plagued the country and anyone, regardless of age, training or experience, applied for open teaching jobs. No prerequisite was required. Some graduates from Normal School offered to work for free just to gain experience. At least they'd have a roof over their heads in the teacherage. Some ads stated "no income" but promised shelter and food. If the school offered an income, often nothing remained at the end of the month to pay them. Families tried to ease a teacher's situation by offering a chicken, vegetables or baking to keep them alive and living there to teach their children.

Louise felt fortunate to gain her first position the following January in northern Saskatchewan at North Beaver River School, Dorintosh. Her parents thought Dorintosh seemed very far from them, now in Alberta, but she had already spent several months searching for work and they realized her good luck. North Beaver River supplied a tiny teacherage, but the school board refused to allow such a young girl to live in it alone and found a boarding place for her. Everyone there lived in desperate conditions, having just left their drought-beaten farms in southern Saskatchewan. Louise contributed her memories to Elizabeth McLachlan's book, *With Unshakable Persistence:*

> Without exception, the farmers of the area had walked away from established farms in the dust bowl of southern Saskatchewan. Incessant wind, grasshoppers, crop rust, and drought had eaten away their livelihoods. In a desperate bid for a second chance, they had sold or packed all they could, abandoned the rest, and trekked hundreds of miles to the more fertile soil of northern Saskatchewan. Truly pioneers, they

cleared the bush, build homes of rough logs, and lived off the land. Hardworking and hospitable, they were civilized people in an uncivilized environment. And they were wretchedly poor.[3]

Most of the tiny log homes had only two rooms and no one had space for another occupant, but a family who agreed to keep her had a teenage daughter with whom Louise shared a double bed. The girl was also one of her students. She fit into the family somehow and later recalled this girl became one of her best friends. They were only two years apart in age.

Fortunately, her new family was congenial, for in such cramped quarters privacy was nonexistent. In the tiny back bedroom there were three double beds. The husband and wife shared one, their two sons another, and their seventeen-year-old daughter and Louise, the third. Nothing more than building paper stood between the beds.[4]

Wilbur feared Louise might marry and stay there, so far away from them. For the following school term, he hunted out a position himself for her and obtained one just a few miles south of them in Alberta.

Millerdale School proved a training ground for disciplining a class of unruly students. She often wrote in her diary of wishing to leave for another school, but the hard times kept her from finding another position and she taught there from 1936 to 1938.

She boarded with the Patnoe family. Saved with her collection of diaries, I found a short record of those teaching days written on pages torn from a school notebook, called a "scribbler" in Albertaspeak, the loose pages saved among her other diaries of a more noble form. Recorded in such humble means, it's a miracle these pages survived over sixty years.

Louise, her parents and siblings spent the last of their 1936 Christmas holidays in isolation because her younger brother and sister, Stanley and Varina, contracted measles. In those days, there was no vaccine and measles could sometimes become a deadly disease. Measles outbreaks took the form of today's Covid epidemics.

The loose pages begin, "Jan 1 to 22: Quarantined for measles. Stanley worst—very thin. Varina seems quite recovered."

They celebrated their release from quarantine by inviting some friends over for supper: "After due preparations, Mrs. Trickerey, Ruth, Muriel McNaughton came to sup."

Louise's dry humor surfaces when she writes: "M is very busy at needlework, etc., for she is leaving the profession to take a permanent position in June." She means M is getting married. In those days, once a woman married, they "left their profession" to become a full-time spouse.

>Jan 23, 1937: Prepared to go back to school on Mon. Made two beanbags (main accomplishment). I dread going back but have only said so once so far.
>
>Jan 24: 20 degrees below this a.m. Visions of two frozen corpses (Daddy and I) in a cutter held up by two frozen horses (Johnnie and Nig). Have only said I didn't care to go back three times. I wish someone would stick a pin in me.
>
>Arrived at Patnoe's about 3:30. Drifts are conundersus (this is not in the dictionary). It means almost insurmountable. Daddy had to walk part way to hold the cutter up. I hope dear old fellow didn't freeze going home. Wind is N.W. We had turkey for supper. It must have been a flighty one for Irene and I couldn't go to sleep until near one a.m.
>
>January 25: 14° F below, wind 5 mi… so sayeth the weatherman. Managed to slip from the warm covers at 8:10. After great difficulty in finding walking places arrived at school 9:25. Met Mr. Palterson, enroller, who gave me my December cash ($68.00). School was rather frosty in corners, but by 10 a.m. we had thawed out some (my feet were like clubs). Thirteen pupils have convalesced from measles or flu and were in their customary places. Contrary to my forebodings, I think the day was a fair success. I really believe I liked it. But I was awfully busy—straightening up after the concert—enduring last article notices.
>
>Gave the kids my New Year Rules and have decided they must obey or retreat. The dear old School Board actually delivered some Science equipment. Now I want a cupboard above the washstand to keep them in. I hope I get it. Here's hoping and praying that this term is a complete success. Wouldn't it be queer if I turned out an "excellent" teacher! I stayed until 5:25, consequently was late getting home as the drifts were still there.

I'd actually rot without Irene to talk to and discuss things. She is frank.
Singularly happy now. I wish I knew more and could spend more time studying and practicing."

Louise's happiest accomplishment at Millerdale occurred in motivating the girls to start a CGIT club for themselves. It built confidence in both her and the girls, and may have begun a turning point in her attitude toward teaching.

The acronym CGIT stands for Canadian Girls in Training, an church club for girls from grades seven to twelve, launched in 1915. Despite a decline, small groups still gather today in churches across Canada, giving girls a place for social development, community outreach and leadership training. In small-town Marwayne, Alberta in the sixties, the group grew so big it had to be divided into two sections by grade, a younger group for girls frim grade seven to nine, and senior group for the high school students. It attracted most of the girls of the area. It was the female alternative to Scouts. My sisters and I began in the junior group called Explorers, graduating to CGIT. James joined Cubs and then Scouts. That was the days before Cubs and Scouts became co-ed.

Despite Louise's determination to nurse, the twist of fate that closed one door opened a window and let in sunshine. She enjoyed teaching. Never having sympathy for a sick child, she loved learning and her enthusiasm inspired her students. She valued getting to know her students and corresponded with many for years after graduation, also developing friendships with other teachers that lasted into her senior years. Perhaps as a young girl, the romantic idea of nursing appealed to her imagination—dreaming of a Florence Nightingale persona—more than teaching. She saw enough of that profession every day in school.

Teaching challenged and rewarded her and she taught most of her adult life. When the provincial government made a university degree compulsory for every teacher, she finished her prerequisites by correspondence, doing lessons at the dining room table every evening while teaching during the day and at the same time, meeting all the demands of raising a family.

She loved travelling, perhaps influenced by her parents' restless life. In summers while single and teaching, she took trips with friends. After marrying Harold, she learned he preferred to stay home on familiar ground but she pried him off the farm to go camping all over western Canada or travelling farther away to Europe and Australia. He regretted none of it, always in wonder of the places he saw, but greeted his own bed at home with thanksgiving, grateful to have survived the trip.

After Millerdale, she taught at Clear Range where she met Harold at a school dance. Restlessness and the quest for higher pay took her to three more schools, staying one or two years in each. By the fall of 1944, Louise felt desperate for a change and went to Vancouver for a year of university.

She kept in contact with Harold and after the declaration of peace in 1945, they decided to settle down and raise a family.

3.
❀ Tumbleweed on Barbed Wire ❀

Differences in upbringing, personalities, philosophies and social skills made Louise and Harold as mismatched as my grandsons' socks.

Alice Hathaway treasured her only son, Harold. She and her husband Edward had one other child, Connie, the oldest, born eight years before her little brother. Alice suffered several miscarriages. Most babies of those pioneer times were born at home but to ensure this baby's safe delivery, Alice stayed with friends in Lloydminster to await Harold's arrival close to to the hospital. On his entrance to the world, his parents named him after three significant Hathaway men: Harold after his uncle, Corporal Harold Hathaway who died in WWI at Passchendaele; Alfred, his grandfather, and Edward, his father. Naming one seven-pound infant after these three ancestors spoke of both the legacy and the expectation laid on his tiny shoulders.

Living far from other neighbours, Harold had no childhood friends and his parents seldom entertained company. He never had a birthday party, nor even a birthday cake until Louise made them for him after they married. His parents didn't believe in God and never took the children to church. While Edward played violin at dances, Alice, the introvert, kept her two precious children home. When she took them across a field for tea with a neighbour, little Harold hid behind her skirt. Gregarious Edward didn't know what to make of his quiet son.

Harold's shyness prevented him from starting school until age seven. On his first day, the teacher tried her best but failed to hear him say anything at all. He always remembered her gentle encouragement, but bigger boys or even boys his own age with more pluck bullied him without mercy. He often heard stories of World War I, the stuff of legends over many a cup of tea. I wonder if he imagined the classroom as his No-an's-land across which he must maneuver every day, the desks his barbed-wire entanglements. "The boys gave me no end of grief," he'd later recall.

When little Harold arrived at school in the morning and stood at the doorway, did his heart pound in his chest? Every time he walked to his desk, did he keep his eyes down, telling himself, "don't trip"? Sometimes as he crept across No-man's land toward his desk, did another boy feint a lunge at him? And if he lurched backward, did he hear snickers? Did he watch for a quick boot to snap out in front of him? If he missed seeing it and went over in the trenches, did he hear laughter and pounding on desks sounding like gunfire?

Often when opening his lunch pail, stored in the boys' cloakroom, he'd find it empty, raided during someone's trip to the outhouse. One more battle lost. The bullying made him quit in the spring of grade eight, not yet fifteen, fleeing to the solitude of the amiable fields. Later he could joke, "I started school as late as possible and left as early as possible."

In his teen years, Harold showed his aptitude for the inner workings of machinery. His father preferred horses and I imagine Edward resented his son's interest in new equipment and modern farming methods. A proud man, Edward thought Harold tried to show him up. He might have turned a passionless stare on his son who, still a teenager, explained in serious tones the new farming methods to his father.

A wall between them hardened like cement. Edward liked to make a fuss over his daughter, Connie. His quiet, serious boy, so different from himself only irritated him. He taught violin to Connie but not Harold. Edward loved a good, hot political argument, often taking either side to promote it, and at those times, Harold disappeared like mist in the valleys ahead of the sun.

Harold never travelled further than a day trip to Lloydminster to sell grain and buy supplies. Twice in his bachelorhood did he ever travel farther: to Camrose, Alberta for basic training as a Reservist in 1940, and to Vancouver for his wedding in 1945. He didn't mind not travelling. In fact, he preferred staying home. He loved the solitude of the fields, watching the steady rhythm of the seasons, the undulating movement of wild geese in fall and crows in spring, and learned to predict weather by the sky. Like a barbed wire fence standing in place, steady and permanent, he belonged to the farm. His choice of a partner in Louise changed him in ways he never imagined.

Louise's childhood contrasted with Harold's like pepper and salt. Her rugged Scottish parents, Wilbur and Gertie McLean, migrated west from Nova Scotia. While Gertie treasured fond memories of a happy life in her Atlantic home, Wilbur's childhood lay smudged and crumpled behind him like an old shirt.

The day his mother went out and left him and his older brother in charge of their two-year-old sister changed his life and forever tormented his memories. Arthur was eleven; Wilbur was five. When little Louisa got hungry, they fed her dried apples. In the boys' innocence, they let her eat as many as she wanted and it resulted in her tragic death.

Their mother never left the house again and died nine years later at age fifty-one. Neighbours whispered she died of a broken heart. When his father remarried, Wilbur couldn't abide his new stepmother and left home at nineteen, landing first in Winnipeg and then Regina. His father called him home once to take care of the farm and he tried, but the rift with his step-mother remained, and he returned to Regina for good.

Obeying the nineteenth century expectation of Nova Scotia's young people to gain training in Boston and return home, Gertie and her sister, Jessie, both trained as nurses and then worked in Boston Malden Hospital. Gertie took specialty training for psychiatric nursing, giving her an edge for better employment if she stayed in the East. She broke with tradition though, following Wilbur to Regina after his proposal.

Wilbur met her at the station, tall and broad shouldered, walking on the platform as if his legs were tree trunks. His thick thatch of red hair almost stood on end for lack of room on his head, and sky-blue eyes pierced out under bushy red awnings for eyebrows. He loved his farming life and his beautiful wife.

Neighbours once told Louise her father's temper could simmer up and boil over in a froth of expletives. Gertie, they said, exclaimed "Wilbur!" making him tamp down the volcano. Louise never saw this side of her father and related the memory with the same feeling of surprise she felt when first hearing it. She always remembered Wilbur as a gentle, committed husband to her mother and a kind and patient father. I think his kindness toward girls and women stemmed from the tragic death of his little sister, followed by his mother's untimely death.

With their little son, Mac, the young Wilbur and Gertie McLeans left Regina, pulled by the promise of cheap farmland. Their search took them first near the hamlet of Senlac in 1915, then Evesham in 1916. On a pilgrimage to escape the city for a comfortable life in the wide Saskatchewan expanse, they found instead, its legendary array of dust storms and rocks. Thus began the nomadic life they sustained until they died.

With each move, Wilbur bought a homestead plus the pre-emption beside it. The Homestead Act defined a homestead as the first quarter of land purchased. The second quarter is called the pre-emption, each at a cost of ten dollars and the farmer must develop both quarters. The homestead quarter must be the one lived on.

He worked hard. At the Evesham farm, he moved the house to a new location, built a new barn, a workshop and chicken house. He nursed the dry earth back to health.

Louise entered the world on August 19, 1916 in the house her father built, and named Louise Lavinia after Wilbur's dear little sister and mother.

Despite her parents' struggle, Louise's childhood rolled along merrily with many friends and parties. Missing old friends and family in Nova Scotia, Gertie encouraged an active social life for her children, keeping the big house creaking with friends and cousins popping in and out.

Wilbur expanded the house to fit a growing family by splitting the roof, installing a basement with a cistern and an upstairs with four bedrooms. The big house often rattled with laughter, groaning with so many people within, threatening to burst. They often invited neighbours for a meal, sharing their meagre existence with whoever would have it. Summers brought relatives from Regina for a few days' visit and Louise's school friends stayed overnight, and she with them.

By some miracle, she took all her schooling in the same school. The Depression forced her parents into a nomadic life, bringing a low price for grain and a high price of everything else. They searched for a pot of gold at the end of a good harvest. The only crops that flourished in Saskatchewan were grasshoppers and cutworms.

Roaming like tumbleweed over the prairies, Wilbur and Gertie drifted northwest into Alberta, settling wherever survival looked possible. For Louise, going "home" for a holiday meant a train ticket to wherever her parents lived at the time.

Like her parents, Louise, became as restless as the tumbleweed that rolled across the dusty prairie. Travel and moving became easy for her. After high school, she took courses in Edmonton (nursing), Saskatoon (teacher training) and Vancouver (home economics). Similar to her parents' search for a more lucrative livelihood, Louise taught in five schools before the age of twenty-six, a restless tumbleweed. One summer, she and an old school friend, also a teacher, took a trip to Vancouver by train, just two single, carefree spirits out on a fling. She enjoyed travelling all her life.

When she began teaching, she first fulfilled her obligation to repay the hundred dollar loan her parents borrowed from Mrs. Loury for her Normal School tuition. She then sent money home for her younger siblings' high school fees. All grades were free in Saskatchewan, but in Alberta, only elementary grades were free. High schools being built only in major centres, students like Louise's younger siblings, Stanley and Varina, left home to attend, adding the need to pay rent for living quarters in addition to tuition. At first, the two attended high school in Dewberry, living on their own in a tiny shack. For one year, they even shared it with another student. For their grade twelve, they went to Edmonton.

Views on faith between the Hathaways and McLeans differed like fire and water. While the Hathaways were atheists, the Methodist faith held an important place in the McLean home. Gertie had regular personal devotions and took the family to services every Sunday, sometimes holding her own version at home if none existed elsewhere. She saw faith as a personal relationship with Jesus. Wilbur was an Orangeman, a clansman of a centuries-old British order dedicated to a Protestant monarchy. He saw faith as a political statement, not a reason to attend church unless Gertie insisted. Amidst her parents' philosophies, Louise learned to see faith as a normal and essential part of life while enjoying many friendships through church, Sunday School and church camps.

One can only imagine the glances across the table if the two families should happen to gather for a meal, but the opportunity never arose. Alice and Edward had already moved to Vancouver a few years before Harold ever started "seeing" Louise. Until 1940, the Hathaways lived in the Clear Range District while the McLeans rambled over the prairies, only landing at Streamstown, Alberta in 1935 and then Riverton in 1938, too far away to make acquaintance with the Hathaways when travel required a horse-drawn vehicle. Wilbur and Gertie moved to their "retirement home" in Marwayne, Alberta in 1951. When Gertie's health declined with a heart condition, they bought a house in Lloydminster in 1955, closer to doctors and the hospital. Gertie died on January 14, 1956.

Louise's diaries hint at Harold's courtship, starting in the same one-room schoolhouse where Harold once attended. The place Louise loved and Harold hated is both fitting and ironic. Louise arrived in the Clear Range School District in the fall of 1938 with three years of teaching on her resume.

Prairie custom dictated that the community put on a dance after harvest to raise money for the children's treats at the Christmas concert. Naturally, the school served as the venue so the planning logically fell in the teacher's hands although some parents also took part. The list of tasks included asking local musicians to play, sending notices home with students, and planning decorations for students to make during free time at school. On the day, either the teacher or a student cleaned the school, stoked the fire, and made coffee. All those attending brought food for the midnight lunch.

On the night of the event, parents moved desks against the wall, often shoving them so hard the books fell out. They scooped them up by handfuls, thrusting them in a pile in a corner. The first day back at class began with sorting and redistributing it all to the correct owner. On her first January day at school after the Christmas holidays at North Beaver River, Louise recorded in her diary, "I was awfully busy straightening up after the concert."

Lamps of either the coal oil type or gas provided the lighting. Gas lamps gave a brighter light, making them preferred in public buildings but needed more technical know-how, something Louise's didn't get in her genes. When she later moved from Clear Range to the Lea Park teacherage, she wrote in her diary, "When I first got a gas lamp, I had to call on Bob or George to light it." The Lea Park teacherage stood in the Hanson brothers' yard, so either of these men could walk over to help whenever called upon. "It used high-test gas and had to be pumped up, turned on and lighted, accompanied by a high, shooting flame which soon subsided and after, sent out a constant hissing sound."

But we're getting ahead of ourselves. For this particular dance at Clear Range, Louise tried her best, but one gas lamp rejected all her efforts to light it. Having run out of ideas, she looked around. She learned long ago how to fix mechanical problems—ask a man.

In those days, schools had a girls' and boys' cloakroom. No one wore "cloaks" but they gave it this name anyway. Prairie people don't quibble over labels; everyone knew the meaning. With no doors in these rooms, they offered only short hallways leading from either side of the school entrance with coat hooks along the walls. Today we may scoff at the idea of segregated areas to hang coats, even if there were no doors. The separate spaces gave less chance for boys and girls to touch while taking their coats off, and that was important.

At the start of the evening, the men gathered in the boy's cloakroom to talk farming, the only activity Harold liked about a dance. Louise squared her shoulders, went to the entrance of the boy's cloakroom and asked if anyone could fix the lamp. Harold loved to help and when a blue-eyed, red-haired "good looker" needed salvation, well, he was the man. He solved the problem with ease, bolstering his self-confidence and Louise's estimation of the quiet farmer. In later years, he liked to joke, "I've been fixing everything for her ever since."

His chivalry with the lamp didn't lead to taking her home that night. Again, his reticence held him back. Holding the wall up with his shoulder, he followed her red hair with his eyes as she and her dance partner wove among the others. He managed two waltzes with her—the one dance he felt he could manage. He didn't trust himself to try a faster number. She went home with the Boyces with whom she boarded, and for the next two years, the schoolmarm was "spoken for"—another young man stopped in at the school for visits after hours. Miserable, on Harold's trips to the Bellcamp Post Office, he took the long way home, checked for the roan mare standing outside the school, and passed on by.

Problems of the heart resolve best when managed by a gentle hand and I can imagine how the ice may have broken between these two. Alice Hathaway realized her son's misery and knew what she must do. She invited Louise for several meals as a normal gesture of friendliness to the new teacher. On their first evening, Alice kept Louise at the table as long as possible, sharing cooking and gardening wisdom with her and Connie while Harold studied the floor, his stomach leaping in his chest. Watching his son, Edward rolled his eyes and rose from the table, put a hand on Louise's shoulder, "I'm so glad you could visit us, Miss McLean." Connie and Alice stopped mid-sentence to stare at Edward, their mouths open. Harold glanced up, meeting eyes with his father across the table, who looked back in wide-eyed meaning. Harold cast his glance down again while his face flooded brighter red than the checkered tablecloth and Edward went out for chores.

More visits followed and, like the April sun melting the ice in spring, so it happened for these two. A halting, hiccupping ramble of a courtship could have been much worse without help from Harold's mother. Alice invited Louise over for supper or tea as often as looked appropriate. It created another friendship in the bargain—Louise listed her best friends in the back of a diary and included the name, Connie Hathaway, among them.

At last gossip carried the news the other guy wasn't seeing Louise anymore. A row had broken off their friendship, said the chatter flying over the prairie like Canada geese. Louise recorded in her diary that she told the poor fellow "perhaps he shouldn't stop in anymore."

I can imagine Harold, light as air and just as unsteady, dropping in to see her one day after school. Halting short at the cloakroom doorway, he may have looked across No-man's-land to where she sat, pen in hand, her brow furrowed over a student's book. His heart somersaulted in his chest the same way it did on his first day of school, age seven.

He removed his hat, fingering the brim, and cleared his throat. "Is that lamp giving you any more grief?"

She looked up and blinked. "What lamp?"

He looked at the floor. 'Don't trip,' he told himself. He walked between rows of desks to the front of the room. As he walked, memories of his own schooldays returned, hearing again the banging of the boys' fists, but it was only his own heart this time. Leaning on a student's desk close to hers, he crossed his ankles and began again. "How are you finding life with the Boyces? I guess living with Charlie must be as hard as putting up with all the scallywags here all day. Are they behaving themselves? The kids, I mean—not Charlie and Irene."

Louise would chuckle. "Oh no, the Boyces have become good friends."

"That's good. If they give you any grief, just nail their ears to the wall, both ears on the same nail. That goes for Charlie too."

She'd gasp but chuckle. "I'll tell them it was your idea."

All right. Laughter always eased his tension and put him on the right track. It sure saved his bacon that day.

Bolstered, an affable conversation continued. He ended his visit with the biggest question waiting in the back of his mind: "Could I visit again sometime, Miss McLean?"

"Yes," she smiled. "I'd like that."

"I'll say goodnight, then. Enjoy your evening." He tipped his hat over his dark hair, turned and tramped outside, wobbling down the school steps on legs like water. Striding to his horse, breathless and shaking as if he'd fallen in the gully in spring, he took in a lungful of air. A meadowlark lighted on a fencepost and threw out its triumphant call. He nodded to it, mounted his charger and turned for home. Victory at last.

He paid regular visits to the school and soon, gossip reported Miss McLean was spoken for again. They played tennis on the new, grassy court behind the school, attended dances, school plays, and whist parties. Louise's diary entry on March 7, 1940 records, "Harold Hathaway here to supper and evening. Played Norwegian whist, bridge, rummy and checkers." Harold didn't like table games, but he never complained. Thus began years of give and take for both. The steadfast barbed wire fence had been caught by the restless tumbleweed.

4.
❀ Reserved in War ❀

The moment Alice and Edward heard the news, they prepared to fight for their son's life. In the fall of 1939, Britain declared war on Germany. It meant Canada also found herself embroiled in the conflict, a country still very much connected to its motherland.

At age twenty-one and single, Harold fit the perfect qualifications of those expected to volunteer without hesitation. His father, however, had other ideas. Edward had already lost two brothers in World War One. Herbert and Harold signed up, ever loyal to their birthplace of Britain and their new homeland of Canada, while also not wanting to be called a coward by the local gossips. Both brothers fought knee deep in the mud of the trenches and died there, never to see another harvest from their quiet homesteads on the Canadian prairie. Edward never forgave the governments responsible and didn't feel compelled to sacrifice his only son to this new conflict. He and Alice vowed to keep Harold safe.

Other events in their lives prepared them for this day. All their lives, they struggled to survive.

As children, they grew up in the overcrowded, noisy city of London, England. Alice recalled living on Windmill Street, a middle-class area of the city. London's severe overpopulation in the 19th century meant citizens shared the streets, shoulder to shoulder with crime and disease, a giant, simmering stewpot of humanity. Fagin's boys portrayed in *Oliver Twist* worked the streets under other names and the real-life grisly attacks of Jack the Ripper, a never identified serial killer, terrorized the city. As conditions worsened, Victorians grew restless for change. When British immigrants came to North America and explained they were seeking a better life, they didn't mean they were after wealth although that too, circled in their minds. They sought open space, peace, and safety from each other.

All the Alices and Edwards of London learned life was hard and they'd have to use both their brains and brawn to survive. Alice, youngest of eight children, was seven when her father died in 1890. Later, she recalled her life as the child of a widow in 19th century England. She remembered running home from school at lunch time as fast as her little legs could carry her, trying to beat her older sisters. She remembers losing the race and finding nothing in the house to eat. Her sisters had gobbled the last crumbs. She remembered quitting school to find work at age eight. The whole family went to work to keep from starving. It's uncertain what employment her mother or siblings found. Little Alice got a job bussing tables in a tavern. She worked long hours, carrying heavy trays and sometimes the customers were loud, but little Alice never thought to complain. She focused on helping the family eat, never returning to school. When she grew older, she worked as a maid for a wealthy family.

She made friends with Martha Hathaway, her future husband's sister. "Martha and I used to pal around to shows and things like that," she recalled in a recorded interview. Cassette recorders arrived in the late sixties and Harold took his recorder on a visit to see his mother and his sister, Connie. "She was supposed to come and work close to where I was working, but she was one of those easygoing types." She paused in reverie and laughed. "Grandpa (Harold's grandfather, Alfred Hathaway) was going to marry her off to some…" she stopped to chuckle, "some rich man, but she didn't fall for his ideas."

Martha was twenty and Edward was sixteen when their parents read posters on lampposts and ads in the newspapers glowing with the promise of a tranquil life as a country farmer in Canada and joined the Barr Colonists in 1903. Alice wanted to go with the Hathaways, but couldn't afford it. This tranquil English lady with a soft voice, precise British accent, and tea every afternoon belied a heart of iron. She scrimped and saved until, in 1910, she paid her fare and wrote to the Hathaways at Lloydminster. By that time, Martha and Edward both "worked out", sending money home to help support the family. It's likely Alfred wrote to both adult children about Alice's future arrival.

The trip remained sharp in Alice's memory sixty years later.

"The boat was the Prince Edward," she told Harold who sat beside her in her kitchen with his recorder. "Four days on the boat and... I'm not certain about the train. It was either three or four days because it stopped off for a day at Fort William and then again at Winnipeg. Then we came right on to Lloydminster. It was three o'clock in the morning when the train arrived there."

Harold gasps. "Who was there to meet you?"

"Grandpa and Grandma," she said in a matter-of-fact tone (Alfred and Annie Hathaway). "They took me to a Chinese restaurant for tea. That was all that was open then."

She meant this restaurant was the only cafe open at that late hour of the night. Prejudice kept many European customers away from Asian businesses during the day, forcing them to work long hours to survive. This restaurant stayed open into the early morning hours to serve any tired customers disembarking off the train. When Alice stepped off her coach in 1910, three restaurants operated in Lloydminster.

"They met me with a team of oxen and a wagon. They covered the floor of the wagon with hay and some rugs, so Grandma and I sat down on the floor and Grandpa drove the oxen. One time—the big beggars—they picked on a slough. They were in the habit of going through it, but Grandpa didn't want them to go into it then, at night, like. And then," she laughed, "all the cussing set out! All the swear words under the sun!"

In 1910, no roads existed yet on the prairies, and people drove wherever they thought was best, usually whichever direction gave them the shortest and smoothest ride in their wagon, cutter or democrat. Pioneer stories often refer to oxen being headstrong and hard to manage. Not as obedient as horses, they sometimes took control and headed into a slough for relief from mosquitoes, likely what Alfred's team searched for in those early morning hours, but since it was still dark and Alfred couldn't see well, the oxen's headlong charge may have meant a dangerous ride, possibly upsetting the wagon. It's possible he regained control and steered the team away from the slough, but Alice doesn't finish that story in her interview.

Alice helped on the farm through August while she visited with her future parents-in-law and planned her next steps. She needed to make her own way and soon went to Edmonton. Edward worked for a blacksmith elsewhere in Alberta but when he received the letter from his father informing him of Alice settling in Edmonton, he moved there and soon connected with her. After courting her for one year, they married. When baby Constance arrived, serious thoughts of where to raise a family had to be faced.

Remembering their own childhood in London, they knew they didn't want to raise their children in the city. They scoured the *Edmonton Journal* for farmland near Lloydminster close to Edward's father and brothers, choosing at last to make an offer to trade two houses in Edmonton (one house had belonged to Edward's brother, Harold, who died in Europe during WWI) for two quarters of farmland belonging to Mr. C.G. Wheeler and a Mr. E.H. Switzer, in the Clear Range School District[5] north of Lloydminster. The land was close to his family, but not too close.

Years earlier, Edward quarreled with his brother, Donald, over a property line between their homesteads and left home in anger, never speaking to Donald again. It seems his older brother had installed a fence a little too far into Edward's land and refused to move it.

Mercurial and prone to blunders as a farmer, Edward endured enough arguments with the prairies and the government to fill a horse trough. Likely, he felt fortunate not to live near his brother as well.

Edward served the community as secretary of the Bellcamp UFA (United Farmers' Union), as a school trustee and one of the first members of the fledgling Alberta Wheat Pool. These organizations gave him joy. Only farming flummoxed him, wrestling with the land and its rocks, weeds, winter blizzards and summer drought through twenty-seven years.

He had a flare for misfortune. He bought house paint at a bargain price, not asking, nor did the hardware proprietor tell him the paint was for interior use. With pride, he painted the house only to see it blister and peel after the first winter.

He bought a new spray called formaldehyde for smut, a disease on wheat. Without taking the time to read the instructions, he applied it to the seed full-strength before first diluting it.

Harold recollected, "When the crop came up, it got about two inches high and then it all died."

Edward bought his first tractor just before the Great Depression. Gas prices soared with the red-tailed hawks, and he returned to farming with horses. Parked in the yard, the precious tractor disappeared behind poplar saplings before he could afford fuel for it again.

He developed a bitter resentment of the land which never offered the gentleman's life of which he dreamed. Rather, it seemed farming resented him, always withholding the income he saw others achieving. He regained lost revenue by blacksmithing, playing violin at dances and giving violin lessons.

He loved music and the jocularity of merrymakers twirling, laughing and sweating in the crowded schoolhouse. His wide smile stretched across his face as he surrendered all his frustrations upon his violin, playing faster and faster music. Pink dawn glowed through the schoolhouse windows as the last party-goers thanked him, put on their coats and went home. Edward collected his wage and returned to Alice and the family, snug in their beds.

A determined survivor, his charm won him credit from friends or businesses. He soldiered on through all his adversities, even enduring the Great Depression which defeated many other farmers, but he gave up when World War II began. Worn out, his greatest fear now looked him square in the face, and he felt helpless to fight against it. He refused to stand by while his only son went off to war, never to return like his two younger brothers had done in WWI.

Over the years, many of Edward and Alice's friends moved to Vancouver and Edward watched them go, wistful dreams playing in his mind of warmer winters, electrified homes with telephones and, perhaps, easier work. For Edward, the best thing about the farm, he thought, meant getting off it while saving Harold in the bargain.

Reading about it in the Lloydminster Times by the light of a coal oil lamp, Alice and Edward saw their big break handed to them. The Schedule of Reserved Occupations arrived, Britain's invention to prevent a recurrence of their devastating mistake of WWI when the government allowed anyone to volunteer for active duty. Skilled workmen signed up in droves and died in throngs. It left Britain crippled during the war and almost unable to rebuild when peace returned. Wanting to avoid the same mistake again, the Schedule listed occupations needed at home to support the country. Canada followed Britain's lead and adopted its own Schedule. Farmers were among those forbidden to enlist. Edward and Alice moved to Vancouver in 1940, changing Harold from a farm worker into a farmer, exempting him from signing up.

Never casting a backward glance to the fields, Edward left the farm in Harold's grateful hands, the greatest gift he ever gave his son, or so they both assumed. At the time, it not only excused Harold from enlisting, at least at first, it also allowed him to farm on his own terms without having to consult with his irascible father.

In Vancouver, Edward found work as a cooper, a maker of wooden barrels, for a jam factory. The work allowed him and Alice to live in relative comfort in their own home, but he could never eat store-bought jam for the rest of his life. Loathing the prairie winters to the end of his days, he asked for cremation "to chase the frost out of my bones".

It seemed as if their plan might succeed. Anyway, they had done their best, and no one expected the war to last long.

Four years later, exhausted in the grip of combat, the Allies needed more men. Earlier, Prime Minister Mackenzie King campaigned on the promise of no conscription, but now it stared him in the face. Controversy and indecision over recruitment wore on the people almost as much as the war. Through a referendum, Mackenzie King asked permission from the people to enact conscription. Without the referendum, King feared Canadians would see him as a second Hitler, the man on everyone's mind. In November 1944, the government at last saw the bill ratified.

Again, Harold stood at risk of recruitment and this time, Alice and Edward could only watch the mail for the dreaded letter from him that he had been called up. He reported for basic training to Camrose, Alberta in December and after one month, the army deemed him ready for combat in Europe's trenches. Now a reservist, he returned to the farm to set his affairs in order.

Edward continued his barrage of, "Don't give in to that madman, Mackenzie King! If you go to Europe, you'll never come back! You wouldn't want to do that to your mother!"

No, he really wouldn't. He loved his gentle mother with all his heart.

He and many others were fortunate. The war ended before the army called him up. Thirteen thousand Canadian Reservists went to Europe. Twenty-five hundred reached the trenches and sixty-nine died in battle.

Questions arise what Harold thought of his parents' plan to keep him safe. There is no doubt he'd rather farm than do anything else and, having heard the stories about his two uncles' tortuous WWI experience and outcome, he understood the consequences. Most telling of all, he hated conflict of any kind, but if needed, he'd have done his duty. The picture of him standing with his classmates in basic training shows a tense young man, uneasy, not knowing where to look. This also best describes his feelings about war. After some families watched their men go off to Europe, they often pressured others to join up and some young men enlisted, going off to risk their lives just to avoid the 'coward' label and sarcastic remarks from neighbours.

After the horror of the WWI, many war-weary families felt bitter toward governments for creating it. World War Two saw many families try various ways to save their sons and daughters from active duty and many found help in the Schedule of Reserved Occupations. Harold's story is only one of many. Other professions listed on the Schedule of Reserved Occupations included dock workers, miners, scientists, merchant sailors, railway workers and utility workers.

Harold avoided war in Europe but encountered other battles at home on the farm.

5.
❀ Louise's War ❀

They called the months from September 1939 to May 1940 Britain's Phoney War. Although Britain declared war on Germany in September, no military action took place until June. A large part of English Canada still considered themselves British, following Britain's lead in almost every part of life which explains why Louise's oldest brother, Mac, looked forward to enlisting as soon as possible, but didn't sign up until July. She wrote on July 13, 1940, "He went to Militia Camp at Dundurn, Saskatchewan," for training in the Saskatchewan Horse Infantry.

There, he saw planes, perhaps for the first time in his life, and talked to pilots. His imagination sparked. When living in his little shack on the farm, flying a plane remained a vague idea—something he read about in newspapers but never imagined he'd be close to one. A year after enlisting, he boarded a train for the unheard of distance of almost 900 km (over 530 miles) from Evesham to Brandon, Manitoba to enlist with the RCAF. Louise wrote on July 14, 1941, "Saw Mac off at Evesham at 6:20 a.m. He went to Brandon." War became serious business, no longer the quick little skirmish everyone first imagined.

On July 19, 1941, Louise wrote in her diary, "Stan's wedding day." Her younger brother married his long-time school sweetheart, Hazel, in Edmonton at her parents' home. Hazel's father was a train station master in Streamstown where Stan and Hazel met. Gertie and Varina, Louise's mother and sister, attended the wedding while Louise stayed home on the farm to cook for her dad and hired men.

Stan and Hazel's first child, Milton, arrived a year later. Following in his big brother Mac's footsteps, Stanley also enlisted in the RCAF in 1942. The Air Force denied his hopes to be a pilot when they found his eyesight didn't meet the requirements and posted him in office work, first in Canada, then England and Germany after the peace treaty.

Hazel struggled with loneliness, poverty and perhaps postpartum depression when Stanley left home for training. War took its toll on all young mothers. Loneliness and an incessant late delivery of her husband's salary meant that wives with children found life insufferable in their husband's absence. While expecting the birth of a second child, she and little Milton stayed with Wilbur and Gertie. They gave her the shack meant for a hired man during the harvest. Baby Valorie was born in Lloydminster Hospital while Wilbur and Gertie kept their little grandson.

They farmed at Riverton, ten miles from Louise in the Clear Range teacherage, but with no vehicle of her own, it might have been a hundred miles. She didn't visit often and or mention seeing much of Hazel or her children.

On September 24, 1941, Louise wrote, "Mac received his wings and sergeant stripes at Brandon." The next day, he arrived home on leave. Mac and Stan's activities seem to be Louise's primary reminder of the war. Europe remained a hazy picture far away from the Canadian prairies, and life carried on pretty much as normal except for the men in uniform on train station platforms and the letters they wrote home to their families. She doesn't mention rationing or any of the other hardships marking a country at war. She bought a radio and recorded some war updates heard in the news. Without television or the internet, the accurate picture of war never quite registered on the average Canadian.

She donated clothing to the Red Cross, whether to help the destitute Europeans or the poor in Canada, she doesn't say. As a young teacher just starting her career, busy with work, friends and social events, life in Europe seemed vague and distant. If she worried about her brothers, she doesn't document it. The general feeling in Canada pictured war in cloudy terms, something far away. The men who served returned with a very different perspective; most found it impossible to explain their true experience to family at home.

The largest change World War II inflicted on Louise's life took the form of delay in her plans for her future. The war held back all life in

Canada, forcing Louise once again to wait, practice patience and this time, watching the years pass by seemed more difficult than in her teenage years. The entire country held its collective breath. Everyone waited. They waited to see if the new conscription laws took effect, to see who came home from Europe, or which mother received a dreaded letter. Most of all, they waited to see which side surrendered.

Louise refused to join the general population and conform to this patient philosophy. This time, no government age restriction held Louise back or her parent's meager finances. Her sister already worked in Vancouver as a telephone operator. Varina's letters sparkled with descriptions of plays and movies, shopping and new friends. Louise looked out at Alberta's flat, somber prairies, and her quiet life seemed as shabby and dull as her father's boots. Bored, restless and tired of uncertainty, she decided she needed a break from teaching and the stolid prairie life.

But what would she do? She'd heard of some friends from Normal School who went to university to advance their careers. Now in command of her own income and not requiring her parents' permission, she wrote to the University of British Columbia asking for a course calendar. Perusing its exciting pages, she enrolled in Home Economics for the 1944-45 term and off she trotted, ready to live a carefree student's life again, sharing an apartment with Varina and turning a cold shoulder to the dreary prairie and World War II.

This news tied Harold's stomach in knots. He'd taken too long, he told himself. Why couldn't this blasted war just end? Lucky for him, he wasn't bereft of resources. He scrawled off a letter to his mother who just happened to live in Vancouver and mentioned Louise's plans.

In her quiet kitchen, a diminutive Englishwoman in a green flowered dress made herself a cup of tea, withdrew a sheet of paper and pencil from the kitchen cupboard. Sitting at her table, she took a sip of tea, and charged into battle for her son.

> Dear Louise,
> I hear you are coming to the coast for some schooling. It would be very nice to see you again. Please let us know when you arrive in the city. We'd be pleased to invite you for supper.
> Sincerely,
> Alice Hathaway

Harold and Louise wrote letters back and forth, Louise pouring out her minutest activities in multi-page epistles decorated with illustrations. Harold slaved over one paragraph in his large, awkward scrawl to fill a page, adding humor in every sentence.

Germany surrendered at last and the world expelled its long-held breath in an explosion of laughter and shouted, "The war is over! Let's get married!" Canadians and other Allies celebrated peace with wedding bells, followed by the fastest growing population explosion the world had ever seen—the Baby Boomers.

Eager to join in on any community event, Harold and Louise decided to take part. She enjoyed her year on the coast, but her mother wanted her home and so did Harold. When the war ended, the promise of a stable, bright future beckoned and the prairies didn't seem so bleak after all. They set the date for Saturday, June 23, 1945, after Louise's courses finished and Germany signed the official surrender. In Hitler's absence, Gen. Alfred Jodl took that hot seat, signing the surrender on May 7th, scheduled to take effect the following day. Since then, May 8th has been 'Victory in Europe Day' (VE Day). Diary entries all over the world describe people going crazy in the streets on May 8th, honking car horns, shouting, waving handkerchiefs or hats, and flying streamers and confetti. After all this, our happy couple celebrated their wedding in typical 1945 Canadian style.

It took place in Mount Pleasant United Church, Vancouver. Harold's parents, Alice and Edward, and Louise's sister, Varina, attended. Having just travelled to the Coast the previous winter to enjoy a warmer winter and visit their daughters, Wilbur and Gertie couldn't afford the trip again. Gertie later told Louise she cried all day on her wedding day, wishing she was there.

Similar to any other that year, the bride wore a knee-length blue dress—something she intended to wear again. Like many with good intentions of that time, she never took it off the hanger again after that day until their fortieth anniversary to show guests. The same goes for her sturdy, serviceable walking shoes, although she skirted some practicality by choosing white.

The wedding supper of a modest meal in a restaurant for the few guests passed in quiet conversation. The three-tier wedding cake, for the sake of austerity, had two false layers formed out of cardboard, covered with icing. When the couple tried to cut it, someone called out,

"Make a wish, Harold!" Harold quipped, "I wish I could cut this cake."

Louise planned a honeymoon of a few days in Victoria and Lake Louise, an extraordinary expenditure at a time of post-war austerity gripping the world. Memories of her earlier vacation with Betty prompted her to want to share the experience with her new husband, although Harold secretly wished only for his bed at home.

The happy bride moved into her husband's childhood home carrying all her belongings in two suitcases. She told herself that as a married woman, she'd never teach again. She must enjoy working at home. I can easily imagine my mother as a young bride telling herself she must settle down and be happy as a farmer's wife, all the while crossing her fingers and squeezing her eyes shut, hoping she could do it.

6.
❁ On Holiday from War ❁

On Sunday, September 10, 1939, Louise wrote in her diary, "Canada declared war on Germany." She doesn't comment on how she or anyone felt about it. The day carried on as any other. Her friend Betty got a ride with the mail truck and stayed overnight. The next day, they went to Sunday School, played tennis on the court behind the school and attended church at Jumbo Hill with friends in the evening.

On September 19, 1939, she wrote, "War news terrible. Russia in fight now," and on November 11, "Armistice and war going on!" reflecting on the irony of a world celebrating the WWI peace treaty of 1918 while embroiled in war a second time. With WWI given the moniker "the war to end all wars", everyone realized the irony when WWII erupted. While old folks glanced sideways at each other, remembering the disasters and hardship of WWI, young people looked forward to adventure and possibilities afoot. The Depression began a tortuous crawl back to a semblance of normality. The glowing promise of higher wages in uniform, packaged up with a chance to learn a new skill at government expense as well as the exciting offer of free travel to far-away lands attracted many to enlist. Louise's brother, Mac, a poor Saskatchewan farmer, learned to fly during his service and everyone hailed it as the chance of a lifetime.

Ignoring the war in the summer of 1940, Louise and Betty added sparkle to their subdued life as a teacher and went on holiday to Vancouver and Victoria. Most considered their trip a very exciting and luxurious adventure. People rarely traveled except to the nearest lake.

Ah, summer! Today, it's a time for Canadians to free themselves and travel while the weather cheers the soul with warmth. Many enjoy a local lake for respite, but no lake saw these two girls that year! These fearless travellers were single, working and saved for an escape to the Coast—two wild and crazy gals, footloose and fancy free!

Their trip differed from a holiday today from start to finish. Today we can plan a trip in a matter of minutes online, but back then, it took months. These two friends lived about 200 km apart (124 m) and long-distance phone calls cost money. They wrote letters. At one time, they both lived near Evesham, Saskatchewan where they became good friends in school. Although both were adults by 1940 and working, Louise and Betty lived with their parents. Stamps cost three cents each and delivery took one day.

Once they agreed on the trip, they travelled to a train station to research departure times and fees. Air travel didn't become popular in North America until the fifties. These two valiant voyagers took the train. Neither girl owned a car, so even travel to the station required some planning since they'd have to arrange a ride. With departure times confirmed, they wrote more letters back and forth until they agreed on a date.

Louise wrote a long letter home from Burnaby where they stayed with family friends who once lived at Evesham. She asked her parents to save her letter as she wanted to preserve it as a diary, and it appeared in her box of diaries when she gave them to me.

In Calgary, Betty met her at the station where their holiday began. They booked rooms at the YWCA and went to a movie called The Leading Citizen, about which Louise wrote, "it is similar to *Helen of the Old House*. We got 2 peaches and some white grapes that night to eat before going to bed."

They kept a close count of their spending: "We had breakfast at The Platter: toast, jam, coffee for 15 cents."

With a free day in Calgary before catching their train to Vancouver, Louise phoned a friend of Gertie's, Mrs. H. Mack who, with her husband and three children, took them "all over Calgary. As we went, Mr. Mack told us the value of all the buildings. He thinks of things in terms of $ and ¢. Mr. Mack made me value conscious."

No doubt their hosts meant to impress and entertain the young women with the size and design of the houses, but Louise only felt annoyed and bored, which didn't improve when they returned to the Mack home. Her dry sense of humor peppered her account: "The children played duets and separately. They take swimming lessons too, at the Y but didn't demonstrate. Before Mr. Mack took us to the station, we had ½ lb. of ice cream each with strawberries, cake and cookies. She invited us to come back on our way home. We don't expect to."

The trip through the mountains was a first for both of them: "In many places, it is a vertical drop straight down. The CPR has great faith in the mountains and rocks. We had dinner in the dining car for the experience. We found out it's the service is what we paid for. The waiter does everything but eat the meal and he stands near and follows diligently with his eyes each bite as it is taken into the mouth and sent to its destination."

At Kamloops, Louise sent a telegram to Mrs. Loury in Vancouver, informing them of their arrival time so they could meet them at the station. Telegraph offices were in railroad stations for public use at a fee. Transmitted by electricity using Morse code, the operator printed the message by hand on a form. Boys delivered telegraphs to the recipient's home. When they arrived, telephones prompted cheers of delight and sighs of relief for their convenience over the telegraph.

This is the same Mrs. Loury who loaned Wilbur and Gertie the one hundred dollars for Louise's training at Normal School. When she loaned them the money, she and her husband lived in Regina, but by 1940, they lived in Vancouver. While reading this diary, I wondered if Louise carried in her suitcase the repayment of the loan or if she had already reimbursed them.

The Lourys met them at the station and took them to their new apartment—so new, they were the only tenants in the building. The young travelers, on the spur of the moment after seeing the apartment, arranged with them to stay there instead of a hotel and "pay them for their trouble." I wonder if, right at the outset, the intrepid vagabonds already worried about their money not lasting through the trip.

Over the next days, they visited many friends from home. Vancouver beckoned all prairie dwellers as the go-to place for anyone wanting a change of lifestyle. Young people went "to the coast" if they could afford it, to attend university and seniors retired there. Many discouraged farmers escaped west hoping for more lucrative work and an easier life. Louise recorded visiting school friends from Senlac, others from Normal School and some of their parents' acquaintances. Mrs. Loury hosted an "Evesham Reunion" at her home to give everyone a chance to connect with them.

The women also took time to be proper tourists, travelling to the ocean for picnics and sight-seeing. "<u>That</u> was our first smell of salt water," she wrote. The ocean held special interest for these prairie daughters, going every day to a new beach or tourist spot.

"We went to First Beach. We could see the new Lion's Gate Suspension Bridge from there." Officially named First Narrows Bridge, it opened in 1938, connecting the city of Vancouver with the cities of North Vancouver and West Vancouver over Burrard Inlet. Carrying three reversible lanes controlled by signal lights, it was a toll bridge until 1963 to help cover building costs.

She included a postcard of the HRSS Princess Marguerite, the boat they boarded for the crossing to Victoria, and a postcard of the Empress of Japan stating, "Empress boats go to other countries; Princess boats do not go far from the mainland."

"Victoria is quiet compared to Vancouver," she wrote. "It is known as the windy city of the Dominion." They visited the Observatory at Saanich and Butchart Gardens.

She remarked how everyone asked about her brother, Mac, then in training. This reminder of impending war sobered their excitement.

At last their trip approached its end and on their way home, she wrote, "We stopped for a very pleasant week of sight-seeing, hiking, and resting at beautiful Lake Louise." I wonder if this trip to Victoria and Lake Louise is what caused her to plan the same trip for her honeymoon five years later.

Snacking wasn't a part of travelling as it is today. Louise doesn't mention snacks on the train or ferry. Snacking while travelling didn't become popular until the sixties, or the importance of drinking water.

A common difficulty while travelling that persists throughout history is running short of money. The difference between travelers of today and those of the forties is no credit card existed to rescue them. While only half-way through their trip, in her long letter home, Louise asked her parents to send money. It's not known if Wilbur and Gertie had any available to send.

After leaving Victoria, the women exercised every form of austerity to stretch their dollars. Of their Lake Louise visit, they stayed in a room over a "cheap restaurant until our money ran out." On their last night in Lake Louise, Betty bought an apple for her supper. Louise told her, "I'll be fine once we reach Edmonton as I can borrow from my sister, Varina. She's working there now." Their return tickets guaranteed their trip home.

Varina met them at the station in Edmonton and blurted out, "Am I glad to see you! I'm flat broke!"

Somehow, they survived.

7.
❧ Married Bliss ❧

On their first morning home from their honeymoon, Harold and Louise slid down off the moon and faced into the bright glare of reality. Years later, Louise stopped me at her door, on my way home after a visit, to describe a sudden vivid memory of those blushing, newly married days. We'd been reminiscing about Harold, now passed away but in the same visit, I tried to explain problems developing with my marriage. I think it was my attempt to inform her of my own troubles that brought forward this memory for her.

"After breakfast on our first day back on the farm after our honeymoon, I brought out my Bible. I said to Harold, 'Let's have devotions.' My parents didn't have devotions, but I imagined how I wanted my marriage to play out. Harold stood from the table and said, 'Never bring that book out in my house again,' and marched outside for chores."

As she related this memory to me, she described how shocked she felt, and as I listened, it had a similar effect on me. The man she described didn't sound like the same man I grew up with, and I wondered how to make sense of this memory. He had passed away by the time and couldn't defend himself.

Knowing my father's carefulness with all things of a sensitive nature, it must have been a shock to him too, seeing he'd react in that way. We all react in unexpected ways under stress. However, knowing my mother's habit of exaggeration, I wondered if I could believer her. As I drove home that day, I tried to imagine how this scenario might play out, if indeed, it was true.

Louise loved to travel and Harold, an incurable introvert, followed her through every vacation with an iron smile welded across his face. After this first trip together, only the second in Harold's life at the time, I think he must have craved a quiet sojourn in his own territory: the house, the barn and fields. His father taught him that Bibles symbolized an ignorant, gullible belief in airy promises from an institution that only wanted to take your money.

I could imagine him thinking, 'Yes sir, I've tolerated enough over these last weeks through the wedding and honeymoon. Now I must set things straight as master of this home.' He didn't know it yet, but things never resembled his single life again.

After calming down, I think he might have returned to the house, sat down again and spoken to his young wife with gentler words.

"I shouldn't have told you never to take it out," he'd say. "You can do what you like with it. Living with my dad though, well, he never allowed it and we never went to church or... prayed at home. Dad never put stock in church or..." waving a hand at the black book still laying on the table "any of that. I understand your parents are regular church-goers, so... I guess you had a different life."

His words may not have stopped Louise's tears—they seldom did—but at least a crack in the door had opened. She could read her Bible whenever she wished. Given the best she could hope for as a 1945 woman in her husband's home, she took it at face value and hoped for more in the future.

One might wonder, over the two years they dated, why they didn't talk about faith but I think, in their youthfulness, they assumed something about the other. Harold's family never discussed religion except in derogatory terms, so if serious discussion should take place, it fell to Louise to broach it, and she never considered it necessary until that day when it forced itself upon them. Her family never discussed religion either; it lived among them as an everyday part of life.

Louise knew Harold's family never went to church, but she may have assumed the scarcity of services in the wide prairie or the constant busyness of farming prevented them from attending. Church counted as a staple of life for most, as did school. While building a new community in pioneer days, after the home, a school and church took the next most important priority.

She also hadn't realized the quiet man she'd promised 'to love and obey' had such a hot temper. Absorbing the shock of it in her kitchen that day, she realized she had taken some things for granted about him. Her Bible remained unopened that morning and for several mornings after, but there came a day when it served as a great comfort to her and she needed to return to the regular habit of reading, meditation and prayer, often petitioning on her husband's behalf. Now came the work of every marriage.

After a few weeks, she told Harold she wanted to give thanks for their meal and he nodded, waiting in silence while she repeated her favourite lines. "For what we are about to receive, may the Lord make us truly thankful. Amen."

Over time, he began joining her, closing his eyes and bowing his head while she prayed.

It may seem strange to some why his own daughter doesn't know how his faith developed, but my family never discussed God or faith. I can only surmise, but I think probably his education in faith developed through music. After Harold and Wilbur wrestled Louise's piano out of her parents' home into their own, she often played after supper. Hearing the music, Harold stood behind her and sang. He renewed a love of singing he had found as a boy in school and he appreciated the chance to continue it. Pianos in homes stood as the same common fixture as computers do today.

The young pair found companionship through music. They enjoyed songs like "Good Night, Ladies" and "Little Brown Jug" along with spirituals such as "How Great Thou Art" and "It Is No Secret." He sang for the joy of singing as he remembered doing in school and gave it his all. He never learned to read music and sang by ear. Louise played a new piece while his eyes travelled over the words and then he'd know it.

As a farmer, the words of "In the Garden" rang true to him and it became one of several favorite hymns:

> I come to the garden alone, while the dew is still on the roses
> And the voice I hear, falling on my ear,
> The Son of God discloses,
> And He walks with me, and He talks with me,
> And He tells me I am His own, and the joy we share as we tarry there,
> None other has ever known.

Any farmer has risen in the morning, tramped across the yard and stopped to look in awe across the east field at the glowing pink and bronze horizon, perhaps thinking, 'Look at that! There has to be a God to make a sunrise like that!' Harold may have spent many hours in prayer while working in the fields. In later years, he needed to pray for very good reasons. Indeed, through those days, God may have walked and talked with him many times while he worked alone in his garden.

It's probable they didn't attend the sporadic church services while living on the Clear Range farm. Their move to the new farm outside Marwayne gave them a fresh start in several ways. It's likely Louise's parents invited the young couple to join them in church. By then Wilbur and Gertie lived right in town and at the end of their street sat St. Andrew's United Church. The McLeans attended regularly and took an active part in all its events. Harold gained a friendly respect for Wilbur for his steady support of them and success as a farmer, making it easy to accept the invitation.

Perhaps Reuben Johnson encouraged them as well. He and Irene attended the same tiny edifice as Wilbur and Gertie. Having bonded as friends through farming, the Johnsons and Hathaways visited together often over a meal. When the Reuben first sat down at the Hathaway table, he may have spied Louise's piano and asked if she played. She'd nod and asked if they'd like to sing after they'd eaten, to which the Johnsons happily agreed. Learning of Harold's love of music, Reuben likely asked him to sing alongside him in the choir. Here was a man of faith, wishing to share a love of music with no criticism—just a simple welcome. This was not the reception that Harold's father taught him to expect from church. He appreciated Reuben's friendship and embraced the prospect of singing.

While in the services, he might have learned to see church as a prominent part of the community, one in which he could contribute. There, he could stand with friends and neighbours, enjoy the music and feel welcome and needed. In the congregation, he saw Andy and Janet Ferguson, their nearest neighbours. On the other side stood Earl Grey with Frances, Garth Midgley and Ollie, and Roy Pinsent, a lifelong bachelor. All sang together and bonded as friends.

> Blest be the tie that binds our hearts in Christian love;
> The fellowship of kindred minds is like to that above.
> We share our mutual woes, our mutual burdens bear;
> And often for each other flows the sympathizing tear.

The Hathaways attended church for sixty years or more. The minister's teaching seeped into their souls, melting and remolding Harold, like softening snow that turns hard earth to pudding. For Louise, it nourished the seeds already sprouted in her heart.

In 1951, Louise gave Harold a Bible for Christmas and he still had it when he died in his eighties—still like new, unread. She wanted him to know the same comfort she enjoyed from her Bible, but his faith grew from his life outdoors in God's creation and while listening and singing in church, not from a book as remained her habit.

Sometimes, Louise asked Harold to lead the prayer at mealtimes and he always gently declined. In his senior years, something inspired him to say a whispered "Amen" after she gave thanks. For him to take part even this much triggered others to look up with wide-eyed surprise. All his life he refused to discuss religion and in reply to these curious expressions, he only looked back without apology, maintaining a reflective, reverent countenance. Whatever caused the change, whether slow like the growth of a Manitoba maple or a jolt of heat like lightning in a storm, he refused to say. Perhaps the event emerged too personal, or beyond his lexis to describe. He let the visible change speak for itself. After all he'd survived by then, faith no longer seemed something to mock, rather had become his lifeline.

> There is no night, for in His light you'll never walk alone.
> Always feel at home wherever you may roam.
> There is no power can conquer you,
> While God is on your side.
> Just take him at his promise; don't run away and hide.

God won my father by inches. His brash arrogance toward religion quietly reshaped into a quiet commitment to church and faith. Respect for others and God's environment became the basis of his life. He served in the church choir, on the church board, and as an all-purpose repairman, donating time and resources to keep both the building and the assembly going. His temper remained his nemesis until the day he lost almost everything important to him.

From beginning to end, he remained considerate and respectful toward women, especially his mother and his wife. Never again after that first day on the farm did he speak to Louise with harsh words.

For the rest of her life, Louise read her Bible often, but alone.

8.
❀ Walking the Clear Range Farm ❀

Sometimes Harold and I walked the Clear Range Farm—that old place nestled in the school division of the same name, that place of my father's natal home. Walking it remained his favourite thing to do in his senior years. Someone else owns the land now. No one lives there anymore; cattle grazing is its only use, although we rarely even saw cattle on it.

I parked on the approach and turned off the car. Harold pulled himself out and approached the barbed wire gate. Someone had tightened the top loop and put a new one on the bottom. Other times, we walked through and closed it behind us even though we never saw cattle there. This time, the new loops gripped the gate so hard, we climbed through the wires of the gate instead of trying to open it. No problem. He pushed a middle wire down with his foot and pulled the above strand up, making a space for me to put a leg in and duck through. I did the same for him.

The two rows of trees standing guard on the east and west ends of the wide yard remained ever faithful soldiers, giant poplars on the east and Manitoba maples on the west. They swept the sky, brushing away the dust-coloured clouds. As ever, Harold looked at the trees and the distant bushes lining the horizon and said, "When I was a kid, no trees grew here at all and a person could see to the ends of the earth. Mother planted the lilacs beside the porch."

I've learned some pioneers planted lilacs by the kitchen door in memory of a lost baby. Harold's mother lost a few babies in miscarriage. She told Louise one day in her senior years but never gave a number. Although I said nothing to Harold on that warm, windy day, I now view those lilacs with a sense of sadness.

We approached the house, grey and tired, relaxing into the goldenrod and buffalo beans, its sightless windows staring past the lilacs that surged higher every year against the house's east side like a green and purple wave crashing against a jagged cliff. The chimney Harold rebuilt when he and Louise married still stood at attention. The decrepit house lowered herself a little more every year like an old woman settling into her chair, gripping her cane, the warm and welcoming prairie holding out its arms to receive her. Peeking in a window, we saw how the floor of the tiny living room sank a little every year into the dirt basement where years ago, jars of canned fruit and vegetables stood in rows on shelves against the dirt walls.

Through a break in the floor, I spied part of the dirt wall and my memory immediately jumped to a time when I rode my bike to a friend's house to play:

> Her mother asked her to go to the basement for a jar of fruit. "Would you like to come with me to the basement?" she asked and I nodded. She bent over a ring, sunk in the middle of their kitchen floor. I had seen that ring in the kitchen floor many times and never wondered why it was there. To my surprise, she lifted and pulled on the ring, opening a trap door. I followed her down a narrow ladder and looked around into the dim light that streamed down through the open trap door. She pulled a chain on a light bulb hanging in the middle of the space, and the yellow light revealed rows of shelves loaded with canned fruit and fresh vegetables. The basement smelled of fresh soil even though it had been dug a century before. We walked across the dirt floor to the shelf where we picked a jar of fruit for our snack, took it upstairs where her mother opened it and served out our portions. We sat at the Formica table and talked to her mother while we ate. I'd never been in a dirt basement before and never have been since.

~

Harold turned away and I followed, completing our circle of the house. We noticed how the low little pig shelter, once looking like a home for gnomes, had at last sighed its final breath and lay flat on the crunchy grass. The barn had long ago disappeared, its lumber taken and repurposed on other farms, and the corral had vanished too, one log at a time. The ice house, enfolded by poplar saplings and wild roses, leaned to the east, away from the wind. The hole under this little building had caved in like the lips of a toothless old man, pulling with it grass and earth so there's a dip in front of the door which hung at a crazy angle like the broken wing of an old crow. We inched open the rickety door for a glimpse in the dirt hole where once blocks of ice stood and sides of beef hung on iron hooks.

We headed out across the north pasture. As we walked, Harold's memories marched alongside us. "One year—it was after Louise and I got married—I got a letter from the government saying all this money was owed on the farm. It turns out, my dad never paid taxes on this place for as long as he owned it. What the Sam Hill!"

Stopping on the rise of a hummock, we watched the grass ripple away down the slope. The prairie was an ocean and we rode the waves. Harold became young again in his memories, farming the old place with a team. His musings thronged together, too many to count or name. He stood silent with his eyes on the horizon while they marched past him on parade. Once they'd dispersed, he could speak again.

"The spring of '47—we bought the new farm just right up against Marwayne and we moved over there."

They kept this part of the story hidden in their hearts. Neither of my parents ever disclosed many details of that troubled time, but knowing their personalities and the nature of their relationships with others in this scenario, I can imagine how it might have played out. I can see a picture of that fateful day in 1946 when Harold and Louise first learned of Edward's secret debt and how they absorbed it:

> Harold returned from picking up the mail at the Bellcamp Post Office. Tossing the few letters on the table where Louise waited with a pot of tea and two cups, he turned back into the porch to hang up his coat and hat. Then he took his place at the table. They looked to see what the outside world brought into their quiet corner. A few letters from family and friends greeted them, but also one with a government stamp on the return address[6]. Louise looked at the address and passed it to Harold who took it, shrugged and pursed his lips. He opened his pocketknife and slipped the blade under the flap.
>
> Before reading, he cleared his throat but read in silence.

Louise glanced up from her letter to study his face.

He frowned. "What the Sam Hill," he said in a low tone. His eyebrows pushed together to form deep furrows between them. He read it again. Louise watched his eyes slide back and forth across the page, then finally held out her hand.

He passed it to her and watched her face while her eyes cast across the paper, then stopped at the spot in the middle where the dollar figure stood out, thumbing its nose at them. She put the paper down and their eyes met.

"What do you make of that?" he asked.

"Your dad must have never paid the taxes, it looks like," she cast down at the paper again.

He leaned back, looking out a window to the fields. "I guess it means we'll have to pay that before the sale goes through."

"It's got a lien on it, so I guess so," she said as she looked at him.

"Heaven help us! Where will we find the where-with-all to pay all that and stay alive?"

Louise shook her head, looking down again. Her thoughts went to the Clear Range schoolhouse down the road. She once taught there, then went to Lea Park School but resigned two years ago, never imagining she'd teach again. She thought of the young girl now pacing the rows of desks, peeking over students' shoulders at their work at that very minute while she and Harold sat in their kitchen with their thoughts churning.

"I could sell cream," Louise offered. "And butter." Their second child made his presence known with morning sickness.

Harold pushed his chair back. "He never said... He never told me this would be coming down the road. How long did he think he could keep this quiet?"

Louise shook her head. "I suppose he never told your mother, either."

"No, probably not. Well, that takes the cake! They sat at our wedding there and I was at their house chewing the rag and I talked to him about buying this place. He never owned up to this. We've been left holding the bag! We could lose our shirt over this."

"He wouldn't have wanted to admit it, I suppose."

Harold looked at the floor, shaking his head. "That money I was saving for a new tractor," he sighed. "It'll go to this now." He looked at her. "And I'll separate the cream and make butter.

He's my dad. I'll pay his debt. I just wish he'd been on the level with me." He pushed on his knees to stand, feeling old. He slapped on his hat and swung out the door.

That evening, as they settled again at the supper table, their conversation continued. They'd both formed more thoughts since the first shock burned off a little.

"I'll have to work tooth and nail until it's paid off," his low voice reflected the embarrassment he felt. "Right to the bitter end."

"I could ask Daddy… for help," she looked down at the table.

"No! Your dad should not be put over a barrel to cover my dad's debt. That's not right." A thick finger poked the table. "No, it stops here."

"I wonder who we can talk to about this," Louise put forth. "If we talk to the bank… but you know… I don't think we should tell anyone. They'll think it was us who caused this. They wouldn't understand your dad did this. So many people liked him, and your parents still have friends here. They'd never believe he could do this and then just leave."

"Yeah. Most people here are vaccinated with a gramophone needle. They're already talking a blue streak about other folks. We don't need to give them a new fodder from this corner, that's for darn sure."

A story of back-breaking struggle is told by the land titles for the Clear Range Farm, first in Edward's name bearing the year 1913 and then Harold's, dated 1947. Edward's title looks like a crazy quilt, patched with stamps representing loans on the farm—or liens. Some state he paid the loan; others remained owing until Harold paid them.

A loan dated 1933 from the Agricultural Relief Advance Act has a lien placed on the land in 1936. Harold's title shows he paid this lien in 1947.

A 1927 mortgage taken out by Edward plus taxes owing appears on Harold's title as paid in 1948, the same year Harold sold the land to the Veterans' Land Act (VLA).

Enacted in 1942, the VLA gave ex-servicemen the chance to buy land, helped by a government loan. So as not to overburden these veterans and help them succeed, they had choices for repayment. Encouraged to pursue small rural holdings worked as part-time farmers, veterans realized a second income or a supplement to their livelihoods with gardens and small numbers of livestock.

Harold and Louise always told family and friends they sold the Clear Range farm to Jim Hardstaff, but there's a problem with this account. The "Hardstaff Family" story in *Echoes of Marwayne Area* states, "Jim joined the Air Force during the war in 1940. He served as a cook, stationed at various training centres in Canada." Due to his war service, it's probable he took advantage of the VLA and purchased the Clear Range Farm from Veterans' Affairs (VA). However, Jim's land title states he didn't buy the land until 1962 and it seems the land remained in possession of VA in the interim. Someone must have rented it, perhaps Jim. It seems my parents were the last inhabitants of the little house with its single-pane windows and hollow walls.

When talking to friends or even their own children about the move to the Marwayne farm, Harold and Louise always gave their reason as Louise's wish to live closer to her parents. This filled part of the truth and all of a listener's curiosity.

Other explanations don't seem as logical. Harold called the Clear Range Farm "the worst pile of rocks in Alberta," stating the Marwayne farm had much better soil. It's questionable if this is true. The Marwayne farm had its own share of rocks. It also didn't have a good water supply and, after a failed well, Harold had a cistern built in the basement. As a child, I loved going into the basement during a rain to hear the water running into the cistern. Rain water from the roof siphoned into it, giving us lovely soft water for washing. Later he had two dugouts excavated east of the house with the necessary plumbing installed to bring water to our taps. By contrast, the Clear Range farm had two wells, providing ample water. Their reasons for moving seem reasonable until a closer look pulls back the curtain on actual evidence.

Neither Harold nor Louise ever told anyone they lost the Clear Range Farm, but the land titles reveal their true experience. Their assertion that they sold the Clear Range farm to Jim Hardstaff simplifies the details of a problematic situation. Harold's title shows he sold the farm to the VLA, so it seems reasonable the government offered a settlement whereby they would take the land, pay off the debt owing and give him the remaining money for a down payment on another farm.

Both Harold and Louise recalled their separate memories of the move to the new farm. Harold remembered Louise's dad, Wilbur, hearing about the Marwayne farm listed for sale and told Harold, who drove over and walked the land for a close look. He recalled expressing concern to Wilbur about the fields being full of weeds and Wilbur agreed it would take a lot of work to restore the land, but being first-rate soil, once he'd conquered the weeds, he'd have a profitable farm. Wilbur spoke from experience in reviving sick farms back to health during the Dirty Thirties.

Louise recalled her own misgivings when she saw the house, a squat little one-bedroom shanty standing forlorn among the scrabble. Its advantage over the Clear Range house lay in having insulation, but with no basement, the floors felt cold in winter. She wrote in her memoirs, "We bought the Tom Stevenson place near Marwayne in May 1947 so I had another house to clean and rejuvenate, having done the Hathaway house before we moved to the new farm."

Crushing debt and a relocation weren't their only worries. Severe hail storms and early frosts peppered the decade of 1946 to 1955. Thinking of those post-war years when it seemed like the weather declared war on farmers, Harold said, "We kept our noses to the grindstone." I was fourteen when my father exclaimed how good it felt to have the mortgage paid off at last on the Marwayne farm.

Our circular walk of memories neared its end on the Clear Range Farm that windy summer day. Approaching the gate where the car waited, he told me, "Later on, we sold the Clear Range farm. We sold it in the spring of '48 and we could make it then until the next harvest."

∼

All these losses took a heavy toll, and on a farmer's income, they needed patience, endurance and determination to restore a level of security. It's unknown if Harold asked his father for help to pay off the debt, but considering their already prickly relationship, Edward's brash and arrogant personality besides his low income making barrels as a cooper in high-cost Vancouver, it's unlikely Harold ever approached him. My parents set to work, saving in any way possible, but it's doubtful they lived in any sense of comfort for a very long time.

"When you're in the basement, the only route you can take is up," he said, swinging his legs into the car.

A fresh start on the new farm and another year of crops forthcoming offered hope for a happier future.

9.
❀ Hailed Out and Knocked Down ❀

Harold withdrew a pencil from a top drawer in the blue kitchen dresser. Moving to the window, he inspected the point. Removing his penknife from his jeans pocket, he moved to the McClary stove and grasped the portable handle and fit it into the smallest of the removeable plates, lifting and setting it aside. Holding the pencil over the opening, he whittled at the point until satisfied. Returning to the dresser drawer still gaping open, he slipped out a pad of letter-sized paper and closed the drawer. Now ready to compose his letter, he cleared his throat and sat at the table, also painted blue. He'd rather pull nose hairs with a vice grip than write a letter, but he'll give it his best shot. He must touch base with his parents now that he and Louise had moved to the Marwayne farm.

With his pencil poised over the paper, he looked at the Wheat Pool calendar on the kitchen wall. Drawing in a long sigh, "Let's see, now," he poised his hand over the blank page, rubbed his forehead, inserted the date, July 17, 1947 and began:

> Dear Mother and Dad,
> We are getting used to the new place. We can go to town and do our usual business and be home again in an hour or less. The crops were looking real good until a week ago yesterday when we were hailed out on both places. We had a terrific wind with it. The wheat was just heading out and the oats were in the shot blade, but now it's shaved off clean to the ground.

Two of the granaries on the old place were smashed to pieces. The one that was moved when you were here, Dad, two of its walls are just a pile of chips. The other two walls, the floor and roof are flat, one on top of each other.

The other granary, the one that I built with the lumber I got up north with Joe Bucyko that winter, its four walls, roof and floor are spread across the field, one wall is split in two from top to bottom. The oats are starting to come up again so I guess it will make green feed. I'll till the wheat under. It's too late to be any good.

Louise and Betty Anne are fine. Mac has just stopped in on his way to town, so I'll close and ask him to post it.

Toodle love.

Love,
Louise, Harold and Betty Anne

The Local News section in the *Edmonton Journal* of July 11, 1947, reported:

> Marwayne: An electrical storm, accompanied by strong winds and hail, lashed this district for more than an hour Wednesday with 0.97 inches of rain falling.
> The rain brought much needed moisture to the area while the hail caused an unofficial estimate of 50 to 100 percent damage in a strip four miles wide. Wind damage to trees and small buildings also was extensive.

On another day of walking the Clear Range farm with Harold, I listened as usual while he talked:

> "The spring of '47 we moved to the land at Marwayne. And I had the crop in there—got the crop in with help and the crop in over on the old place too. And then, the 11th of July, it was all up—standing there nice, swaying in the wind. A big hail storm came through and mowed down everything at Marwayne. (His laugh is like a gasp.) Everything! So, the only time over on the old place when Dad had been there, he'd only ever lost ten acres of oats with hail.
> "So I thought, gosh, it's sure lucky we got the crop in over

on the old place, so I should be alright. Cranked up the ol' Model A and drove over there and before I got within a mile of that place, here the crops were all mowed down! Got over there and all the crops were mowed down and three of the old bins were blown over and smashed all to pieces. Terrific wind! Devastation!

"So, I went up north to work in the bush. I stacked trees, cleaned up, just did whatever the boss told me to do. And I had been there awhile when I got this phone call from the doctor in Lloydminster Hospital. He said, 'If you want to see your wife alive, you better come home now. She has a strangulated hernia and has a fifty-fifty chance of living.'

"So, I collected what pay I had coming to me and went home. Louise's parents were taking care of Betty Anne. Louise somehow survived and came home. I looked for whatever work I could find in town, but we had no money and Ted Rea, you know—he's married to Louise's cousin, Helen—he gave me a job at the Beaver Lumber in Marwayne. He didn't need help, but he felt sorry for me. I stacked lumber, stocked shelves, swept the floor… just did whatever he could think of to keep me busy. Later on, we sold the farm at Clear Range. We sold it in the spring of '48 and we could make it then until the next harvest."

Ted paid him fifty cents a day, about one third the normal wage. Likely he paid him the most he could afford and Harold knew it, grateful for Ted's generosity.

Louise also held those memories close. She never shared much of those days. Hail damage of 100% hit Harold hard, but its consequences knocked Louise off her feet when Harold went north for work:

"Harold going up north to work in the bush was really hard. I couldn't stand living alone on the farm. I asked my parents if I could move in with them and they weren't happy about it, especially Mother, since she believed every wife should live in the home her husband provided. She wasn't sympathetic, but I was desperate. She told me I could live upstairs, and I moved everything myself. It was the sewing machine that did me in. I don't know why I thought I had to have it. I guess I didn't know how long Harold would be away. Moving that sewing machine upstairs in its cabinet did me in… pretty grim."

A wall of muscles line a person's abdomen. When those muscles become weak or damaged, they don't hold everything inside as they're meant to do. Part of the intestine can slip through, called a hernia. Sometimes, those muscles can tighten and close in on the protruding part, becoming a strangulated hernia. In extreme circumstances, it can cut off the blood supply and constrict movement of food through it.

Louise's pregnancy entered the fifth month in July, creating a perfect storm for a hernia to develop. If she didn't already have a small hernia caused by the pregnancy, the strain of moving the sewing machine upstairs while pregnant created a more likely chance of one occurring.

Considering the strained relationship with her parents, she bore her pain in silence, possibly waiting until her condition worsened, perhaps vomiting and developing a fever. Even today, a strangulated hernia is life-threatening, so it's probable it presented a greater risk in the forties. It's also possible the doctor may not have wanted to operate due to risk to the fetus, trying instead to push the intestine back inside and then wait to see if she could overcome the infection. No medical records exist at the time of this writing. This is circumstantial and probable guessing.

It would have taken several weeks for Louise to recover from her ordeal while her parents cared for one-year-old Betty Anne when Harold went to work at the Beaver Lumber or tended to his farm chores.

With or without government aid or insurance money, by 1950 Harold and Louise remained in a desperate financial situation. The "District News" in the *Edmonton Journal* of November 25, 1950 for Marwayne reports, "T. Dowdle and H. Hathaway have gone to Slave Lake for winter employment."

Losing their livelihood took its toll. A long journey of scrimping and hard work passed before they got back on their feet. An old photo illustrates this: two little girls sit on the back step in the winter of 1950. Four-year-old Betty Anne is wearing Louise's winter boots since there was no money for her own pair. One-year-old Marilyn got Betty Anne's hand-me-downs, so she wears boots that fit her. It's a picture that, without words, describes those difficult times. The disasters of consecutive storm years left scars on their memories.

Farmers can thank the Great Depression for one thing, at least. The Prairie Farm Rehabilitation Act (PFRA) of 1935, followed by the Prairie Farm Assistance Act of 1939. Both designed by the federal government, they eased the great hardships of this time. However, an all-risk crop insurance program delivered better help, controlled by the Crop Insurance Act of 1959. Harold never forgot those hailed-out years and subscribed every year to crop insurance. The risk of hail damage haunted Louise and topped off her list of reasons for accepting the offer to teach in 1956 at Marwayne School.

If Louise had died in 1947, the three younger siblings would not have been born, and Harold and Betty Anne would have lived a very different life.

Everyone has done things they regret. Moving the sewing machine upstairs on her own while pregnant filled that role for Louise. She remained fearful of staying alone on the farm all her life and felt relieved when the kids grew old enough to take care of the cattle for the few times Harold went away, while keeping her company as well.

There will always be risks of damage from weather. A plan of action can help reduce total failure and prevent exacerbating the calamity by making wrong choices under stress. Buying insurance can reduce loss. Most important, the help and support of others forms the strength of a community in times of need.

The year 1947 hadn't finished with Harold and Louise after destroying their crops and almost taking Louise's life. It had one more disaster to throw at them of another kind, one they had to bear alone.

10.
❀ RICHARD ❀

One summer Sunday afternoon, the Hathaway family went to the Marwayne Cemetery to wander among the graves and remember those precious ones resting there. After wandering up and down a few rows together, our parents went on ahead and stopped at a small headstone. When my sister and I caught up, they turned away and walked ahead again. Marilyn and I stopped to see which grave they had just visited. I had just learned to read, and the name made me give a questioning look to Marilyn, three years older than me.

"Mom had a baby boy who died," she told me. "She doesn't like to talk about it since it makes her so sad."

And that is how I learned about Richard, his birth and death so traumatic for my parents neither of them could talk about it until thirty or forty years later.

Richard Wayne Hathaway's arrival on November 12, 1947 formed part of another kind of storm. Their poverty played a part in a way no one could have foreseen.

After Marilyn became a mother herself, Louise related the experience to her. "There was a car accident that night," she recalled, "and Dr. Cooke told the nurses that since they knew how to deliver a baby, they should take care of me while he attended to the accident victims."

In her nineties, the hours of her labour remained clear in her memory and she described Richard's birth in her family history book, *The McLean-Hathaway Story*:

Richard was born November 12, 1947, lived just a few days, and I only saw his poor battered little face once after he was born, facing upward and weighing almost ten pounds as he had gone overtime even though I had stayed in the hospital several days early. There was no ultrasound then and very few C-sections done and I was 'green'. It was a very sad time—our first. Harold, Dad (Wilbur) and the minister buried him as I was hospitalized two weeks or more, paralyzed from the waist down.

Louise's medical records have been destroyed following standard hospital procedure, so the reasons for her paralysis can no longer be stated definitely. However, a case study of a similar occurrence suggests the probable cause being *cauda equina syndrome* where the nerves exiting the lower end of the spinal column become ineffectual for a time, perhaps because of complications resulting from the epidural. The study also suggests *myelopathy,* an injury to the spinal cord caused by the nerves being pinched. The patient in this study experienced paralysis for a few days, not the two weeks as Louise recalled. Considering the year she gave birth, it's possible she endured more damage because of less medical knowledge of the staff or poorer resources available in drugs and equipment. In its final conclusions, the case study states, speaking of complications from the epidural, "neurological damage during delivery is most often caused by peripheral neuropathy from the obstetric process."

In all likelihood, Louise's temporary paralysis most likely resulted from Richard's position being face forward (occiput posterior position) as well as his large size of over ten pounds, making it a grueling and dangerous delivery for both mother and infant.

The baby born to the modern-day mother in the study showed poor physical condition and performed below par on the Apgar scale (a list of routine simple tests given to all newborns to determine their cognitive ability). Richard's death certificate states he died of seizures due to hydrocephalus—too much fluid around the brain causing pressure—so it's reasonable to assume he also showed poor response during the Apgar tests.

Richard presented severe brain damage, but Dr. Cooke's decision for him and the way he told Louise affected her for the rest of her life. His words to her still rang clear in her memory thirty years later. After holding Richard once, she never saw him again nor informed of any details of his condition. She asked the doctor if she could see the baby.

"You need to let that baby go," he said to her. "You and your husband don't have the finances needed to care for him. You need to let him go and move on with your life."

They transferred her into a private room to shield her from seeing the luckier mothers caring for their babies. For three days, she lay in bed, hearing a baby cry, sure it was Richard. She couldn't move, being helpless with paralysis, but her parental instincts to help her son and her helpless condition made her miserable and desperate. After three days, she remembered the crying stopped and someone told her Richard had passed away.

Then she had a nervous breakdown.

~

The fact the doctor decided the baby's future without consulting the parents may seem appalling today, but this happened before awareness of patient advocacy or patients' rights. Society held the general opinion that a doctor stood above reproach—almost god-like—able to make better decisions than their patients. This doctor made his decision based on the baby's condition and his understanding of the parents' financial level. Of course, that year when they were hailed out, left them in the worst financial position of their lives.

There is another aspect that may have come into play—the Eugenics Movement. Francis Galton coined the term *eugenics* in 1883, describing it as "a moral philosophy to improve humanity by encouraging the most able and healthiest to have more children". The concept of increasing a vigorous population is positive eugenics. The other side of that idea promoting the practice of sterilizing the "unfit" is negative eugenics.

Sterilization of criminals and the mentally challenged became law in the United States in 1907. Although the idea of eugenics sometimes came up in Canadian government discussions, "Alberta and B.C. are the only two provinces that enacted legislation, allowing for sterilization in the 1930s. They phased the laws out in 1972 and 1973, but the practice persists in Canada," said Dr. Karen Stote, an expert witness in the proposed lawsuit discussing the recent case of enforced sterilization of Indigenous women before they could see their newborns.

Carried to the extreme, execution of "undesirables" led to Hitler's extermination camps of the Holocaust. It's understandable that government interest in eugenics faded during and after WWII, feeling the idea had gone too far.

Euthanization of infants never became law, but verbal testimonies of some nurses of the early 20th century confirm this occurred often under doctor's orders for infants in poor health.

Ceilidh Auger-Day, a researcher of the History of Medicine at the University of Saskatchewan replied to my query for her perspective on my mother's traumatic hospital memories. The following are her comments:

> It was likely considered the right thing to do under the Eugenics Movement that swept North America between the 1880s and WWII, though much of the furor had already died down by the 1930s, especially as far as negative Eugenics goes. The late date of your mother's experience suggests too that some amount of farmland 'practicality' was at play as well, that one made choices about animals and even children based on what they could reasonably support in the future, (time and money wise). That the doctor decided for her doesn't surprise me, this being after physician professionalization but before patient advocacy or patient rights, so many doctors were in a comfortable position to call the shots. The doctor's own moral compass or feeling on the matter would certainly have been the final say during this period, except perhaps if there was strong resistance from the father (and maybe even so). That they were unwilling to actively euthanize the baby but left it to suffer also would have been consistent with the line between Eugenics (improve the human stock) and Christian morality (thou shalt not kill). That they left the baby where your mother could hear it die seems unusual cruelty for any era, especially if she clearly wanted to see the baby and was upset.

Another aspect of Richard's birth before universal health care points to no government aid available for his care. The irony that Alberta instituted a medical insurance program in 1948 just one year later must have tasted bitter for Harold and Louise, still mourning the tragic death of their son. The program might have made medical care easier to bear under their desperate circumstances. However, financial issues aside, the care of a child suffering from severe mental disabilities in the forties would have been mediocre, requiring him to be institutionalized. Richard's birth occurred at the worst possible time in history and in the harshest imaginable way.

Babies that could not be birthed easily were often delivered by forceps, ending in a high injury risk. Considering Richard's large birth weight of almost ten pounds and his anterior presentation in labour, it's an understatement his was a difficult birth. Just one year before Richard's birth, Dr. Cooke used forceps to bring Betty Anne into the world and it's probable Richard's delivery also occurred by this means, considering Louise referred to "his poor battered little face." Betty Anne's delivery resulted in the ends of two fingers caught and pinched so tightly in the forceps they turned black and fell off, leaving permanent damage.

Considering Richard's overdue birth which caused his large size of almost ten pounds and in the dangerous face-forward position, and considering Betty Anne's difficult delivery, it remains a mystery why no Caesarean section was ordered for Louise. Even without ultrasound, methods of palpitation existed to determine the baby's size and position. In her memoirs, Louise seems to imply the fault was hers that she didn't have a C-section, saying, "I was green." To think she carried guilt for Richard's death throughout her life is tragic. C-sections were common in those days.

Dr. Cooke's summation of Richard's poor health and death created guilt for Harold and Louise, adding to it their inadequate finances to provide proper care for him. There may have been additional circumstances surrounding this tragedy, but I think Dr. Cooke didn't react with nefarious intent, but only acted within his understanding of the power of his position at the time. Nevertheless, to realize one of their children died in part due to their poverty must have been a terrible burden. Louise's decision never to see Dr. Cooke again declares loud and clear her feelings on the matter. She and Harold saw Dr. James Hemstock for all their subsequent health needs and named their second son James in his honour for his honesty, respect for them, and compassionate care.

Today, we have more understanding of the mourning process. Following the doctor's orders, Louise saw Richard only once and not at all after he passed away. Between his birth and death, no one informed her of the status of his health, following the doctor's advice to forget about him. Today, family members can sit with the body of a deceased loved one if they wish, acknowledging this is an important step in the grieving process. They also receive counselling, but the general feeling of those days asserted, "get over it and move on." Louise and Harold and many other grieving parents of that time struggled to recover their loss as best they could on their own, often carrying guilt and remorse throughout their lives, as did Louise.

It's uncertain how long she stayed in hospital for her nervous breakdown. Even before marriage, Louise occasionally experienced bouts of depression, writing in her diaries, "DEPRESSED" in large letters across two or more day's pages. Later, with the country in its post-war recovery years, the general feeling focused on progress with the emphasis on strength and vitality, and the word 'depressed' became taboo. In her diaries of the fifties onward and in all conversation, she explained to her occasional spells in terms of feeling tired.

With the general attitude being now that the war is over, let's move on and get ahead in life, admitting someone suffered from depression pointed to a condition from which one may never recover. Perhaps she feared being seen as an unfit mother, another byproduct of losing Richard. "I just need a rest," remained all she'd say on the matter.

Harold gave Richard his name and prepared his grave. I believe Wilbur made his small coffin, having skill with wood. He made coffins for two of his own babies in the past. Harold, Wilbur and the minister totaled all the attendants at Richard's graveside service in the Marwayne Cemetery. Today one would expect Louise's mother, Gertrude, to attend, but having lost two babies of her own, perhaps she couldn't face the memories this service might resurrect. It's reasonable she used the excuse of caring for Betty Anne, and society supported this idea, believing they should protect children from the knowledge of death, even though at her young age of one year, she wouldn't remember or understand the event. Later, Harold poured a cement slab, now removed for easier grounds maintenance, but the plaque and headstone still memorialize a tragic event in the lives of an unfortunate child and two young parents.

The Marwayne News section of the *Edmonton Journal* dated November 20, 1947 states, "The infant son of Mr. and Mrs. Harold

Hathaway died soon after birth" closing the chapter on Richard's death, leaving Louise and Harold to cope with their loss alone.

∼

The year 1947, a year of sequential devastation and despair for Harold and Louise, transformed their innocence into sober maturity. Deception from Harold's dad, Edward, loss of livelihood by hail, rejection of Louise's parents in a desperate and lonely time for her, her own close brush with death from a strangulated hernia, and losing a child—five tragedies in one year—left its mark, defeating, testing, and in some ways, remolding them.

After 1947, things such as differences in views on religion no longer seemed important, and they found themselves bound together, now understanding the true meaning of the words they spoke in their wedding ceremony, "for richer or poorer, in sickness and in health". They learned to work, rejoice and grieve together, forever cementing their marriage.

11.
❀ A Big Change in Harvesting ❀

October 13, 1948

Dear Mother and Dad,
    I'm still kicking. We were glad to get your letter the other day. Yes, it's sure great to have some good fall weather so as to finish some work. I just have a half day's tilling left and I'll have all the stubble tilled. Then I'm going to go over the summerfallow with the cultivator. I'm hoping the nice weather stays awhile yet. I have a lot to do in the breaking yet.
    Mina, Jim, and Maud were here today and had dinner with us. It was the first time Maud has been here. Alex Castel has bought a house in Edmonton. They are moving about the middle of next month. They are selling all their stock and if they can't sell the place, they are coming down in the spring and put the crop in. If Harold Boyce can find some kind of a job, I don't think he intends coming back to the farm.
    Harvesting is a big change from 20 years ago, Dad, or even five years ago. Now I go out with the swather and cut about 50 to 60 acres a day. Then about 12 days later, with fair weather, we come along with the combine, old truck and three men and put it in the granary at about 40 to 50 acres a day. The twelve-foot combine can do as much in a day with three men as a 28-inch thrashing outfit which needed ten men and twelve horses.
    There are two new elevators going up in Marwayne. Federal is building a new one. It's 20 feet higher than the others and holds 50,000 bushels. The Pool is building another one. I

don't know how big it's going to be.

    Mr. McLean is in the Lamont hospital. He had an operation yesterday for rupture. Mac has started cutting brush again. He's on his last hundred acres on his own place. He broke 90 acres on it this summer.

    Well, kids, I guess I'll tune off for now and hope you're both just fine.

Toodles love.

Love,
Louise, Harold, and Betty Anne
XXX
XXX
XXXXXX

    Today's combines collect anywhere from 100 to 200 acres a day with their 34-foot wide headers for picking up the grain. In the twenties, huge teams of twenty horses pulled the first combines, but as machinery improved, twelve horses filled the bill and by 1948, Harold used a tractor. The name *combine* arose from the fact that one machine accomplished the work of cutting, threshing and separating; jobs that earlier required three machines.

    Harold mentions three men for the job because post-war combines required a man on the combine to operate its levers while another drove the tractor and a third delivered the grain from the combine to the granary for storage. He may have meant he needed three extra men besides himself, in which case a second man helped shovel grain into the granary, augers not invented yet.

    Not the round metal bins of today, granaries of the forties stood as square little shacks looking much like small houses with no windows. Some vacant houses found a new use in storing grain after having its windows and doors boarded over, but the farmer built most bins especially for the purpose.

    As a teenager, Harold worked on threshing crews in the area. As he bent over his letter that evening in 1948, the old days of threshing drifted through his mind. Upwards of ten men on a crew needed to be fed, causing a state of panic in every farm kitchen at the site of the threshing gang pulling in the yard. It took a lot of food carried out of the cold cellar to feed so many hard-working bodies.

Best described in a blog post on *Wessels Living History Farm*, "Women teamed up with neighbours to feed threshers a huge noon meal, most often of fried chicken, mashed potatoes, bread and biscuits with homemade butter and jam, green beans, lettuce, peas, onions, tomatoes, ham or roast beef, pies and cakes of all kinds, iced tea, and lemonade." Dean Buller remembers the desserts. Caramel pie and chocolate pie were his favorites. That was only "dinner," as prairie people called the noon meal. Many men slept overnight under wagons or in bunk houses, also requiring breakfast and supper. Someone lit the fire in the boilers of those first tractors at 4:00 a.m., then returned to the farmhouse for their five o'clock breakfast. Gasoline powered tractors replaced steam engines in a gradual metamorphosis as fuel became easier to access and farmers saved money to purchase them.

Ten men also needed to be paid, and every farmer hoped for a bumper crop, leaving money for him after all was done and dusted. According to writer Bill Ganzel, labour costs for a threshing crew in 1921 cost the farmer between $86 to $116 a day. The threshing crew often consisted of neighbours who donated their work in exchange for harvesting their own crops, making a payment in money unnecessary.

Combines are one of the most important labor-saving inventions in agriculture. The speed and economy to complete the harvest changed the landscape of the prairies in physical and social terms. Gone were the big straw stacks on the field after the threshers finished their work. Despite the labor-saving advantage, combines reduced opportunities for neighbours to work together, building friendships and a network of mutual support. Also gone were the big neighbourhood parties held after the harvest stood secure in the bin. Six or seven families often worked together to do the threshing and separating, giving all a chance to visit while working and then celebrate together when done.

Ganzel explains, "In addition, the combine worked faster. If a wheat field, for example, averaged 15 bushels per acre, it took over 4.5 work hours to bind, stook and thresh the wheat. The same field needed 0.75 work hours with a combine. Even if you figured in fuel and repairs, an estimate calculates a farmer using a combine could cut an acre of grain for around $1.50. The same acre would cost $4.22 with a binder and thresher."

At one time, grain elevators stood proud every eight to ten miles along the railway lines on the prairies, allowing easy delivery in one day with a horse and wagon. The railway offered free land rental to private companies. Numbers of elevators peaked at almost 6,000 in the 1930s. Improved mechanization enabled hauling larger loads at faster speeds, resulting in a reduced need for so many "icons of the prairie." Elevators today hold 1 - 2 million bushels, but inland grain terminals manage millions of bushels.

12.
❁ Connecting Neighbours ❁

The next time you slip your cellphone in your pocket and walk out of your home for the day, give a nod to your predecessors who worked hard for any small advance in communication on the prairies.

In the first century or so of settlement on the prairies, the only communication for farmers with neighbours involved someone on horseback or on foot. Telephone service to the prairie provinces crept west at glacial speed, beginning in Manitoba in the 1800s. Winnipeg, Fort Garry and neighbouring St. Boniface across the river represented the gateway to the West. A telegraph operator and electrician named Horace McDougall gave Winnipeg its first telephone in 1878. Most considered telephones novel gadgets, but McDougall's forward thinking moved them to a place of serious use. He installed one in his home and one in the telegraph office so he could call back and forth. Primitive, awkward devices that worked in pairs, each communicated only with its partner, similar to walkie talkies of today. Tapping the receiver to make a noise at the other end notified the recipient of someone calling them. McDougall charged new subscribers $60 a year for installation and service.

By 1880 he sold his interest to the new Bell Telephone Company and the next year the first switchboard appeared, enabling connection between many homes within Winnipeg, then boasting 26 subscribers. Telephone lines looped from roof to roof, installing posts only when a shortage of roofs demanded it. Each person with a building used for line installation received a payment for "roof privileges."

Each office, called an exchange, over time numbered three switchboards in Winnipeg. They operated during business hours, staffed by boys. School usually ended at age fourteen when most children started working. School wasn't compulsory for any age and free only to grade eight in most areas.

Since the days of Morse code and the telegraph, boys aged twelve to fourteen worked in telegraph offices. It seemed natural to staff them on telephone exchanges, calling them "telephone men." However, the altered environment of the exchange caused problems for these boys. The new telephone exchanges, in rooms where they worked alone all day, presented a new environment from the former telegraph offices in train stations or businesses where other staff and customers milled about. It meant their only contact with people involved communication with private homes or each other over the lines. During quiet times, they got bored and amused themselves by playing pranks on each other as well as customers. Sometimes shouted arguments ensued loud enough to be heard on the streets, often ending in challenges to "come up and fight like a man".

The problem resolved by hiring women. The "voice with a smile" created a new culture of emotional attachment for customers. In the days before radio, operators supplied information such as weather, the time, hockey scores and important news. Some subscribers refused to deal with any but their own operators and sent them flowers or candy at Christmas or for a special service, such as waking them in the morning.

Bell's patent in Manitoba expired in 1883, leaving an opening for other companies to move in, creating chaos. When a company moved into a community already serviced, residents had to own a separate phone for each company. Competition incited destructive activities: linemen of one company knocked down lines or chopped down the poles of a rival. The high fees charged by Bell, as well as inconsistent service and complaints from customers, resulted in the idea of government owned telephone service. Legislation followed in 1906, 1907 and 1908.

Government owned telephone service solved one problem, but not all. The prairie's open spaces with sparse population made it expensive for governments to run wire to every farm, making them reluctant to do so. Homesteaders realized if they were going to connect with each other, they'd have to do it themselves.

As the new barbed wire fences snaked across the prairies, a second use for them arose. Farmers with an abundance of ingenuity but a shortage of cash soon discovered that the steel wire transmitted telephone signals and invented barbed wire phone lines. By ordering a phone from the Sears catalogue and a length of smooth wire from the hardware store, stringing the wire from the closest fence into their home gave them a connection to their neighbours.

One sunny June afternoon, three fourteen-year-old boys overcame the problem of their homes still not having telephone service by installing their own barbed wire setup over their summer holidays. Glen Lorenz described it this way in his recollection called "Bridging the Communication Gap" in *Echoes of Marwayne Area*:

> I think the idea of a barbed-wire telephone line was first jolted into our brains when Lew Young and I were riding home from school in the proverbial school bus and wondering just how we could keep in touch throughout the upcoming summer holidays. We were lucky to have in our grade a newcomer who knew a little more about electronics than we did, Bernard Weighill, and it was from him we gained enough confidence to tackle those two miles of barbed wire. This was the summer of 1964 and after we spliced, what seemed to be a thousand splices, in the barbed wire (to ensure conductivity), dug under roads and gates, and buried clothesline wire and sent for three old crank telephones, we were ready. Lucky thinking too, for it was now about time for Old Man Winter.
>
> It was quite a day when we shouted the first words across the wires. But like all good ideas, it still had a few bugs in it and until we got all the splices fixed, wires dug out of trees and the weeds beaten down under the wires (all to prevent short-outs) it was liable to go dead in the middle of a sentence. All in all, we were more than satisfied with its performance and I know our mothers appreciated the opportunity to talk to someone else since AGT hadn't been invented for us yet.
>
> But there was no keeping down a couple of fourteen-year-olds after initial success flushed our pride. So the next year we built a spur line, using up our third telephone, up to Asberry Fords place. Now we had a party line and if memory serves me right, Youngs was one ring, ours two, and Fords three, posted

on the front of the phones to avoid confusion.

Every good deal has its problems and the barbed wire phone line proved no exception. If a piece of wet grass touched the wire or if a bull scratched himself on a barb or laid down with his rump against it, the contact grounded the signal. Also, during a lightning storm, the phones might jangle for its duration and it has been said, a bolt of lightning sometimes shot out of the phone and across the room.

Most times, though, barbed wire lines worked pretty well for everyday purposes, but somewhere along the line (that's right, pun intended) somebody realized they'd prefer something more reliable. I'm guessing it happened the first time a farmer had to deliver his wife's baby on his own without passing out. That's when he decided he'd rather haul pig manure, pick rock in a dust storm, or deliver calves at three a.m. than stand by, watching his wife in labour ever again without medical help. Barbed wire systems appeared here and there all over the prairies. The Warwickville School division southeast of Marwayne kept their barbed wire line going until 1970. The Alguires, owners of the little country store at Alcurve, acted as a sort of central, passing on messages from the regular phone customers to the barbed wire users.

Farms in the Clear Range District where Harold grew up acquired the telephone as early as 1921 when Alberta Government Telephones (AGT) installed lines north of Lloydminster. Charlie and Irene Boyce had a phone when Louise boarded with them in the thirties, as did Harold's parents. They were the lucky ones who didn't have their phones removed during the Depression, as happened to some not able to pay their bill.

Early telephones comprised a big wooden box with a ring loud enough to wake the dead and frighten most babies and small children. Big, brown, and angular, it protruded from the wall, most often installed in the kitchen. It had a crank handle on the right and a button on the left. The earpiece rested on a hook, its cord dangling so you could lift and place it against your ear. The mouthpiece projected from the front like a miniature giraffe's head, reaching out to say hello.

A party line comprised a string of farm homes on the same road, all connected on the same telephone line. This system saved the expense of stringing separate lines to every home, but it also meant only one person at a time could use their phone. Let's say you needed help in a hurry, but Martha down the road yammered away to Stella in town. You'd lift the receiver, interrupt her account of the pigs getting into the garden by saying, "Sorry, Martha, to interrupt but I need the phone right away," and Martha, like a good neighbour, replied, "Oh sure, Dear. I'll call you back, Stella," and you'd listen for two clicks, indicating Martha and Stella had hung up. Of course, chances are, they both lifted their receivers again with the stealth of a cat after a mouse to hear all about your emergency.

The temptation to listen in on someone's call held a strong pull, too much to resist for a bored and lonesome housewife with the phone standing right at her elbow in the kitchen. Someone gave it the moniker "rubber necking" from the idea of a listener stretching their neck to eavesdrop on someone's conversation on the street. When growing up at Evesham, Saskatchewan, Louise remembered a particular lady on their line, Mrs. Smith, who loved to rubber-neck but often forgot to be discreet and joined in on the conversation, especially if the topic swam with controversy. Rubbernecking endured a risk of the party line. Those who engaged got fodder for lively conversation and giggling around the supper table.

Louise recalled the McLean's phone number at Macklin, Saskatchewan as 16-2-1. The 16 stood for the number of the party line. Living on a party line meant all phones rang when one house received a call. Code rings given by the phone company signaled which home was being called. For example, three short rings for one house, one short and one long for another and maybe two shorts and one long for a third. In Marwayne, Alberta at Harold and Louise's house, the phone number was RR707. The double R meant we were on a party line—a rural route. Our ring was two shorts and a long.

Finishing our lunch, James and I headed for the door one sunny Saturday. Our parents and sisters planned to leave soon for Lloydminster. As he and I passed the kitchen table, bearing down on the door and general mayhem outside, Louise turned from conversation at the table like an owl on her perch and faced us.

"Oh, yes! Stop a moment while I tell you something." She had just remembered a box she wanted to tick in her head. "You're old enough to start answering the phone if someone calls while we're away."

We froze in our tracks and stared. The news that we now somehow qualified to take charge of the rhinoceros on the wall never passed through our happy little heads. Furthermore, our mother clearly imagined we'd be in the house to answer it. We said nothing and listened while we adjusted to our new promotion. We soon realized the heavy responsibility that came with such a lofty elevation.

"You know our ring—two shorts and a long—so, when you hear our ring, just lift the receiver and say hello."

Fine. This much, I knew. "OK," I said and resumed progress to the door.

But wait! There was more.

"Now, if you have to make a call—if you need help and have to call Mrs. Ferguson—just lift the receiver and turn the crank one short and one long. Mrs. Ferguson is on our line—you know—and that's how you call someone on our line. That is, if you know their ring, but you already know the Ferguson's ring, so call them. They're the closest neighbours and can come over right away."

Being on a party line, we knew all the rings of the other members. We'd hear the phone ring and Louise or Harold might say, "Oh! I was just going to call the Johnsons but now I'll have to wait since someone just rang the Fergusons" … or Allens, or whoever ring sounded. Then they'd hang around, listening for the short, sharp ring signaling the call had ended, leaving the line free.

"OK," I said and took another step. Behind me, James mimicked my movements, but our mother hadn't finished with us.

"Now, if you have to call someone not on our line, that's different. Then you press the button on the side and turn the crank all the way around two or three times. Wait for Mrs. Lucas to answer. She'll say, 'Number please,' and you tell her the number you want. The list of numbers is on that paper beside the phone. Or you can just tell her the name of the person and she'll connect you."

Behind me, James said, "We can do it." He sounded as if we'd just accepted a mission to accompany Laura Secord on her mission to warn the British army of impending American attack. I looked at him. His eyes swiveled back and forth from Louise's face to the door.

I glanced across the table at the monstrosity on the wall. The once innocuous brown wooden box now scowled at me—big, hostile, and imposing. I wasn't sure I'd remember all those instructions and furthermore, that I wanted to talk to anyone on that beast. Any other time it rang, answering always fell to our parents or older sisters. I think I even saw it grinning at me.

"OK, you can go." Our mother ticked the box in her head.

We raced outside, our freshly minted passage into adulthood floated away in our slipstream exiting the door. After an hour or so, we heard the car doors slam, the car drive away, and we continued our play. We didn't make it into the house until suppertime when someone called us. The idea of listening for the phone to ring never entered our noggins. I didn't have courage to answer the phone for another year. Without doubt, I never made a call for another couple of years, probably not until after dial phones took over. No one felt more relieved to see them arrive than me.

Talking to our grandparents who lived in Vancouver remained the only time my brother and I used the big wall contraption. After our parents talked to them awhile, they'd call us over to take our turn. When we were four or five, they let us stand on a chair to move our faces close enough to the mouthpiece and held the receiver to our ear for us. "Speak louder," they reminded us. As we grew taller, we took charge of the receiver, but since we only saw our grandparents every three years, conversation remained stilted on both ends of the line. Long-distance calls cost money, rarely done. Most often, Christmas and birthdays endured the extent of it.

In cities, switchboards stood in rows in downtown office buildings, but in Marwayne and other small towns, a single switchboard stood on a wall of the operator's living room. At Marwayne in the fifties, the switchboard lived in the home of Mr. and Mrs. Lucas who shared the job. One day I went with my mother to deliver a cake which Mrs. Lucas promised to take to a church bake sale. My mother knocked on the back door while she explained to me, "Mrs. Lucas said we should just knock and go in. She's working on the switchboard and can't come to the door."

We entered the kitchen. We could see through to the living room where Marian Lucas, wearing her headpiece, turned in her chair to smile and wave while she talked to a customer. Louise placed her cake on the table and we passed through to the living room, where we sat on the couch and chatted for a few minutes. Very soon though, a call interrupted our visit and Mrs. Lucas returned to her switchboard. She and Louise exchanged goodbye waves and we let ourselves out.

Work on a switchboard afforded the ideal job for women, but if she wanted to go out, a substitute had to be called in and someone with training might be hard to find. Often the operator remained a person not seen in public very often. Working from home meant she was always available when someone wanted to make a call. In the middle of the night, she served as an important contact for help in times of emergency.

Central alerted the entire community of an emergency such as a fire with one very long ring. Hearing it, everyone lifted their receiver and listened as central stated the location and nature of the disaster. The entire community made up the volunteer fire brigade. Hanging up, they'd rush to their vehicle, throw in shovels, pails, boots, gloves and anything else needed, and sped off to help. Gunny sacks, either dry or dipped in water, beat out small run-away flames.

In the thirties, governments gave farms the option to form their own phone companies. Each area organized their own company when they felt ready to take on the responsibility and expense. In December 1934, five members, all farmers, held the first meeting of the Marwayne Mutual Telephone Company around the kitchen table on L.C. Milne's farm. They voted to buy Circuit Number 1 Rural Line and seventeen poles from AGT for $324.30. In 1936, the hamlet of Marwayne joined the company. Later, three more small enrolled, making it big enough to hire operators. Mr. and Mrs. Lucas worked from 1945 to 1963 and then Mabel Craig filled the position.

Over the years, Harold and other members took their turn as director. He served on the Bellcamp Rural Telephone board in Clear Range and after the move, served five years on the Marwayne Mutual board.

In 1967, dial telephones and underground lines replaced telephone poles with their overhead wires and the friendly local switchboard operator. Some lucky operators got positions in large centres to assist customers.

In 1989 the first cellphones arrived, enabling direct connection between individuals instead of locations. We may always have problems with our cellphone service, but it's come a long way from delivering a message by horseback.

13.
❈ Throwing Rocks at the House ❈

The clouds, like a herd of white bison, thundered over the prairie. Big, ponderous, they pushed each other forward— giant silver heads and grey bellies plunging above the farms. Had Harold seen them, he'd understand what it meant, but as they advanced, he sat in Louise's parents' home, enjoying Gertie's Canada Day meal and Wilbur's conversation, comparing each other's crops. Into the midst of this idyllic scene, the hail storm rumbled.

Someone threw rocks at the house. That's what it sounded like when the hail hit. All conversation ceased mid-sentence, like turning off a radio. They listened. More stones—sounded like someone knocking on the door.

"We'll need pillows." Gertie stood and turned to the hall in one motion. Chairs scraped as Harold, Louise, and Wilbur stood at attention. Their Canada Day meal now forgotten, food on plates, forks poked in meat, a glass tipped over. No one noticed the water dripping on the floor.

The knocking changed to a barrage of gunfire. Gertie whisked in, her arms full of pillows, passing them out on her way past the table. Each member took one and turned to a window. They stood silent, holding their bolsters against the glass, eyes closed, waiting for the attack to end. Not Louise though, standing frozen at her chair, holding her pillow. She looked at the others but couldn't move, watching them head to their stations, then collapsed back into her chair, helpless with sobbing. She had seen this movie before and didn't like the ending.

"We'll get hailed out again!" she sobbed.

Three little girls stood staring at her. For Marilyn, then four years old, this picture remained clear in her memory—seeing our mother collapse in her chair, helpless with grief while the other adults took up sentry at windows. Seven-year-old Betty Anne stood beside Marilyn, holding my hand. I was one-year-old. Baby James lay asleep in an armchair.

Hail storms were frequent and ferocious in the decade from 1946 to 1955, often causing severe damage to crops, livestock, buildings, and electricity. Eight storms of the decade appeared in the *Edmonton Journal*. On July 4, 1953, the *Journal* reported, "On Tuesday, July 1, hail lasted for thirty minutes in Marwayne. Damage to crops totaled at least eighty per cent although some fields suffered much more."

The spectators and players in the Canada Day ball games on the town's north end ran for cover. One inch of rain fell and lightning knocked out a transformer, cutting off power for twelve hours.

This scene in my grandparents' home represents a snapshot of my parents' entire lives: my father, Harold trying to hold things together, guarding his family while my mother, Louise, fell victim to herself, imagining the worst, paralyzed in fear. In earlier years, other storms like this one caused particular hardship for Louise and Harold. Memories of those storms overwhelmed Louise on this day in 1953.

On this day, I can imagine Harold standing at his window. He'd wonder how much damage the hail beat on the crops or if the cows and their calves found shelter in the open back section of the barn. He'd wish he were home.

Back then, my grandparents lived in the little prairie town of Marwayne, Alberta, calling it their retirement home, finally done with roaming from one farm to another in search of something they never found. Gertie's health steadily declined with a heart condition—time to take it easy, or that's what they called it. Wilbur still farmed one-quarter acre southeast of town. Family coming for a meal kept him home but on a normal day, he'd be out there repairing machinery or doing some rogueing—the custom of walking the crop to pull wild oats or Canada thistle—a common practice before herbicides came into use. On this July day, the grain would be half grown.

Harold worked that day too, before driving the family to his in-laws. He worked every day unless Louise dragged him away. She loved a drive in the country, an excursion to pick berries, or to drop in on someone for a visit. On Sundays, she loved to entertain at home. He preferred his solitude in the fields or tinkering with machinery in the old garage. To mollify her, he sat in the house with the friends she had invited, trying to think of something to say. Often, the guests took charge and he followed their lead. Of course, if the visitors farmed, well, that was just the ticket. He could depend on Wilbur to talk farming.

Holding her pillow against her windowpane that day, Gertie might have called Louise to take the children into the hall away from flying glass shards, but the noise of hail on the thin walls drowned her out. The old houses had meager insulation if at all and single panes of glass except in winter, with storm windows fastened to the outside. Ever stoic like her Scotch ancestors, Gertie quelled her own jumping heart into submission while she held her pillow. "Crying never helped anything."

Wilbur glanced at his daughter and wished he could stop the storm just for her. He survived enough to know life moves on after any disaster, but he hated to see his children also endure tragedy. After all, hadn't these two already suffered enough?

So when the storm receded and they lowered their pillows, maybe there'd be glass falling. Cool, fresh air might drift in and they'd hear water dripping off the roof. No doubt Harold asked, "Is it over?" glancing heavenward out his now broken window.

Louise cried for several minutes, convinced this time life had defeated them for good. Silence flooded the room as each looked into each other's faces, wondering what damage awaited them, tallying in their minds the work needed to restore everything once again.

We'll leave them standing in Gertie's dining room for the moment as they glance across at each other, listening and wondering. This scene has stories preceding it that demand a telling and others following, each offering a contrasting view, like walking around this house on the outside, looking in those broken windows, each scene offering a different observation of the same souls inside.

14.
❈ Choosing to Laugh ❈

To survive the many trials in their lives, Harold and Louise relied on their mutual love of laughter. They looked for humor in the many frustrations of life while accepting that they too, might be the object of a joke.

Once, my sister got two baby ducks and named them Harold and Louise. The next spring, an egg appeared in the duck pen. Being in about grade four, she reported this event for her "news of the day" at school.

"I have two ducks named Harold and Louise," she said, "and this morning, Harold laid an egg."

Marilyn's story travelled to the staff room where Louise heard it and brought it home to share at the supper table. Then the human Harold laid an egg, laughing so hard he lost all strength, leaning over sideways, almost falling out of his chair, with his mouth sagging open, silently laughing, taking all his strength away, leaving him gasping for breath.

In most of our family photos, Harold is talking, trying with mediocre success to make us smile or even chortle if he could be so lucky. He did it to prevent what he coined the "McLean smile." He coined the term when, while taking a picture of Louise, the former Miss Louise McLean. "Come on now, Mother, don't give us that McLean smile. Show some teeth for the camera." She remained straight-faced, either because of his teasing, or in spite of it.

At a later event and another chance to pose for the camera, Louise held her usual solemn face. It was one of those times when we sat around joking and giggling, wearing wide grins for the camera except for the former Miss Louise McLean.

"Mom, smile! You never smile for a picture!"

In cool composure, she replied, "I am smiling: I'm smiling inside."

We all hooted louder than ever and even Louise broke into a chuckle, unable to hold it in. After that, we insisted, "Mom, don't use the McLean smile. Really smile this time!"

Harold tried to crack some good corkers until she smiled just a little. "Be careful now! Don't scare the camera! All those teeth showing will make too much glare! Throw the flash away. Somebody get my sunglasses!" His corny humor helped ease the tension of Louise's constant terror of sure disaster lurking around every moment.

"Don't go near that dugout! You'll fall in and drown!... Don't walk down the train tracks! You'll be run over!... Don't go near the gulley, you'll be swept away!" We heard all of it often but sometimes, even she laughed at herself.

The time Aunt Mary visited us from Edmonton is one of those times. Mary Hathaway Hoye, Harold's aunt, came in July one year in the middle of haying season. At the lunch table, Harold told us kids to come out and tramp the hay down on the stack. Every July, he borrowed Walter Kvill's mower and hay rake. After mowing and piling it in windrows with the rake, he hoped for dry, sunny days to roast the hay to a crispy grey-green treat the cows relished in winter. On this day, the time had come to gather it with his long tines, attached on the tractor, and pile it into a stack. When Harold asked us kids to go out and help after lunch, Louise and Aunt Mary glanced at each other. I knew they wondered to themselves what on earth they would do all afternoon to pass the time together in the house. While other conversation circled the table, Louise studied her plate in silence. Finally, her face brightened and she looked at Aunt Mary.

"How would you like to go along with the kids and help on the haystack?"

Aunt Mary looked uncertain but said nothing.

"You used to live on a farm and maybe you'd enjoy reliving farm memories again. I'll come, too. It'll be fun!"

Aunt Mary grew up on a farm outside of Lloydminster and also lived for a few years on another farm with her husband. She agreed and the matter seemed settled for the two women. They both smiled.

All us kids exchanged looks across the table. We'd never seen our mother help in the fields and we knew Aunt Mary's character was not the type to do rough, outdoor work. We saw an amusing spectacle afoot. Before us lay the curious prospect of two inexperienced women pretend to be farmers. We would not be disappointed.

Aunt Mary was a good sport. She had no "farm clothes", but that didn't matter. She always wore a dress, pretty shoes and jewelry, even to her own tiny garden in the city.

We slapped on our hats, shoved our feet into boots (rubber boots, of course) and walked to the hayfield at the end of the yard. Harold lifted us kids onto the haystack first with the front-end loader, a height of about seven feet. We were old hands at this. We were demonstrating how it worked to Louise and Aunt Mary. We stood in the loader, leaning against the blade with our hands in our pockets, showing off for Louise and our aunt from the city.

"Hang on or you'll fall off! Everybody hang on to something!" Louise called, shading her eyes with her hand.

We obeyed to ease our mother's blood pressure. Having lifted us and waited while we walked off onto the haystack, Harold lowered the front-end loader to the ground for the two women. Louise gripped the back of the fork with both hands and scanned about while Harold lifted them up. "Oh!" she gasped. He lifted them up and waited for them to disembark. Then he swung the tractor around and set off to begin picking up hay.

With every new load of hay dropped, we tramped on it. With each step, we'd sink in, forcing us to raise our knees for the next step. Goose-stepping and grinning, we paraded around on the hay, even Aunt Mary in her heels, necklace sparkling and earrings dangling. Louise called out, "Don't go near the edge! You'll fall off and break your neck!" Her hysterical warning punctuated the entire afternoon the moment she thought one of us moved too close to the verge of death.

Between loads, we sat in a circle on the stack and rested, talking, joking and sharing a snack. Our breaks lengthened over the afternoon since Harold had to go farther into the field for a full load. In one of these breaks, James broke into the conversation with, "Where's Mom?"

We looked around, mystified since it seemed she had vanished. He leaned over the edge just in time to see her red face rise up the side. She had fallen off backwards, landing on her head so fast while we passed the cookies around, no one noticed. She bruised her pride more than anything, made worse by the presence of Aunt Mary there, witnessing the spectacle. After that, Louise focused more on her own position on the stack than ours. Eventually, she could laugh over it, but at the time we kept silent as she scaled the slippery stack.

Late that summer, Louise ordered new linoleum for the dining room, the room where the heat register sat in one corner of the floor. This three-foot square sheet of iron with rows of little square holes in it allowed the heat to rise from the coal burner in the basement. I sometimes stood under it in the basement and watched through the holes at people's feet walking over my head. It allowed heat to rise to the main level.

The new linoleum arrived in the fall, but the fields beckoned. Harold installed it—except for cutting the hole for the register. Late summer arrived, preoccupying Harold with thoughts of combining and bushels per acre. A calendar page full of warm, sunny days put the coal burner at the bottom of the to-do list. Harold turned to harvesting, determined to work until the crops reposed safely in the granaries or it rained. He explained to Louise he'd cut the hole for the register once he finished the harvest. In his distracted state, he miscalculated his wife's hyperactive imagination.

The new linoleum remained over the hole, sending Louise into a continual state of panic. "Don't go in the dining room! You'll fall through that hole!"

Two routes got us upstairs from the kitchen—through the kitchen and past the bathroom, or through the dining and living room. The latter route was the one we normally took, but for the next few days, Louise skulked in the kitchen keeping watch, so we took the other way.

One Sunday morning, we all came in from church, eager to change out of our good clothes. With her mind on making lunch, Louise hurried through the dining room and—you guessed it—dropped through the hole. As she fell, her natural response made her throw out her arms, catching the sides of the hole. Her skirted ankles and church shoes pedaled air while dangling into the basement. She gasped and struggled to save herself. She didn't dare call out, and we kids had gathered in the kitchen talking, unaware of her dilemma at first until one of us, forgetting orders, walked into the dining room, saw the spectacle of Louise's head and shoulders rising out of the floor and swung back to the safety of the kitchen. The haystack fiasco was still fresh. We couldn't help her, afraid we'd burst out laughing, and for some reason, Harold had vanished. We hid in the kitchen, hands over mouths, eyes shut tight, holding back giggles.

Harold somehow found time to cut the hole and replace the register that very afternoon, restoring tranquility once again in the house and our mother's mind.

Johnny Cash's "Ring of Fire" reached its height on the radio and when we heard him crooning, "I fell into a burning ring of fire," we hooted, "They're playing Mom's song!"

Louise giggled along with us. Sometimes the best thing a person can do is laugh.

15.
❊ Empowered by Electricity ❊

We take it for granted today. Without thinking, our hands move to the light switch on entering a room. Electricity went to cities early in the country's development, but it wasn't always presumed that farms would get it. In fact, in the thirties, people assumed farms would never have it at all. Politicians felt the cost of taking it to the prairie's widespread farms when farmers had very limited finances seemed ridiculous.

Farmers also at first felt reluctant to spend money on electrification, saying they couldn't afford the new labor-saving appliances and didn't see a reason to install it. However, the increased prosperity of the fifties allowed them to look toward an easier life with electrical machines and household appliances that became commonplace.

At the time, farm women benefited the most from electrification. Prior to the fifties, women on farms worked extremely hard, carrying gallons of water to fill wash-boilers on laundry days, heating several irons on wood stoves to iron their family's clothes, and mending them by lantern light.

The first prairie province to connect farms to power, Manitoba almost completed its hookup program by 1955 to all of its 50,000 farms.

In 1949, the Alberta government had no interest in entering the power business, but the people felt electricity should be a public service to farms in the same way the province supplied telephones in the thirties. Farmers had to take an active part in overseeing their power and at last, an arrangement emerged from government meetings. From 1949 to 1953, Alberta worked with farmers in cooperatives called Rural Electrification Association (REAs) to bring power to farms. Each REA had to have at least ten farmers and raise at least half the cost of installation. The remainder could be borrowed from the bank, backed by the government.

Dick Robertson recalled in *Echoes of the Marwayne Area:*

> At that time we had quite an active Farmers Union at Durness, and after a good many meetings (we decided) to proceed with the forming of an REA, the name to be the Durness Rural Electrification Association. The cost of installation stood at $1,000 per farmer.
> Many farmers said their entire house wasn't worth that much," remembered Robertson. "Others felt it was an outrageous price just to have two or three light bulbs in their house. Many houses were wired with from two to four plug-ins, as our people never expected to have enough money to buy equipment to use them.

Electricity arrived in the Durness area in 1951, the president of the Durness REA throwing the switch at the substation south of Streamstown, Alberta changing life forever for Harold and Louise and many others. They never had power on the old Clear Range farm but had it installed at the Marwayne farm in 1952.

However, Saskatchewan, the last province to achieve power because of economic and geographic factors, has the most colourful history of its rural electrification due to the personalities involved: Father Matthew Michel and Tommy Douglas. (Novecoscky 1994)

The Power Commission Act passed in 1929, but the Great Depression, distance between farms and limited access to a water supply made it impossible to move ahead with installation. Late in 1948, before passing Saskatchewan's Rural Electrification Act, Father Matthew Michel of St. Peter's Colony exchanged his priest's cassock for overalls to bring power to farms in the Annaheim district. The successful "self-help" pilot project he initiated played a key role in the expansion of service by the Saskatchewan Power Corporation. At a time when towns and cities in Saskatchewan took electricity for granted, farmers still used lanterns to light their way at night. In the summer of 1948, Father Matthew organized a delegation to meet with officials of the Power Corporation in Regina. He so impressed Chairman H.F. Berry with his offer of local farmers to install power poles that Berry approved his plan to proceed and build Annaheim's power line.

He toiled through months of hard labour in the daytime and tedious note-taking at night. "There was no curling for me that winter," he said in a later interview. By February 8, 1949, Annaheim boasted electricity. Father Matthew and his crew of about five Power Commission men and eight local men then began the work of taking the lines to farms. The success of the pilot project in the Annaheim district inspired more line construction projects. Nineteen forty-nine remains a year of accomplishment for Father Matthew and his team.

Harold Hathaway read his newspaper every evening, keeping track of proceedings in their neighbouring province with interest. "It says here that by 1949 one percent of Saskatchewan farms had power," he told Louise, who still kept in contact with many friends and relatives farming in Saskatchewan. "It says Tommy Douglas and his CCF promise: '40,000 farms electrified in 4 years.'" Harold and Louise shared a wan smile. It meant an average of 7,000 farms to receive power each year.

After regaining leadership in 1952, Douglas wasted no time connecting farms to power speeding up the process by using aerial surveys. After a flurry of activity and political persuading, Douglas achieved his election promise, right on time in 1956. After that initial push, expansion slowed but still continued with about 1,000 Saskatchewan farms per year receiving power until 1966.

Reporting on the development and impact of electricity on farms in the fifties, Joan Champ of the Western Development Museum described it this way:

> Fifty years ago, before electricity, life on Saskatchewan farms offered little in the way of convenience, comfort or leisure time. Hardship and backbreaking chores characterized rural life. With the flick of a switch, the central yard light lit up the farmstead; electric lights shone in the farmhouse, barn and all other buildings. Radio, and later television, brought the outside world to the farm.
>
> In addition to lighting, power in dairy barns included ventilation, livestock watering systems, milking machines,

clippers, sprayers and other aids to cleanliness so important in milk production. In poultry farming, electricity was used for the automatic regulation of drinking water, the lighting of poultry houses in winter to increase egg production, feed crushing, and electric incubators and brooders.

In short, rural electrification produced a revolution on farms—one that, before its arrival, few farm families ever dreamed possible. Yet, within a few short years, the modern amenities electricity brought to the farms were taken for granted. It wasn't long before people couldn't imagine having lived without the advantages of electric power—advantages that quickly became commonplace.

16.
❧ MILTON ❧

The fifties turned out to be a decade of change for Canada and America as they emerged from two disasters, the Great Depression and World War II. The economy struggled to recover and social ideas shifted, transforming social institutions.

Milton and his siblings were orphaned during these years of change and hardship although neither of the afore mentioned tragedies caused it. Without a home or parents for a stable base must have seemed like tumbling into a sea of humanity without a boat.

Milton's father, Stanley (the Stan mentioned in Louise's diaries) was third of Wilbur and Gertie's children and Louise's little brother. Louise remembered him as good-looking but often sick in childhood. "We were disappointed several times when plans had to be cancelled because of Stan being ill," she wrote. His frail health caused Gertie to hold him back from starting school until age seven, but he seemed to thrive in subsequent years. After finishing grade twelve in 1940, he attended Alberta College and then Henderson Secretarial School, both in Edmonton. The first of his siblings to marry, he exchanged vows with Hazel, his schooldays sweetheart from Streamstown, on July 19, 1941, age 20.

Wishing to "do his bit" for the war, Stanley enlisted in February 1942, leaving behind his bride of seven months. His eyesight didn't meet the standards for a pilot like Mac as he hoped, but he served in offices in Canada, Germany and Britain. Hazel was pregnant with their first child when Stan enlisted.

Milton entered the world on July 20,1942, the same year Canada shifted into high gear in the war effort while citizens at home tired of war news, just wanting it all to end. By then, WWII groaned on through its second year. The government began showing signs of desperation, interring its Japanese citizens to refugee camps and confiscating their homes. The government passed the National Resources Mobilization Act (NRMA) in 1940 to define conscription and later repealed it, thus stirring the pot of indecision around recruitment.

The nation focused on strength and resilience, but young mothers like Hazel felt forgotten as they struggled to cope with childcare while living alone, trying to survive on their husband's paycheck, the meagre income of a new recruit. Louise reported Stan's posts in several locations: Edmonton, Trenton, Calgary and Moncton. He received Harvest Leave to return home and help his dad, Wilbur, every fall and Hazel stayed in the hired man's shack on Wilbur and Gertie's farm.

Gertie, a sturdy Scotswoman, didn't show compassion for Hazel's situation. I've seen a couple of hired men's shacks. Most had no insulation, not built for year-round living. Milton's little sister, Valorie, was born in 1944 in the Lloydminster Hospital during that time.

Loneliness and exhaustion haunted Hazel, and she moved back to Vancouver where she and Stan lived before to he signed up. In 1945, Stan received his deployment to Europe during the aftermath of peace declared. After his discharge, he took employment in real estate. Baby Ian completed the family in 1948.

No one could have predicted the tragedy of Hazel's sudden death in 1953. During this decade of change and rebuilding, no provision existed for parental support. Out of necessity to earn a living, single parents took their children to orphanages for care if no family could help. Stan's sister, Varina, and her husband lived in Vancouver and took five-year-old Ian. Not wanting to over-burden a young couple already raising their own three children, Stan took Milton and Valerie to an orphanage in New Westminster.

Just three short years later, Stanley passed away from a heart attack at the young age of thirty-four. He had just married his second wife, Peggy, one year earlier. The children lived as a family unit for a brief few months. New to her role as mother, Peggy decided she could keep one child but not three, especially considering her need to return to work. Ian returned to Varina, but what's to be done with Milton, then thirteen? It was a time when foster homes developed into the alternative for orphanages. The thought of sending him back to that life seemed too cruel in any of the family members' view.

At first, Gertie said she would keep Milton, her oldest grandchild, but like her son Stanley, she had a heart condition. No one realized her heart weakened a little more every day. Milton stayed a few days with his grandparents over Christmas 1955, giving them a true picture of the task ahead in raising him. It would be a tougher job than they expected considering Gertie's poor health. They lived in Lloydminster close to our place near Marwayne, and on New Year's Eve, Wilbur drove to their farm to discuss his dilemma and ask if they could keep Milton. They agreed, and the next day, Wilbur delivered their new charge to their kitchen door.

They made a hasty bedroom for him at the end of the L-shaped kitchen by hanging a curtain across the bottom leg of the L and furnishing it with a bed and small dresser. A curious four-year-old, I whisked the curtain aside to go in and look around. Satisfied, I came out, but Louise had seen me. She explained the space behind the curtain was now Milton's bedroom and I no longer had permission to go in. Soon after, they made a bedroom for him in the basement. He had two windows down there, a closet and a proper door—more than we younger kids had in the big, open space on the second floor. He had a pleasant room, I thought, with the furniture added and curtains hung on the windows.

Many years later, Louise told me Harold and Milton didn't get along. Harold thought any kid should pull their weight on a farm, and no consideration of the trauma this particular kid had just survived entered the mix. She remembered on Milton's first day there, Harold told him to go out and feed oats to the cows, and Milton replied, "What are oats?" Milton had lived in the city all his life.

Harold replied, "Oh for heaven's sake, don't you even know what oats are?" and thus began their turbulent relationship. Harold didn't have a good rapport with his own father so, I suppose, had no frame of reference for how to raise a boy already a teenager. His own son, just three years old at the time, had not yet revealed he might cause him a similar enigma.

It seemed to me Milton appeared almost grown up. Already very tall for his age, at my height when four years old, I suppose any teenager looked like an adult. He paid little attention to me or James. I guess in the same way I thought he towered over me, he must have thought we looked pretty little.

One evening stands out in my memories, though. He had laid on the couch and dozed off. I noticed his pant leg had moved, showing leg hair and I whispered to James and pointed. Without hesitating, James pulled up Milton's pant leg, scrubbed his leg with his hand, saying something like, "I can see your leg hair! What's all this hair doing here?" Then he pulled it down, turned to me with his hand over his mouth and we both giggled. Of course, we woke him up. He lay there, watching us and chuckling.

He became good friends with two boys from town, Eldon Giles and Johnny Bell. Sometimes these two rode their bikes down to our farm. We lived a quarter mile out of town and they whizzed around our yard on their bikes, showing off and racing. After they'd gone, James and I took out our trikes, going as fast as our little legs could peddle, pretending we were Eldy and Johnny.

Milton had a girlfriend too and gave her his dad's Air Force ring as a going steady ring. Ian later told me a miraculous story of this ring that shows the caring and honest character of this girl. Ian recalled he'd been working for an auction company in Vancouver in charge of liquidating some equipment. A young couple came in and started browsing the things on display. "The girl looked at me and said, 'Did you have a brother named Milton?' When I said yes, she said, 'I have something for you,' and she came back the next day with my father's air force ring."

One summer day, the Hathaways went to the Lea Park Rodeo—still a minor affair compared to the professional event of today. The following evening at the supper table, Milton asked Harold if he could ride one of our cows, as he'd seen at the rodeo. Like all us kids, his head echoed with the excitement and action we saw the previous day. At first, Harold scoffed at the notion, but when the idea sparked excited suggestions around the table even Louise pressed Harold, saying our cows were so tame, if he supervised, it wouldn't end in disaster. At last, he agreed Milton could try one of the milk cows since they were the tamest.

That evening, Harold led the unsuspecting cow beside the gate where Milton waited on the rails so he could slide onto her back. Soon I heard the jangling of the cow bell as she lumbered away with

Milton on her broad back, his legs akimbo and arms out for balance. He lasted a good three seconds before sliding off and the cow stopped to look back, ears flopping, trying to understand what had happened. Milton picked himself up and returned to chores, a sheepish grin stretching across his face. I don't think the rodeo ever returned to the Hathaway farm again, but it was fun while it lasted.

He started sneaking out his basement bedroom window at night to ride his bike downtown. He'd get into trouble and word always got back to Louise and Harold. Harold yelled at him in the kitchen, but to no effect. I remember one time, as we kids played in the living room after supper, Marilyn called out, "There goes Milton!" We all rushed to the window to watch him ride his bike down the lane in the dark. Even Louise stood with us, watching in silence. I think by then our parents might have felt perplexed to know what to do for him. I don't remember if that's the night he ran away.

He disappeared, and we learned he'd been sent money for bus fare to Cold Lake where his Aunt Alice lived, his mother's sister, Hazel. I remember one afternoon after that, coming downstairs to stop to stare at Harold who bent over a big metal trunk placed in the middle of the living room floor, carefully putting several things in it I'd never seen before.

"What are you doing?" I asked.

"Milton is living with his aunt and I'm sending his things to him," he said.

I looked at the things, thinking about Milton, wondering how his new life had turned out. I wondered how Harold felt about it but when I looked into his face, it didn't tell me what he was thinking. Being five, I didn't ask.

Ian and Valerie also went to live with their Aunt Alice at Cold Lake. Ian remembers Milton as a kind and caring big brother:

> "I believe he tried hard to be a big brother to me in the brief year we were together in Cold Lake. I wanted to play hockey, so he volunteered to coach a team for kids my age and he bought me a complete Detroit Red Wings uniform with skates and all the equipment. We played on an outdoor rink and travelled to other towns to play. I was a terrible hockey player, but he encouraged me.
>
> "He had quit school at that point and was working as a

laborer building the Cold Lake Air Base.

"One day, as winter was coming on, he took me to Pinsky's General Store (potbellied stove and all) and bought me a pair of deerskin moccasins out of a huge barrel there. I loved those moccasins—the way they felt—walking in the snow and how warm they were."

⁓

I don't remember hearing much about Milton in the following years. I don't know how his life unfolded, but I always felt sad for him and his siblings and the unpleasant life they must have had growing up. Later, I learned when he turned sixteen, he lied about his age and joined the navy. I wondered if he enlisted to become part of a kind of family. I wondered if he liked the navy.

It came as a shock to hear one day in 1965 when Harold hung up the phone and told us Milton had died by falling asleep in his car after he'd had too much to drink. In the blur of intoxication, he'd parked in his garage and died by carbon monoxide poisoning. He was twenty-three. I felt the tragedy of his life then and still do now. If he had lived in this century, there might have been more support for children grieving the loss of their parents. My parents might have received support while filling the role as foster parents. I'm sorry he didn't have a happier life.

17.
❊ Getting There ❊

Jim Adamson farmed in the Clear Range district close to Harold Hathaway and they worked together often for the harvest. Jim recalled those days of working with horses in the local history book, *Echoes of Marwayne Area*:

> Transportation in 1947–48 still involved horses and we had a lively pair of grey Percherons who delighted in periodically running away for no reason at all and, in the process, often completely demolished a hayrack and several hundred yards of fence-line. As I recall, Harold Hathaway had a nice little team of bays who from time to time were known to escape on their own also, but they were no match for the greys when it came to sheer destructive power.[7]

It may have been Jim Adamson's destructive greys but it's more probable Harold's own nice little team of bays motivated him to turn to machinery as soon as possible for farm work. For short distances, most often his own two feet got him where he needed to go but for longer travel, he used the team and democrat, that simple conveyance with a seat attached over a shallow wagon-style bed with four large wooden wheels. Offering no protection for the passengers, heavy buffalo robes or feather quilts covered the shivering passengers (two only) in winter. I can imagine the joy and relief when the chance for his first car arrived, a used Model A Ford.

The brilliant designer, Henry Ford, gifted the world with his first car, the Model T, built for durability and easy upkeep. Then he enamored car owners by lowering the $800 price tag at its inception in 1908 to $300 in 1925 by inventing the assembly line in his factories. These qualities made "Tin Lizzies" the car of choice for 40% of all American car owners and doubtless the same ratio of Canadians and Europeans. No longer just a possession for the rich, every family could afford a car. The Sunday drive and family vacations became popular when earlier, a rarity. Travelling no longer required time to feed and rest the horses giving people a new sense of freedom with the easier mode of travel. City dwellers rediscovered their rural countryside and farm dwellers enjoyed easier access to shopping, medical aid and entertainment.

The Model A rolled out from 1928 to 1932. The "A" had improvements over the "T," most appreciated by customers of no mechanical sense having the electric start, thus eliminating the crank and manually adjusted spark.

However, through the Great Depression, the durable "T" reigned supreme, in particular with persons of low incomes. In those desperate times, they turned many cars of all types into "Bennett buggies"—cars with motors and windows removed to enable hitching them to horses since the owner couldn't afford gas, and naming them after the prime minister of the day. The Honorable RB Bennett appeared to ignore the average person's desperate situation during that time of great hardship.

Harold didn't purchase his Model A until the 1940s, so never needed a Bennet buggy. Louise recalled him courting her in the A and he drove it until 1956. Henry Ford would be proud.

> I recall when we drove to or from town on Saturday night a part of the Model A might drop off, but Harold threw it in the back and we'd continue on our way. A sure sign of spring was the stripping down of the car to be re-assembled for another year. Never daunted, if we couldn't climb a hill going forward, he just backed down to the foot of the hill, turned the car around, and reached the top with ease, going in reverse.

By 1956, the need for a new car became urgent, but as usual, money remained in short supply. Once more, Wilbur stepped in to help. He and Gertie had just moved to Lloydminster and, in a conversation with their new neighbour, Wilbur learned she owned a car she'd like to sell. Her husband had passed away and, like most women of those days, she didn't drive. Wilbur looked at her car and recommended it to Harold.

Given the name Champion, this dark green 1950 Studebaker had the style of back doors later called "suicide doors" because their hinges fastened at the rear of the doors. The back doors opened at the centre of the car. The door would injure anyone falling out of the back seat with the car in motion and the open door swinging over them. Suicide doors went out of use in road-legal cars after instances of air currents forcing them open at driving speed.

One might wonder when anyone would fall out of a car, but in those years, everyone strove to adapt to automobiles and how best to manage a road trip. Car manufacturers focused on how to design a model that attracted customers but kept them alive. Falling out of a car happened more often than anyone with sunburned faces and ankles sporting white bobby socks liked to admit. That's just what happened to my brother, James.

We didn't own the Studebaker, yet. Good thing too, or he wouldn't have seen sundown. It's possible Harold's Model A had already died, making it necessary to take Wilbur's car or perhaps it was just a rare treat and an honour for Harold to be given the wheel in his father-in-law's 1948 Plymouth DeLux sedan. The two men took James and me along to give Louise a break in the house James was three-years old and enthralled with the push button locks, a new concept to us kids. Harold's Model A had no door locks at all.

Of course, it had no seat belts, either. The usual speed for normal driving remained around 40 mph. That's about 64 kph in metric terms; Canada still used the Imperial system then. The expression to describe someone speeding exclaimed, "Going like sixty!"

We'd taken a trip to Lloydminster to see the car for sale that Wilbur recommended. All the way into town, James played with the lock on the door beside him. Whispering to himself, he lunged forward, thumped the button down, dodged back against the seat, more whispering, lurched up, pulled up the button, and so on. Harold turned backwards two or three times, telling him to "Leave that lock alone!" James sat still for about five seconds before starting his play again.

On the way home, he continued his game. Harold had either given up reminding him or his head now churned with numbers and dollar signs after looking at the woman's car. At last, even the lock had had enough. James lurched forward, yanked on the lock, the door opened and he tumbled out, rolling and into the ditch, head over heels like a ball. He must have pushed on the lever handle.

It was a warm day meant we opened all the windows. Air conditioning wasn't a word yet, never mind an invention. Harold continued talking to Wilbur and didn't notice the drama unfolding in the back seat. The air rushing past him camouflaged the road noise from the open door. I looked out the back window at James in the ditch, then forward and called out, "Dad! James fell out of the car!" He turned onto the shoulder and ran back to James, sitting up in the weeds. I watched out the back window. Harold seemed to talk to James, no doubt checking him over for injury. He carried him back to the car, put him back in his place, went around to the driver's seat and from there turned to us, shaking his finger.

"And don't play with those locks!"

James sat in the spot Harold had placed him, white-faced and silent for the rest of the trip. I couldn't see any scratches on his face and Louise had dressed him in long sleeves and pants. I'm not sure if he had bruises or scrapes anywhere else.

The trip continued in silence until we got home. I remember Harold standing in the kitchen telling Louise what happened while James went into the living room to play on the floor. Louise stood in silence, watching Harold's face while he talked. I can't remember her checking James for scratches, but I like to think she did. No one in the family ever talked about it to my knowledge. No one ever said, "Remember when James fell out of the car?" Perhaps it was something we all wanted to forget. Anyway, new events waited just around the corner for us to live through, so why spend precious time dwelling on the past?

Harold bought the Studebaker they went to see. I was four years old but even then, I thought the dark green colour and rounded shape made it the ugliest car I ever saw. It got us where we needed to go, so for my parents, it fit the bill and looks didn't matter.

Having a newer model gave Louise freedom to travel every summer. One year we took a trip to the Calgary Stampede while visiting at the home of her friend, Betty Miller and family. On several summers we went to Evesham, Saskatchewan, her childhood home where she reunited with old friends and we drove out to the farm where she grew up so she could reminisce. The Evesham Reunion happened at regular intervals and the Hathaways always attended.

She bought a big, green canvas tent, an obdurate monstrosity requiring all six of us to put up, grunting and puffing. We camped at Whitney Lake often but also other campgrounds from Peace River to Regina and all points in between.

Cars changed everyone's life the world over. New words entered our language like *learner's permit, driver's license*, and *speed limit*.

School buses made centralized schools possible. Larger class sizes meant more and better school equipment available to more students. Motorized travel ended the need for one-room schools just down the road and nine grades taught by one teacher.

Centralized high schools remodeled the culture for young people more than any other social class. More education became easier to achieve. Young people no longer quit school at fifteen or sixteen to work and marry. The word *teenager* entered our conversations as this age group defined itself as a different stage of life between childhood or adulthood. A new culture specific to teenagers developed with a focus on sports and social activities. Words like cruising and dating became popular.

The big green Studebaker kept us rambling for about ten years. It was a great day in the early sixties when our parents, wearing wide grins, came home from a what we thought was a routine grocery trip to Lloydminster driving a brand new red Rambler, made by American Motors. It gave them modern transportation but also a sense of accomplishment—their first brand new car they had ordered—a point of pride. They began to feel freedom from the doldrums of poverty at last, in a large part due to Louise's income after she resumed teaching in 1956.

Harold never wanted to buy from the big car companies. In all his business, he tried to support a new start-up company except for the Co-op. If the Co-op sold cars, Harold would have bought from them. He did buy from Co-op Implements—tractors, a swather and combine. The German company called Deutz built equipment for Co-op Implements (CI) in Canada from the late fifties into the mid-seventies.

Before ordering the Rambler, they talked in secret together, researching the model, the features, and even the colour. Louise wanted red to make us visible in the dust she imagined hid us from other drivers, forgetting that paving made most roads almost dust-free by then. The white roof was to repel the sun's heat in our hot prairie summers. Air conditioning hadn't arrived, so keeping a car cool remained an important consideration, but white roof or not, the car still became so hot we rolled down the windows most summer days.

Oh yes, the Rambler had push-button locks on the doors. By then, James enjoyed junior high school, long past the age of playing with buttons. It also had seat belts.

Seat belts were first invented back in the 1800s but didn't come into common use until 1958. No one saw the need for them until cars rolled out with higher speed capabilities and people started wondering how to stay alive while driving. In 1966, the US invented the National Traffic and Motor Vehicle Safety Act, which mandated the wearing of seatbelts. Canada didn't follow suit until 1976, with Ontario leading the way, and then Saskatchewan in 1977. We welcomed higher speeds—only our acceptance of safety laws advanced at a snail's pace. Manitoba got on board in 1984, Alberta buckled up in 1987 and the Yukon in 1991.

"Going like sixty" went out of fashion in the fifties since by then, everybody reached that speed for normal highway driving. A 1930 Maclean's article states, "In Canada, thirty-five miles per hour is the usual maximum speed, although Quebec and some other provinces still stick to thirty miles per hour and twenty through towns and cities." By 1959, a proposed 65 mph limit in Alberta on four-lane highways would be the highest in Canada, stated in an *Edmonton Journal* of the day. By 1977, the metric system entered Canada and, while switching speed limit signs, the newly posted speed had increased. Expressions like "this fast-paced world" entered our language. Before the 1960s, no one worried about hurrying.

Louise and Harold's next car sported air conditioning, cruise control and power windows—the last Rambler my parents owned. AMC struggled to compete with the bigger car companies and folded in 1987, bought out by Chrysler. The next car came from Datsun makers. When Nissan phased out Datsun, Harold switched loyalties to Toyota.

Harold wanted a pickup for everyday farm errands for many years. It was a happy day in 1960 when he could afford both a car and a truck and came home with a '55 International Harvester (IH) half-ton. He kept it even after buying a new truck, first choosing a Ford for a few years, but returned to IH models.

Besides farm errands, the newer trucks came in handy for pulling a fifth-wheel trailer whenever Louise itched with the camping bug. The fifth-wheel offered an enormous improvement over the canvas tent, much to Harold's relief. All us kids had left home, taking with us the help needed to erect the big green monstrosity.

Harold's diligent care of his vehicles reflected his pride in them. He followed the advice in the car's manual to the letter and kept them spotless. He kept meticulous records of gas expenses, dates of oil changes and other maintenance in a little notepad in his shirt pocket. Somewhere in his life, he began buying new cars and keeping them only as long as the warranty lasted. Gone were the days of taking the Model A apart in the spring and re-assembling it for another year. The complexity of modern car design along with his advancing age put him in the position of choosing the convenience of paying a licensed mechanic instead of saving money by doing the work himself. When he passed away in 2001, his 1995 Toyota sat pristine, in like-new condition in his garage, his longest owned car since the days of the Ramblers.

A long and winding road took him from the days of the nice team of bays who enjoyed the occasional run-away jaunt to the 300 horse-power red Toyota Camry—computer-driven with automatic transmission, power steering, cruise control, air-conditioning, CD stereo, and a long list of other features. Driverless cars and other advances of today's vehicles would have mesmerized him, but he felt proud and blessed to see the changes his life revealed to him.

It is true we live in a fast-paced world compared to the way of thinking and travel of the thirties and forties. Since speed increased for vehicles, people focus more on getting there in the shortest time possible, ever striving to reduce it.

18.
❃ Finding Childcare in 1956 ❃

Finding suitable childcare when both parents worked away from home has plagued every family in history. While living in rural Canada in the fifties, it presented an almost impossible challenge. Married women didn't often work outside the home and childcare options were few. My parents faced this conundrum in 1956.

Sometime in my childhood, Louise and I had a conversation about why she quit teaching and then returned to it. "After I married Harold, I put teaching out of my mind, thinking I'd never do it again. I focused on my family and becoming a farmer's wife. Once a woman married, society thought she should never work outside the home again. People thought it was an insult to the husband's ability to support the family if the wife worked."

Even as Louise said these words, I couldn't imagine my mother spending her life doing farm work. The machinery and animals were foreign to her, in spite of growing up on a farm.

Her imagined future changed when a grade two teacher position opened in Marwayne School. At first, the school principal offered the position to Louise over the phone.

"No," she said, "I'm married now and have a family." At the time, the four Hathaway children ranged between the ages of three to ten. In addition, Marilyn would be one of her students and she didn't think it would be good for a teacher to have one of her children in her class.

Later, the principal came to the house and, while sitting in her kitchen over tea, gave her the blunt truth. "If you won't teach grade two in school, you'll be teaching it to your daughter at home, as I can't find anyone to fill the vacancy."

Now realizing his situation which also had consequences for her own daughter, Louise said she'd think about it and talk it over with Harold.

Many factors weighed on their decision. Louise enjoyed teaching and the prospect enticed her. Driving to school involved a mere quarter mile through a quiet village so even though she feared driving, the challenge wasn't too much for her. She and Harold also recalled the hailed-out years, realizing this extra income promised a financial cushion if it should happen again. They both never forgot Dr. Cooke's words that they didn't have the financial resources to care for one of their children and never wanted to hear those words again. They also had Milton living with them, a fifth child to provide for and no financial support as foster parents. The extra income shone on the horizon like the sun after a storm.

However, the care of James and I posed a problem at a time when no one asked someone outside the family to care for preschool children. The situation might have resolved easily if Louise's parents still lived in Marwayne. Perhaps she thought of this, but that option no longer remained. Wilbur and Gertie had moved into Lloydminster and Gertie's heart condition took her life in January just before the principal's visit. In earlier years, Gertie had sometimes babysat Betty Anne and Marilyn after school.

At last, our parents worked out a plan. Harold would keep us during the winter, but harvesttime loomed when he spent long days in the field. They needed someone to come to the farm during the day in fall and again for seeding in spring.

In those days, few women drove a car much less had access to one. Finding this singular jewel in a small village who also agreed to the job seemed impossible. At last, this gem appeared as a senior lady who now enjoyed a quiet retirement.

Although she agreed to the position, it soon became obvious she wished to maintain her quiet life. Her ideas about child rearing differed from my mother's, often scolding us to be quiet. She must have thought we were two little hellions. She took care of us for a short time and then called Louise one evening to give notice.

Until they could find someone else, the position fell to Harold. From dawn, he worked in the fields until eight-thirty—time for Louise to leave for school—then returned to the house for the day.

Louise came home as early as possible in the afternoon and he'd take supper with him to the field, working until late at night. Later, he described those days to me as the most exhausting of his life. "I felt like I was almost asleep on my feet."

At last, Louise hired a young girl, just graduated from grade twelve. Since she lived some distance from us and didn't drive, our parents worked out a new arrangement; she would live with us during the week and return home for weekends.

A flurry of activity filled the house while men thumped up and down the stairs, carrying boards and hammers, looking important. Louise told us to stay out of their way. She didn't need to worry. When we heard them tramping in their big boots, we jumped up from the floor and stood back, staring in awe at such noble giants in pursuit of their solemn mission.

The new bedroom occupied half the upper floor space, walled off and used for storage before the mayhem moved in. The other half opened in a cavernous space where all of us kids slept. Louise painted the new room her favourite colour—pink. Its closet alone made it the envy of us kids, even if it closed with a curtain. The room already had a door and a window, and my grandfather, Wilbur, used his woodworking magic to create little box-like shelves built into the walls. We kids admired this spectacular room and Louise hoped Catherine, the new girl, might also think the same.

At last, Catherine arrived, delivered by her boyfriend, holding one small suitcase. She entered the house, shy and quiet, and we all adored her on the spot. Considering how much I worshipped her, I think it's strange that today I don't remember how James and I spent the days with her. She must have at the very least fed us and perhaps even played with us, but none of it sticks in my memory.

I just remember her boyfriend, tall and fun-loving, coming to visit in the evenings. His visits weren't something agreed upon with the job, but Louise accepted it since finding Catherine proved to be a miracle. He positioned himself on a stool in the kitchen and joked with Catherine and my sisters as they washed dishes. He liked to tease me and, being very shy, I didn't know how to respond. I stayed out of the kitchen if he was there. One day, I forgot and ran right past him from the living room. He grabbed me as I steamed 'round the corner. Embarrassed, not sure what to do, I went limp, closing my eyes. After an eternity, he let me go. I was more careful after that, during his visits.

While all this went on, Louise marked school work at the dining room table. She must have found it challenging to concentrate.

Sometime later, as I played in the living room on a quiet afternoon, down the stairs came our beloved Catherine carrying her suitcase. I eyed her suitcase, knowing it spelled trouble. It was only the middle of the week and anyway, when she went home for weekends, she didn't take any luggage.

Louise came out of their bedroom, rounded the corner, and came face-to-face with a nervous young woman. I watched, slack-jawed and gopp-eyed. Looking down at the suitcase, then up at Catherine's face, Louise asked, "Are you leaving?"

"Yes," Catherine said in a quiet voice, turned and passed through the house. As she headed for the kitchen door, the other kids stopped and stared. The house fell silent except for the creak of the screen door. Her boyfriend drove up, she got in and we never saw her again. If Louise knew the reason for Catherine's leaving, she never told us. Once more, childcare duties passed to Harold and he worked in the fields before and after school.

The next sitter was another senior lady, Mrs. Hayes. Grey-haired and tall, she reminded me of our first babysitter. I imagined she'd be strict, and I felt apprehensive the moment she entered the kitchen door, but she smiled and talked to me in a kind way, putting me at ease. She brought knitting in an old cloth bag, I remember, but again, specific memories of our days together have floated away with time. Her kindness and gentleness to everyone remains in my memory. She took care of us until Harold finished the harvest and other times when needed.

James and I, always each other's companions, didn't take notice of, or have much contact with the adults in our lives. Louise and Harold always had work to do, and we kept busy as heroes of our own adventures. The barn, the bale stack and trees teemed with dangerous villains, raging wild animals and even outrageous and rare monsters that demanded our immediate attention. The daily business of our high adventure kept us oblivious to the real-life drama swirling around us, or the knowledge that we took centre stage to any of it.

Harold took care of us in winter, but in fact, giving us lunch remained his primary responsibility. I remember we ate a lot of Campbell's tomato soup or leftovers warmed in the frying pan. One day, he forgot to call us for lunch. We heard the noon ringing of the fire siren from town, that ritual test of the fire alarm, and continued playing, keeping an ear open for his call to come inside. After playing quite a while, I realized he hadn't called and, using my authority as the older sibling, asked James to go to the house and investigate the delay. He returned with his matter-of-fact report, "Dad forgot to call us. He's sitting at the table eating lunch. We're supposed to go in and he'll give us something."

When we entered the kitchen with rumbling tummies, even to my childhood eyes, I could see embarrassment written on Harold's face. I wonder if he ever told Louise about his mistake, but without doubt, James and I never did. We had more important things on our minds. When your life teeters every day in peril from criminals and villains, a late lunch is much too paltry to think about. It must have been one of those days when, as he described it, he almost fell asleep on his feet. It was tomato soup again that day.

Louise enjoyed teaching and taught grade two for two years. The year I started grade one, she stayed home with James, then five-years-old. When he started school the next year, she returned to teaching in grade seven this time. She taught for twenty-nine years until her retirement in 1983.

We never had a caregiver again. We kids went home from school on the bus to an empty house, never thinking our life should be different, never locking the door until the day we heard of other people doing it. Harold invented a secret hiding place for the key in the carport. If Harold was home and not in the fields, we knew he'd be in his shop repairing machinery or inventing. He always came inside for his four o'clock tea and talked with us about our day.

"Well, what did you learn in the great halls of learning today?"

"Nothing."

"Nothing! Well, I know where there're rocks needing to be picked on the back forty. At least then you'll be doing something useful!"

We rolled our eyes. "I'd rather do nothing at school, thanks."

Harold laughed.

The spectacular pink bedroom upstairs became the room of the oldest child still at home until they moved away, then transferred ownership to the next one in line. You can imagine the looks the second in line gave his or her older sibling, knowing they were biding their time until their turn in the *big bedroom* came up, unless we had overnight company in which case, we had to give it up, often sharing a bed with a sibling or sleeping on the couch in the living room.

Our mother often worked late at school until almost six o'clock and we all had our turn to make supper, starting at about age eleven or twelve. On Saturdays we all pitched in to finish the housecleaning, laundry and baking done for the week. Over the years, we became a close-knit family, working together until each chore got done. Everyone was always expected to help if someone needed it, following our parents' example as they supported each other through every dilemma.

19.
❀ Aunt Mattie ❀

Aunt Mattie's Brown Sugar Fudge

Brown sugar fudge makes a welcome gift for Christmas or birthday, reposing in an attractive container.

1 ½ cup brown sugar
1 ½ cup white sugar
3/8 cup corn syrup
Pinch salt
¾ cup whole milk
3/8 cup margarine or butter

Melt margarine in pan and then add the other ingredients. Put on range at medium heat (number 6 on dial). Bring to a rolling boil and keep at rolling boil for 7 ½ minutes or until a firm soft ball forms in cold water. Set the pan in cold water until it is quite firm. Add 1 tsp vanilla or maple flavour. Beat until you see sugaring forming around the edge of the pan. Add chopped nuts if you like and turn out on a flat sheet.

Aunt Mattie cringed to see Louise scraping a pan until almost clean when making anything. Louise always tried to save as much food as possible but for Aunt Mattie, it spoiled the look to see the pan scrapings sitting on top of the glassy smooth surface of the fudge. If you're a pan-scraper like Louise, maybe scrape it into another dish for the cook or children to enjoy. After all, you'll need a professional taster to ensure it's good enough for guests! When Aunt Mattie wrote out a copy for Louise, she added this note: "Do not put pan scrapings on top of candy."

~

Someday I hope to visit Tatamagouche Mountain Cemetery in Nova Scotia where Mattie Terry Harris McLean rests, and I will thank her for her influence on our lives. I remember the day I met her. I was five years old, colouring at the dining room table with Marilyn. My grandfather walked in with a strange lady on his arm.

"Hello, girls," he said, "I want you to meet my new wife and your new grandmother."

She smiled at us. "You can call me Aunt Mattie."

I stared slack-jawed and gopp-eyed. Maybe someone should have told me. I didn't know grandpas could remarry and without doubt, didn't know mine had done it.

"He could never live without a woman," Louise summed up her father later to a friend with cool composure.

After Gertie passed away, Wilbur found the house too quiet. She died in January 1956 and he tried to busy himself outside the house, away from memories of her. After the harvest, he felt at loose ends, not wanting to rattle around the silent house through another winter alone. He travelled to Vancouver to visit his daughter, Varina and family, but the power of home for comfort pulled him back to his natal place in Nova Scotia. He told his family he was going on holiday.

It turned out, while visiting old haunts and old friends, he also looked up old girlfriends. Rumor has it that before asking Mattie, he proposed to another former girlfriend who turned him down. No doubt she lacked Aunt Mattie's spunk. We'll never know if it's true.

Often, when Louise asked her to our farm for an overnight visit—Christmas or a special weekend—she'd respond, "I can't see any reason why not." We heard her say it often. I wonder if that's what she said when my grandfather, Wilbur, proposed. At sixty-seven years old, this was her one marriage.

She wrote in her memoirs that they planned a quiet wedding service in her home church, Tatamagouche Mountain United, with just her family and best friend as guests but the entire community felt so pleased for her happiness, they filled the church to wish them well.

Louise told me Wilbur wrote a letter from Nova Scotia to each of his children, informing them of his new wife and ordered, "You kids be nice to her!" And so, they welcomed her to the family with open arms. Of course, they were adults with families of their own. They understood his need for companionship—a partner for growing old together. Mattie's open friendliness and grace soon won everyone's hearts.

Wilbur returned to farming his quarter southwest of Marwayne and she plunged into the life of a farmer's wife with enthusiasm, not knowing much about farm living and nothing at all about farming on the prairies. She'd led a full life in the east but retired when Wilbur proposed. His modern house in Lloydminster no doubt gave her some peace of mind, knowing she wouldn't be living out in the sticks on the farm. She was too genteel for that although she would have accepted it with grace.

It broke her heart when Wilbur died just eleven months after their wedding. In her memoirs, she relates she went through a period of agonized indecision, trying to decide whether to stay in Alberta or return to Nova Scotia. She described the Lloydminster United Church women welcoming her with such warm friendship, she decided to stay—"for a while, anyway."

She had little time to grieve, however, as her own health problems arose. Her doctor diagnosed breast cancer soon after Grandpa's passing. She was sixty-eight years old, and the doctor told her she had six months to live. With her usual aplomb, she overcame the cancer and carried on for another thirty-seven years.

After her recovery from a double mastectomy, the United Church women asked her to take on a monumental task, but one in which her work in the east had given her experience. They asked her to manage the amalgamation of two women's groups within their presbytery, the Women's Association and the Women's Missionary Society. Willing to try anything she thought she could do, she seemed to think all life was an adventure, welcoming it but treating it with the greatest care.

She didn't like to talk about herself or former accomplishments. I didn't know about her life before marrying Wilbur until I read her memoirs, written at the age of 102. She began her career as a teacher at age sixteen with a Permissive License, not old enough to teach under the province's mandate of age seventeen. She didn't attend Normal School until she had already taught for several years. On her graduation, she at once accepted a position as secretary of the new Division of Rural Education, operating under the Provincial Department of Education. In this position, she learned the steps to forming a new organization.

As she recalled in her memoirs, "a much broader insight into education began for me under the umbrella of Professor DeWolfe and his assistant, Miss Dora Baker." Dr. L.A. DeWolfe is chronicled in Nova Scotia's history for his work in education reform. She worked with Dr. DeWolfe for twenty-three years. When the time came to amalgamate all the Home and School Associations across the province, her intelligence and professionalism at the first meeting so impressed the members, they voted her the Executive Secretary-Treasurer, a position she held until retiring in 1951.

Her retirement turned out to be a quick retreat. A few months later, she agreed to fill the position of Executive Secretary of the National Home and School in Toronto in its infant stage, promising to fill the vacancy for three months while they looked for someone else. She didn't leave for three years.

After all her experience in forming new organizations and amalgamating smaller groups, she became well equipped to shepherd the unification of the United Church women's groups. With her leadership, the United Church Women (UCW) took shape within the St. Paul Presbytery. A 1962 article in the *Edmonton Journal* of the title "UCW is Organized on Presbytery Level" states, "United Church Women, which at the first of the year supplanted the Women's Association and the Women's Missionary Society was organized on a presbyterial scale here recently at a meeting in Wainwright United Church where officers of the St. Paul Presbyterial were installed." At the celebration, Mattie received a charter presidency in gratitude.

She thought every task should be finished well, not fast. Louise had a different philosophy and I think these two had their silent clashes, but resolved to remain polite. While raising four children, a garden, sewing all our clothes and teaching school, Louise thought speed in housework prioritized over perfection. Aunt Mattie must have cringed at some scenes in our house, but always said nothing.

To a family meal she brought homemade after-dinner mints, so light and sweet with melt-in-your-mouth goodness, they tasted better than any store-bought version. We asked for the recipe and made them often ourselves. Her brown sugar fudge was a work of perfection—crunchy on top, soft inside. Everything she made materialized with scrupulous care—unhurried and presented in an attractive container. She made the best marmalade, taking the time to slice the fruit paper-thin. We marveled at the wonders she brought with her on every visit. These recipes are at the end of this book.

I remember some gifts she gave me at Christmas, chosen with care. I could tell she thought of me personally not choosing anything to pass for any little girl's gift. This meant a lot to me. Once she gave me a green ceramic Christmas tree, sprinkled with glitter and gold rhinestones. At about ten years old, it seemed a strange gift but I value that tree today. She gave me a gift I could appreciate all my life, not just something to entertain me in childhood. Another gift was a silver jewel box in the shape of a Dutch clog. Decorated on the outside with tulips and a windmill, lined with red velvet, I have always treasured it. I appreciate her thoughtfulness. Her gifts preceded me in my childish years, but I appreciate her wisdom and care now.

She drove east every year, either to Boston or Nova Scotia to visit family and friends, travelling alone in the little Chevrolet she herself bought. Later, she concluded that too many friends and relatives had passed away and she was too old for such a trip.

She became a great influence on us all for poise, decency and a willingness to try our best. She passed away—in tranquil dignity, of course—in her sleep at age 105, just three months short of her 106th birthday. I can imagine what that event must have looked like—God holding out his hand saying, come with me, and her reply, I can't see any reason why not. She was always up for adventure.

20.
❀ Working with Neighbours ❀

For Harold and many other farmers, working alone remained the thing he liked best about the small family farm. Louise never understood how he could stand it, but it suited him. He loved rising with the sun, making his own plans without coordinating tasks with someone else—just doing it his way—not having to agree with a co-worker. He'd had enough of that when farming with his dad, Edward.

He farmed at a time when one didn't always need money to accomplish a task. When in need, neighbours worked together, creating friendships in the bargain.

Harvest is always a labour-intensive time but, in the thirties, each piece of machinery required two or more men to operate. A binder or hay mow needed at least two men, one to drive the horses or tractor, and one to operate the implement. Threshing machines, the precursor to the combine, required a crew of many men, one for each of several tasks. Neighbours helped each other.

At age twenty, Harold worked on Matt Alsager's threshing crew in the Jumbo Hill area for $1.50 a day in the Great Depression. Matt's nephew Ted remembered, "The Dirty Thirties were tough years, but the Jumbo Hill district fared better than other, more southern areas of Alberta and Saskatchewan. Many from those areas left their farms and came north to find work."

Harold often recalled the following story which illustrates a threshing crewman's life in the thirties:

"One day, we worked late into the night and in just a few hours, morning would dawn, so rather than spend precious time walking home, I grabbed a blanket and lay down under a wagon. Soon the mosquitoes got so unbearable I made a smudge to drive them away. After just a short sleep, I awakened to learn my blanket had caught fire. Between feeding the mosquitos and extinguishing fires, I got very little sleep and morning came early."

The combine came into common use in the forties, bringing an end to the large threshing crew, but like the thresher, the cost of a combine proved prohibitive for some. Harold owned a combine and helped neighbours to finish their harvest. He helped Walter Kvill for several years, who owned a small farm. In return, Walter helped Harold with his grain harvest or haying. He picked up grain from the combine and delivered it to the granary or for haying, he stacked bales of hay while Harold drove the tractor and baler. The Kvills and Hathaways became good friends, visiting over supper in winter.

He also helped Alex Kettles, a farmer with one arm. He always spoke with great admiration of Alex's grain shoveling skill, telling us he got the job done as fast as anyone with two arms. When Alex retired, Harold bought his quarter.

For several years, Marsh Franklin, a cattle farmer, made an agreement with Harold to bale the straw left after combining. When finished harvesting a field, he called Marsh, who soon arrived with his tractor and baler. As payment for the bales, Marsh stacked a few on the field's edge for Harold's cows; an agreement of mutual benefit for both.

Sometimes, Harold had to harvest alone, running the combine until its hopper registered full, then driving it to the bin on the edge of the field to empty it. Of course, this way took longer to finish a field.

Without help to move machinery from one field to another, he made a train with the small tractor pulling the auger, wagon, and half-ton truck. The combine required a separate trip. He moved machinery in the evening when someone home from school could drive him back.

Having help during harvest held other advantages, too. With no cell phone in those days, everyone had more reason to pray they didn't injure themselves, as hours may pass before anyone realized they should have come home.

He tried to hire a retired farmer if possible—someone with experience and enjoyed a temporary return to their old life. Herb

Lafoye worked with him a few years until he moved away and then Tom Burke helped him for many years until Harold himself retired. Harold and Tom formed a lasting friendship.

When illness or an injury prevented someone from finishing their field work, neighbours made sure it got done. Everyone pitched in, doing whatever they could as still happens today.

Distance between homes, limited communication and other non-existent services in earlier days created a cooperative spirit and, while working together, many friendships formed. Farming alone is great most days, but certain times call for a helping hand between neighbours.

21.
❈ How We Spent Our Summer Holidays ❈

I sat cross-legged on the tingling grass, my hands laid palms up on my lap so the warm sun and cool breeze could work their comforting salve on them. I had just chopped down another slim poplar and now James worked at cutting it into pieces. On this day, we were into the second week of building the fort.

Earlier that July, bored and restless, I decided to go for a walk in the pasture. As I headed out, James caught up with me.

"What can we do today?" he asked.

"I don't know," I said. "I thought I'd go for a walk in the pasture and see if I can find something out there."

"I'll go with you."

The pasture gave us our own private playground where we spent many summer days exploring and playing. We enjoyed nature all around us and reveled in our adventures. On that day, near the banks of the dam we saw a poplar tree leaning over, clasped in the arms of its neighbour. A storm had left us a gift that sparked James' imagination. "We can cut down other trees and lean them against it. We can nail them on. We can call it our fort."

"That's a good idea," I said.

"I'll go home and get the hatchet and hammer and nails," he said.

"Be careful Mom and Dad don't see you," I reminded him.

Our parents wouldn't approve of us having the tools, so every day we snuck them out of the old red garage, careful no one saw us.

When we had the fort big enough to shelter them, we left them out there, making sure they were covered against dew or rain.

As I sat with my palms turned up I watched the bees and dragonflies. The clear, pungent fragrance of fresh-cut poplar added to the cleanness of the air. A crow sailed overhead, cawing out its lonesome strain. Busy sparrows in the branches overhead twittered like gossiping old women at the grocery store. Far away, a meadowlark burst with joy.

We talked in soft voices as we worked. We had no need for louder tones in this peaceful spot. The poplars laughed low in whispery voices, their leaves twirling like copper pennies on strings. The water in the beaver dam rippled in low murmurings and the duck family prattled around on the water, dabbling after water bugs and gabbling to each other in their funny, croaky voices. Once we saw a whole family of toads on their bumpy journey to new homes over the dam to the slough beyond. We stopped our work to watch—a parade of so many undisciplined soldiers—all heading in the same direction, each marching out of step with his neighbour. Jump, bumpety, hop, jumpety. We laughed.

Although we felt pride in our accomplishment, we learned the cost of our project. Blisters grew on our hands from gripping the tools hard enough to take effect. Our backs and arms ached from bending over a new-fallen tree to cut it in pieces. The hatchet wasn't very sharp, forcing us to swing it with all the strength our nine- and ten-year old arms could muster.

Surveying our progress, we thought we had quite a nice little shelter. James lay on the ground and put his head inside. Looking up for a minute, he pulled out. "Have a look," he said.

The bumpy, twisty poplars left large holes between them even though we fitted them together as tight as possible. Some spaces gaped big enough for our hands to fit through. We hadn't considered those spaces opened that big from the outside. We decided it needed clay in the spaces. It scooped like pudding from the banks of the dam, its smoothness cooling our sore hands and this work became our favourite activity.

We enjoyed the work more than the product. We loved the warm, quiet spot next to the dam, backed by the poplar bush and we felt pride in our accomplishment. Full of purpose, our labour among nature's people was our pleasure. Once finished as much as our puny muscles allowed, we lost interest in it, too old to pretend anymore and our attention turned elsewhere.

On later walks through the pasture, we came across our old fort and always took a good look, noting how nature reclaimed it, remembering those warm and pleasant days when we built it.

Today we'd be called free range kids but at the time, we just thought of ourselves as farm kids having fun with whatever came our way and almost never told our parents. Their days kept them occupied with seasonal work: haying or harvesting for Harold and gardening, canning, and sewing new school clothes for Louise.

It took us two or three weeks to finish our fort. We left in the morning, came home when Louise called us for lunch, and went out again for the afternoon. We never told anyone what we were up to and no one asked. If we had told one of our parents, in all likelihood they'd deny us the fun because of the danger of using the hatchet. As long as we turned up for meals, no one wondered how we spent our time.

I loved climbing trees and led James into adventures with the birds. Between the house and barn grew a variety of trees in a moderate semblance of order: huge black poplars dotted the yard, a row of Manitoba maples bordered the lane, the ever ubiquitous caragana hedge stood behind the house, and a group of small elms abutted the garden. My curiosity with birds led me to climb many different trees to see if eggs or babies reposed in a nest.

I often climbed alone when James was off on his own adventures. The black poplars offered perfect climbing prospects that I couldn't pass up. Some presented low branches to get me started and off I'd go, one at a time, looking for the next branch to take me as high as I dared. What a gift if a bird lighted on a branch in the same tree! I'd sit still, enjoying activity around me, smiling to myself if someone walked below, never looking up. If the wind blew as it almost always did, the swaying of the tree I sat in gave me a ride of a modest degree. If it blew with ferocious speed, I didn't tempt fate and stayed safe on terra firma. Once while sitting in the fork of a tree during a strong wind, I didn't realize my leg would be pinched between the trunk and the branch—not hard enough to injure me, but it taught me to respect the strength of both wind and trees.

My parents sometimes saw me in trees but I didn't think they knew how high I climbed or of my adventures, and I never told them in case they forbade me from continuing. One evening I had a vague feeling I had been seen in a tree. While I played in the living room, my mother's voice drifted from the kitchen. She and Harold remained at the supper table while all the children went their separate ways.

"The kids need a treehouse."

My father didn't reply right away. After a pause, Louise said, "You should build them one."

Harold still hesitated, but finally said, "I'm no carpenter." Our grandfather Wilbur had built all kinds of things for us children—small tables and chairs, a horse swing in the yard (two horse heads facing each other on a frame that moved back and forth when we "pumped it" by swaying to and fro, and he helped build many houses and barns. He had a gift with wood. By comparison, Harold must have felt foolish.

I'll never forget, to my surprise, the next day when James and I climbed down from a big poplar, turned around and saw our mother coming out of the house carrying a hammer and pail containing old nails. Work with tools quartered firmly in Harold's domain so this sight stood out as a true anomaly. She hurried out, sizing up the trio growing snug together we had just descended and said, "That would make a good treehouse." I stared in disbelief. Had hell frozen over?

She put her things at our feet and went to Harold's junk pile in the bush behind the garage, returning with boards of moderate length. "Find me some straight nails in that pail," she ordered and we set to work. It seemed to take a matter of minutes for a floor to take shape with a hole where James and I later climbed into our treehouse. She then attached walls and a ladder of three short boards nailed to a trunk. My amazement in seeing her use a hammer and the ease with which she planned and built it superseded my delight in having a real treehouse. She then retrieved a wooden box that once held Christmas oranges and nailed it inside one wall. "There," she told me, "you can put your doll dishes in there and it will be your kitchen cupboard."

We felt very special knowing she had gone to all that trouble just for us and we spent many hours in that treehouse at various forms of play that enters a child's head. Looking back, I wonder if she really did notice at least some of our outdoor play and tried to give us a distraction from climbing trees before we injured ourselves.

That night at supper, Louise set the last dish on the table and took her seat. "I made a treehouse today," she said, looking across the table at Harold. He showed the same degree of surprise as I felt earlier and after a moment, he said, "How did you do it?"

"With old boards from the garage," she answered with a matter of fact tone that told Harold he'd been a dolt for rejecting the idea. He could think of nothing more to say, and we children kept quiet as well, focusing on our plates.

If the treehouse was meant to keep us from injuring ourselves, it didn't perform as intended. I did injure myself in a tree one day and got no sympathy for it. James and I were thick in our adventure at a time when the rest of the family were away somewhere, maybe to Lloydminster for errands or taking my sisters to piano lessons.

While climbing on this particular day, I noticed a dead branch and a fleeting thought came to me that I shouldn't put my weight on it. Our imaginations occupied us and we talked as we climbed, describing new scenarios as we thought of them. We both started to descend, talking as we went. I forgot to avoid the dead branch and let myself down on it. With a crack, it let go. I was quite high up and another branch caught me across my ribcage. In one sense, I was glad the branch stopped me from crashing to the ground, but it knocked the wind out of me and a terrible pain stung across my ribs. I moaned and James grabbed my arm, pulling me to safety. I managed to tell him I had to go inside because of the pain.

The family returned and Louise entered the kitchen first. I waited at the door to tell her what happened and receive what I thought was my due sympathy and attention. The pain still burned my ribs, making me wonder if something inside me had broken.

Instead of the concern I expected, Louise walked past me, appearing not to hear me, wearing a serious face. I knew from past experience that something had happened to upset my mother and this was not the time to tell her any more bad news. My sisters and Harold then entered also wearing a sober expression and ignored me standing there. I never told anyone about my injury. My ribs hurt for about a week and I never learned what upset my mother that day.

Our play didn't always involve risk-taking. One summer we became interested in the local aquatic life and caught tadpoles with a small aquarium net bought at Fisher's Department Store in Lloydminster, dropping them in jars of water from the same water. Our mother told us to feed them wheat germ. Some lasted long enough to develop legs but some died. We lost interest in them and let them go back to the gully where we caught them. While poking around in the water, we noticed snails and scooped them up into our jars. Not as interesting as the tadpoles, they still entertained me for a time, watching them open their little mouths for the wheat germ. I soon let them go again.

After Dad had the two dugouts built, we realized the banks offered nice clay and we scooped it up in an old pail to take it under the maple trees in the yard. We had an old wooden table under the trees where we sat on old chairs or a bench to make our creations. When the sun dried them hard, we took out paints and decorated them: little dishes, vases or sculptures. All that ended when our mother decided it was too dangerous to go near the dugouts and ordered Dad to build a fence around it, then forbidding us to climb the fence when she once saw us attempt it.

On other walks in the pasture or down the train tracks, we collected different flowers and took them home to press in a big book. If we remembered to take them out a couple of weeks later, we glued them in a notebook and labelled them. Often, we forgot about them and they surprised us by falling out while working on a school assignment in winter, a reminder of warm and delightful summer days.

Even though it was the summer holidays, I never tired of books and enjoyed the interesting ones our mother put on shelves in our living room for either her use in preparing school lessons or for us to use. *The Book of Knowledge* and *World Book* held the most interest with their beautiful pictures of nature or other countries.

In spite of our mother wishing to educate us through a variety of reading material, we learned not to sit in the living room while availing ourselves of the books or magazines she supplied for us. If she saw us there doing nothing (in her view) she'd give us one of the many errands she kept running in her head. If we wanted to read, we'd go upstairs to our room. *Out of sight, out of mind* goes the expression and we learned the truth of it at a young age.

Summers brought freedom for us kids and lots of work for our parents. We enjoyed the liberty to do what we wanted without parental supervision (or their knowledge) and they made use of time alone to get as much work done in as short a time as possible.

22.
❀ Janet and Andy ❀

"You're supposed to come in the house," Marilyn told me.

"Why?"

"Mr. Ferguson is moving cattle to his field on this side and Mom doesn't want you to hear what he might say if he gets mad."

Well, now I wanted nothing more than to stay outside. In the dining room, I stationed myself at the window, watching for the Great Ferguson Cattle Drive, straining my ears for anything I could hear from the tall man wearing the big, white Stetson, riding his white steed he had the good sense to name Silver. The Lone Ranger rode into every child's imagination then and became one of the most popular television shows. Everyone knew about the masked man and his adventures chasing bad guys on Silver, his magnificent white charger. "Who is that masked man?" we heard every week at the end of each show as he rode off into the sunset. The rider of this particular Silver at Marwayne posed no mystery to anyone. Everyone knew and liked him.

The frantic calling of the cattle drowned out any possibility of hearing any questionable language. What a disappointment! What a waste of good play time outside! I never heard Andy use bad language for as long as I knew him, but it doesn't mean he didn't.

Janet and Andy Ferguson lived across the road from us. Most of Andy's farm lay to the west of their house and outbuildings, but he owned one field tucked between our land and the town on our side of the train tracks. In those days, the train chugged twice a day past our place, alongside the gravel road.

The cattle drive ended and Andy and Silver returned home for lunch. I sighed and washed my hands, resigning myself to more time wasted indoors.

Andy and Harold formed an amiable friendship, but Janet and Louise bonded in a special way two women of similar temperaments can. No longer having living parents, Louise enjoyed the friendship of a surrogate mother who gave her support and a voice of experience. To us kids, they became substitute grandparents. We shared many meals at each other's tables, in particular, birthdays and special holidays. They had one daughter, Joan, married and living at Turtleford. At ten-years-old, I thought Joan the most beautiful person I had ever seen. Perhaps I embarrassed her for staring. She was also one of the nicest people I knew. To add to my fairytale, she married her high school sweetheart, Johnny, also very handsome. They lived a good hour-long drive from us. Janet and Andy had their family, but we also claimed them as ours.

I remember visiting the Fergusons when they lived in their old house, a quaint little elf-house nestled in the trees beside their lane. People in those days didn't worry about a lawn and they had none to my knowledge until I found one behind the house. Out front, poplars crowded up to the house and their lane swung past the door. One day in summer, I went outside to play while the adults visited and surprised myself by finding a neat circle of grass at the back. An odd place for a lawn, I thought. Apparently, no one else thought much of it either, sitting forlorn under a stand of tall grass, huddled between the house and the trees.

Visits at their house lingered as relaxed affairs. While Janet made tea, Andy opened a cupboard and brought down a box of store-bought cookies. His favourites were also mine—those chocolate-covered marshmallow variety with the dot of jam inside—Viva Puffs. "I baked these just this morning," he'd say, holding out the treasures. We never had store-bought cookies at home and they made my mouth water. Still do today.

We spent many hours in that quaint little house. Mrs. Ferguson let us come over to watch TV one day when ours broke down. Suffering withdrawal from missing so many Lone Ranger, Roy Rogers and Bug's Bunny adventures, I appreciated the reprieve.

One summer, we asked if we could show Mrs. Ferguson our new kittens. After calling Janet to make sure, Louise agreed. Janet fed us her usual store-bought cookies. I felt only a little disappointed she didn't seem to care about our fluffballs of cuteness. We'd had them for just one hour—long enough to steal our hearts.

Later, I learned of her fear of cats. She had come over to visit Louise at five o'clock after school as she often did. I walked in the house in time to see my Fluffy wander up to her, smiling, purring with all her might, and holding her tail high in the air. Mrs. Ferguson watched and began drawing up her knees. Louise turned from stirring something on the stove, saw Fluffy advance on Mrs. Ferguson, and charged to the rescue. Whisking my cat off the floor just as she gathered herself to jump into Mrs. Ferguson's lap, she swung around and planted her in my arms. "Take this cat outside." Later she explained to me our neighbour's ailurophobia.

We always got Christmas and birthday presents from her and she always signed the card "From Aunt Janet and Uncle Andy." I think she preferred we called her that name, but Louise insisted we use the proper title, Mrs. Ferguson.

Mr. Ferguson may have used coarse language with his cattle, but he always practiced the epitome of decorum with people, being kind and generous to a fault. If we did a small errand for him, he paid us far more than the real value of the chore.

He never locked his door. After they built the new house out in the open on the hill, Harold warned Andy to lock his door. Andy followed Harold's advice, but left the key hanging in plain sight on a hook at the top of the door frame. He followed the old prairie philosophy that if anyone needed shelter, they were welcome to his and anything inside if they needed it.

At harvest time, he hired local unemployed men to help him, giving them his little bunk house to sleep in. Like all farmers, he kept a supply of gas in a tank in his yard from which to fill his car and tractors. One year, he noticed the level of gas often showed a lower level on the gage than it should and mentioned to Harold he thought someone might be stealing gas from him. Harold worried about this news and kept a close eye on his own gas tank. The problem continued, but always from Andy's tank, never anyone else's. Later, Janet told Louise they learned the identity of the culprits. Hearing noises in the yard one night, she and Andy stood at the kitchen window in their housecoats and slippers, watching men fill their cars with gas out of his tank. In the glow of the yard light, he recognized and named each one—some of the men he hired to help with the harvest, but he refused Janet's request to call the police, allowing them to take gas from him whenever they wished. He never spoke of it to anyone. We would never have known if Janet hadn't told Louise.

As a retired nurse, Janet filled our need as a First Response contact. When James complained for an entire morning of having a stomach ache, Louise called Mrs. Ferguson out of exasperation. It didn't take Janet long to diagnose a case of appendicitis, sending Louise into a state of panic and the house into an uproar. Louise had only called Janet in frustration, tired of James's complaining, sure he had a simple stomachache. She shouted to Harold to bring the car up to the door and wrapped James in a blanket. They whisked him off to Lloydminster Hospital where he received emergency surgery and stayed a few days.

Janet's good intentions could cause both relief and anxiety for our family. Several years later, on a sunny June day in 1970, she called me. "How are you managing at home alone?"

"Oh fine," I said. At eighteen, I felt quite comfortable staying home alone.

Then came the real reason for her call. "Your parents' twenty-fifth anniversary is coming up."

"Yes," I said, "but I don't know what I can do when Betty Anne and Marilyn live so far away."

"You could have something. Just a small party, couldn't you?"

I gulped. "I suppose so. What should I do?"

"Just make a list of friends and call them. If everyone brought something, you wouldn't have to do all the baking yourself. June twenty-third is a Saturday this year so that would make the perfect day to have it."

"I suppose so." I doubted I could manage a party by myself.

"You make a list of their friends to call and I'll think of some people. I'll call you tomorrow to compare lists."

The next day, we reviewed our lists. She named the people she would call and gave me the others. I felt as nervous as a hen on a nest of eggs but kept it all secret from my parents when they returned from their vacation.

On the morning of the party, Saturday, June twenty-third, Harold stood from the breakfast table to answer the phone. After a brief conversation, he hung up and turned to Louise and I. "Uncle Donald has passed away and there's a small service for him in Lloydminster this afternoon, one o'clock."

While they planned their trip to Lloydminster for Uncle Donald's funeral, I changed my original plan to make their anniversary party a surprise and told them. I worried they might spend all afternoon visiting others at the funeral and running errands in town. They said they'd come back as soon as they could after the service. The funeral started at one o'clock and we invited the party guests for two, so it seemed possible they could be home just in time if all went well. They left for the service at noon.

With my heart leaping into my throat, I straightened the house and set out Louise's best dishes, pulled down her big coffee perk, added water and coffee, all ready to turn on. Some early birds turned down the lane at one-thirty. I welcomed them, told them about the funeral, and invited them to make themselves comfortable in the living room. I flicked the switch on the coffee perk and boiled water for tea. With my eyes glued on the clock, I welcomed more guests and started setting cookies and squares on serving dishes.

When Mrs. Ferguson arrived, the house had filled from wall to wall with people and I circulated from kitchen to living room with a frozen smile stretched across my face. I greeted her at the door as if someone had thrown me a lifesaver.

"Hello," she purred as she entered the kitchen.

"Hello!" I said, "Am I glad to see you! I could sure use a little company and some help."

She looked startled. "Oh no," she hissed, "I'm not here to work. I'm visiting with the guests. This is your party."

I gaped as she strolled into the living room, smiling, mewing to each guest, and holding her tail high in the air. When I served another round of goodies on a tray, I found her settled on the couch between two other women, almost purring with contentment. I was grateful when another lady offered to help serve while I worked in the kitchen, even if she made a tsk noise and gave me a withering look.

Now some guests frowned at me when they saw me coming on my rounds and asked, "When will your parents be coming?"

At last, the guests of honour returned at almost three o'clock. They progressed through the house chatting with everyone and Harold made a brief speech, thanking them for coming. People started trickling out around five o'clock, time to make supper by prairie time. The house didn't empty until almost six o'clock and my head buzzed. The leftovers for supper should have tasted good, but for me, it took effort to eat with my stomach in a knot.

Life resumed in the usual way. I tried to tell myself the party had been alright, but I was never sure if my parents appreciated my efforts. The next day, Louise asked me where I got the idea to have it and I told her about Mrs. Ferguson's phone call. Later, I overheard her thanking Janet on the phone.

For all of her medical knowledge which helped many in the community, Mrs. Ferguson couldn't solve her own problems with arthritis and emphysema. She wore hard, strange-looking casts on her hands at night to keep her fingers straight. None of the pills she took for emphysema seemed to help. In her later years, she had little breath left to talk. She passed away, leaving Andy rattling around in the house alone for a few years until he joined her.

Louise and I visited the cemetery one afternoon and we stopped at Janet and Andy's graves. "I sure miss Janet," she said, pulling a few obstreperous weeds from the edge of Janet's headstone. She'd been gone several years by then, but no one else filled the empty space of lost friendship and substitute mother for her. Much as she wished Janet wouldn't drive over or phone at 5:00 when she needed to make supper, it remained one of the awkward inconveniences she permitted in order to enjoy the benefits of a close and amiable friendship.

23.
❁ Ten-year-old's Letter ❁

This letter is copied just as James wrote it, warts and all.

Marwayne, Alta
April 7, 1964
Box 123

Dear Betty Anne,
Well guess what! I'm in the Loyd Hospital. I had my appendix (part of my stomach) taken out because it was hurting very much. Mom and Dad came in with me on Sat. nite, the same nite they operated (poked around in my innards).

I have two room mates one is five year old boy named Jerry and the other is a part indian who had her teeth taken out. The nurces are all quite pretty. The first nite when I rang the bell a crabby old nurse came in and said, "there are other people in this place too, you know!!!!!"

I didn't sleep to good last nite. I guess I was walking along the halls until a nurse took me back to my bed. So they rolled bed and all to a place where they could watch me.

The hospital is quite a nice place for people walking in and talking to you when you don't even know them.

Well that's about all I can tell you.

Yours Truely
James

24.
❁ Kids and Cows ❁

"Old Dandelion came up behind you and sniffed your head. Then out came her long tongue and licked up the back of your hood. You were only about two feet tall and your little body being so stiff, packed into that thick snowsuit, you just tipped over into the snow. Dandelion just stood there staring at you. I stood you up again. You couldn't bend in that suit. It was the funniest thing I ever saw!"

This is one of Harold's many well-worn stories he called the funniest thing he ever saw. It's a prime example of our close relationship with the cows. He kept six or eight that became like big sisters to us kids. We knew their names and personalities. We walked among them as children, pushing them around, and they always moved for us. When they had a calf, we rejoiced with them, but we knew some had their grumpy side and stayed out of their way.

We knew which would hide in the pasture to give birth and who would go to the edge of the straw bed around the wagon where all the cows congregated. Sometimes a young mother came in from the pasture at feeding time, finished eating and then remembered her newborn calf she'd hidden in the pasture. We'd see a panic-stricken bossy lumber out of the gate, bag swinging, knees creaking, calling her baby. We'd open the gate again and off she'd go. Most often, she found it by herself, but sometimes we'd have to help her. Curled up in a bush like a new fawn, it waited, not having learned its mother's voice or the meaning of her frantic calling. If we found it first, we'd start pushing it toward home and call the mother. She'd shamble up, sniff it all over while grunting to it. We'd have to keep pushing them home before the calf started sucking or this trip would take forever.

Star reigned as the boss of our small herd. When she moved in for her share of hay or grain, the others gave her room. Some were her daughters, making Harold's cow-calf operation a real family affair. We gave them pretty names: Dandelion, Daisy, Buttercup, Lucky… all Herefords—good producers of both milk and meat—gentle animals for the most part. Wild Cow earned her name, but to be fair, her place at the bottom of the butting hierarchy made her skittish.

Star and Dandelion each wore a collar with a cow bell so we could hear them and know the herd's location in the pasture, or whether they happened to be coming in at end of day. They came in by themselves for their grain. If they were late, we'd stand at the pasture gate and call, "Come on!" Sometimes we'd bang two grain pails together to remind them why we called them. Soon we'd see them sauntering through the trees, heads and tails swinging, taking their time. We didn't expect the old girls to run. It wasn't a rodeo we had here; it was a family farm.

Harold milked two cows for the family's use and these old girls were tamer than the others because of the extra attention they received. During the milking, their calves went into a loose box where we'd visit them, talking to them and putting our fingers in their mouths to see if they'd suck. I didn't like doing that. They had a strong suck and sharp teeth. We never named the calves. We knew their destiny. The cows though, were family.

Each cow had their stall and when Harold opened the door, they walked in and took their place. More of a routine than precaution, he put a short chain around their necks but there wasn't much need. They came in for their grain, a nice brushing and the relief of being milked. If something made Harold late to the barn, they'd stand at the door calling him, their swollen teats spraying milk on the ground.

Milking time holds a special place in my storehouse of happy memories, a time to sit on the extra milking stool, pet a cat on my knee, and talk to Harold. Most often his replies involved "Mm-mm," "Yup" or a chuckle. Sometimes I'd brush the cows, making fancy designs on their sides or my initials.

The milk cows were the most attuned to Harold's cues. If he wanted one in the barn at an unusual time, he'd stand on her left and push on a hip bone with two fingers of his right hand. She'd turn her enormous head to look at him and he'd hold out his left arm toward the barn. She'd hoist herself on creaking legs and start off. Harold followed, holding two fingers on her hip.

Sometimes, he kept a neighbour's bull for a visit. The reason might the neighbour wanted the bull out of the way for a while or some of our cows needed his services, a compatible arrangement resulting in the happy outcome of calves gamboling among the mothers. During these visits by the big stranger, Louise warned us to stay out of the barnyard. We never knew the big fellow's personality. He might not want to be disturbed by gawky children. Harold did all the feeding chores during these visits. Other times, we kids took our turn carrying pails of chop through the throng of hungry old ladies to pour it in the troughs, then climb into the hay wagon and push bales over for them.

Artificial Insemination (AI) eliminated the need for a bull, making life safer for us kids and offered the chance to choose the sire's breed. Harold tried for a Holstein heifer, a promise of greater milk production in a future milk cow. The heifer that resulted we named Lucky—lucky she was a girl, I guess.

When Harold called the AI man, he announced to the family, "The AI man is coming today, so you kids stay in the house out of his way!" He slapped on his hat and headed out to the field. We all knew, or at least suspected Louise had asked him to relay this message to us. Harold wouldn't have cared if we went outside, risking contact with the AI man, and the AI man didn't care if we saw him.

Louise stayed in or near the kitchen all day, guarding the door. "Stay indoors today," she'd say if she caught us passing a little too close to the door. "The AI man is coming today."

I got the impression we should fear the AI man. In one sense, I was right. While on my way back to the house one day, I spied a small, red Datsun whizzing around the corner of the house, heading through the yard as if a banshee chased hot on his heels. Then I remembered the morning's announcement of the AI man coming. Being a teenager by then, I suppose the fear of the AI man was wearing thin for my mother. Somehow, I had escaped outside without being seen.

Full comprehension of Louise's fear of the AI man dawned on me a year or two later. Walking through the yard one day, I saw the little red Datsun parked at the barn and the barn door standing open. I recalled the morning proclamation of the AI man's arrival. I continued to the house, but at a point where some trees stood between me and the open door, I glanced inside.

The cow stood munching grain, surprised by the treat the stranger gave her, left in a tin can earlier that day by Harold. I watched as the AI man began his work, pulling on a long, plastic sleeve up to his shoulder and then bending over his kit for the essential equipment.

The cow relished her surprise gift in sublime oblivion of proceedings at her nether end. The man eased his arm in under her tail, it seemed to me as far as his arm could reach. Now I understood the truth behind the terror my mother held of the AI man.

Several times she told us that, although she grew up on a farm, she never saw a calf being born, never helped feed or care for the cows, and with certainty never helped with branding, a much too cruel practice for her sensibilities. Her mother, Gertie McLean, feared large animals and didn't want her children near them, in particular her girls. She recalled Gertie often told her and Aunt Bunny, "The barn is no place for a lady."

Now a mother herself, Louise struggled to decide whose opinions she should adopt, her mother's or her husband's. Gertie had passed away long ago, but Louise still wondered if she should honour her mother's sentiments while Harold felt kids should be out there working and she understood the practicality of that, too. We kids and Harold tolerated Louise's indecision and tried to satisfy her fears as much as possible. Sometimes she seemed relieved when we went outside and left her in peace. Other times, she tried to keep us hidden safe in the house.

Liz, Lucky's calf, lived up to her Holstein heritage as a good producer of milk, but with that benefit came an unpredictable personality. We learned when she was still a calf to respect her personal space, and even more so when she gave birth. Of all our cows, *bossy* described her better than any other.

One day, she rested in the loose box with her own newborn calf and I decided to have a look. Of course, I didn't go inside the box with her. I climbed the side and peeked over the top, pushing an elbow through the boards to hold me in place.

Liz and I stared at each other for a few moments. She didn't move and when I thought she'd remain calm, I turned my gaze to the calf. In a flash, she swung her head and bumped my elbow so it knocked the board above. My elbow throbbed, but I didn't want her to think she had the upper hand. I pulled my elbow in but hung on with my fingers while we continued to face each other. When I thought she understood I remained my own boss, I lowered myself to the barn floor and walked away. I had to give her credit. She could swing her enormous head with precise aim, hitting my skinny elbow clean and clear without bumping her nose on the boards. I left the barn with new respect for her skill and a pulsing elbow.

One day, the quiet farm routine faltered, upsetting Liz, but more so, Louise. It revealed the degree to which Louise had detached herself from farm life. Something prevented Harold from milking the next afternoon, and at the supper table, he asked Marilyn to milk the cow, Liz. Marilyn often helped Harold milk when two cows gave milk at the same time, she taking one while he took the other. She felt very proud of her farming achievements.

Unaware of Marilyn's ability with milking alongside Harold, Louise exploded. "Marilyn's just a little girl! She's too young to milk a great, big cow!" She squared her shoulders, "I'll milk the cow!"

Harold looked at her in disbelief, but shrugged and turned for the door. Louise sniffed and returned to her sink of dishes, the matter settled, in her mind at least, but we kids shared silent looks around the kitchen. We all doubted she'd know the first thing about milking. She hadn't been to the barn for years.

Harold had tethered Liz to a stake to eat grass between the buildings. The next evening, Louise marched out, determination in every step, carrying the milk pail. Harold may have been willing to let the matter drop, but Marilyn remained defiant. She followed behind Louise with arms crossed and chin set, feeling displaced from an opportunity to take charge. Louise retrieved a milk stool from the barn and placed it beside Liz, still tethered to the stake and now gazing with suspicion at this stranger, her ears flopping back and forth, signaling her confusion. Louise placed the stool beside Liz and sat down. Liz stepped away sideways and Louise followed, standing to move the stool and pail. Each time, Liz retreated. The two circled the stake, looking as if they'd invented a new game of leapfrog.

With arms crossed, Marilyn watched this dance before asking, "Why don't you put her in the barn?"

Exasperated and embarrassed, Louise stood, handed the pail to Marilyn. "You put her in the barn," she said and retreated to the house.

Marilyn led Liz to the barn, milked her and put her back on the tether.

In the safety of her kitchen, I can imagine Louise banging pots as she dried and shoved them in the cupboard, tossing a cloth on the counter and staring out the window. Seeing her little not-so-little girl walking to the house with a half-full pail of milk, she might have sighed and hurried out to help her. No one said anything again about a young girl being too small to milk a cow.

We always owned a dog, more for a companion and watchdog than herding cattle. Spike knew this and spent his days snoozing on the front step or following us on our adventures, never bothering with the cows. However, after old Spike died, Louise decided since we had cattle, we should have a real cattle dog.

We didn't ask why we needed a cattle dog when the cows came in by themselves. Thoughts of getting a new puppy filled our excited little heads. Louise studied the ads in the *Western Producer* and ordered a month-old pure bred border collie from a farm in Manitoba at a cost of $13.13. He arrived by COD in a crate on the train on Friday, July 13, 1961.

"I sure hope this dog isn't bad luck," Harold chortled after meeting the train. Late by four hours, it arrived in the middle of the night in pouring rain. "Any dog with the price tag he had and arriving on Friday the 13th has either got to be good luck or bad! Let's keep our fingers crossed."

The glory days of *Lassie* had taken hold, the famous book and then a movie about a collie in Scotland swept across North America. The new puppy was a border collie, not a Scotch collie like the famous dog, but close enough to us and we wanted to name it after the canine movie star.

"Yeah! Lassie! Just like on TV!"

"But he's a boy," Louise reminded us, "and Lassie is a girl dog's name." After some silent thought, she suggested, "Maybe Laddie."

"OK." We had compromised, but the name seemed close enough to the Hollywood star. Little did we know we had just welcomed our own initiator of high drama onto our peaceful stage.

Our entire experience with dogs involved a likable, easy-going chump named Spike, and we knew nothing about purebred border collies. In a few short months, Laddie taught us. He followed the natural inclination of his breed and started chasing the cows, bursting into their serene life in the pasture. Without training, he careened all over and everywhere. Harold said the cows would become so spooked they'd go wild or the milk cows might go dry from stress. He became almost wild with anger himself. Even worse, he worried one might break a leg or push their way through the fence and escape. He said he knew how to cure Laddie and tied him to our small corral with a couple of steers. He theorized the pup would tire of cattle and leave them alone. We moved his food and water dishes out there and he remained in the corral with the steers for about a week.

As soon as he regained his freedom, Laddie's genes overpowered Harold's dog psychology. His few days with the steers made him more comfortable with them than ever and continued chasing the herd around the pasture.

This couldn't go on. No one wanted to leave Laddie tied, nor did we know how to train him. One day, Laddie disappeared. Without asking, we knew Harold had taken care of the problem. He had an impersonal view of dogs, as many people did in those days. A farm dog should be useful. We understood Laddie posed a risk to the cows and accepted his fate.

A few weeks later, Louise announced we'd go to Mrs. Dale's farm to pick out a new puppy. Mrs. Dale, another teacher at our school, told Louise one day after school she had a litter of puppies ready to go to new homes and we could pick one out. We chose a tri-coloured little thing—black, brown and white. This time, being a girl, we could name her Lassie and much to our parent's delight, she was absolutely free. She turned out to be gentle and loyal, following us everywhere on our exploits and slept at the kitchen door at all other times. Too timid to go near the cows, I have a feeling even they adored her.

Although the cows seemed powerless against an energy-riddled pup, we learned of at least one time when their natural instincts for defense proved successful against a coyote. Harold told us the story one evening at the supper table. He'd been working in the field next to the pasture and witnessed them in action. Noticing the cows running across an open space and bunching up, he slipped the tractor into neutral and stood for a better look. Amazement tinged his voice as he described how they formed a circle around their calves, turning their heads outward as if they were muskoxen on the northern tundra defending their young against a pack of wolves. He then spotted a coyote trotting across the pasture. He supposed the coyote had given up on an experiment to try catching a nice veal dinner for himself. Age-old instincts still flourished in the cows through thousands of years in domesticity.

One day while playing in the living room, I spied Harold through the window, walking down the lane with Dandelion on a short lead. As calm as if a jaunt through the yard happened every day, she paced alongside him. I dashed to the window for a closer look. It was the first time she ever wore a halter, but that didn't seem to matter. She trusted Harold and would go anywhere with him. The two strolled down the lane, two friends going for a walk. I asked my mother where they were going and she replied he was taking her to the stockyards.

"He's going to sell her?" If she said Harold was taking Dandelion to the moon, I wouldn't have been more surprised.

Louise smiled. "She's getting pretty old. She's too old to have a calf."

We lived a quarter of a mile from the yards and Harold knew walking her would be easier on her than loading her in a truck, something she had never done. He made her last day on the farm as gentle as possible. I felt sorry to see her go. Taking the calves to the stockyards was a normal part of farming, but I never thought this might also be the cow's destiny.

As with all things, times changed. We kids grew up, moved away. The cows got older still. Harold didn't need milk cows, and the markets changed. I came home one weekend to find the barnyard silent of ringing bells and low conversations of the old mothers I used to know. The pasture became a cultivated field. A few months later, a new fenced yard replaced the old barnyard and eight bright-eyed youngsters grouped under a new red shelter—feeder steers—easier to care for than cows but wild, not the pets of our childhood.

I accepted this as the normal course of events in the farming business, but I'll always cherish the cozier days of a real family farm.

25.
❧ It's A Farm Dog's Life ❧

Today, almost every farm has a dog. Their loyalty and intelligence make them a valuable resource as companion, security guard and in some cases, farm laborer. In pioneer days, a dog on a farm either meant the farmer had achieved a level of success, or he needed defense from so much predation by coyotes on the livestock. More often, with no extra food to give a dog, most didn't have one.

In the thirties and forties, the country struggled to recover from the Great Depression and then WWII. The farm dog began a presence but received very little care, receiving table scraps or, if that wasn't available, porridge. Even in the fifties, I remember my mother sometimes cooking a pot of porridge after supper for Spike.

If given shelter, the dog often preferred the front step anyway, the closest spot to its family. Spike claimed the front step as his favourite place. Most farm dogs descended from the English Shepherd, a hardy, intelligent and gentle breed that manages well in our Canadian winters. You still see English Shepherds on many farms, similar to the Scotch collie. Spike was all gold with white markings, but most are predominantly black with white and gold.

Spike always seemed old his whole life to me, but maybe his massive size and gentle, complacent personality gave that impression. He looked more like a Scotch collie than the English variety. Whatever his ancestry, his thick coat of under-fur topped with an outer layer of long, coarse hair served him well in winter and he never suffered from frozen ears or toes even though he slept on the front step in all weather. The lack of brushing produced a layer of mats on his back. As we kids got older, we tried to remedy this and bought him a brush out of our allowance, but it was tough going and failing to be consistent, the mats stayed.

Spike, like many farm dogs, proved his versatility. In his role as companion, he patiently allowed a child to dress him in a baby bonnet, but without hesitation gave ferocious chase to a coyote in the yard. Curious and loyal, he followed us everywhere except inside the barnyard, having learned from the cows it was their domain and he wasn't welcome.

Ever notice the dog has joined a family photo? They know they're part of the family, even if their owners disagree.

Two significant events caused many dog owners to change how they viewed their dog and improve their care: the production of commercial dog food and publication of *Lassie*, both occurring in the 1940s. A businessman named James Spratt introduced the first commercially prepared pet food in England in 1860 after watching dogs being fed leftover biscuits after the ships returned from voyages. Storage of bread being non-existent, sailors ate hard, non-perishable biscuits called *hardtack*. Regular trade in dog food didn't come into common practice until 1941.

I remember the novelty of canned, store-bought dog food and the revulsion at the terrible smell. It took some changes in our thinking to become accustomed to this innovation. One day, one of us kids fed the dog and left the spoon on the counter. Louise came along, swept up the spoon in the act of straightening up the kitchen and put it in her mouth to clean it off. She turned a pale shade of green when we told her she'd just eaten dog food.

Lassie first appeared as a short story in a 1939 edition of the *Saturday Evening Post*, written by journalist Eric Knight. The *Post* sent Knight to England to report on the country's desperate situation during World War II. Moved by the terrible state of the people having to sell their beloved dogs to keep going. When he returned to the United States, he wrote the story based on his own collie. It received so much response in the *Post*; they asked him to flesh it out into a novel. When the book hit the best-seller list, MGM bought it for a movie.

The story of the famous farm dog influenced farmers to feel a new appreciation of their animals at home. I remember the day in the fifties when, at the supper table, Louise and Harold gave our new puppy we named Lassie (of course) her own house. Taking the roof from the old outhouse (no longer needed because of the new running water in the house), Harold gave it low walls of scrap lumber. Lassie never used it except in the coldest winter days, still preferring the mat at the kitchen door. In fall, Harold piled straw bales on the roof and loose straw inside. Being low to the ground, the snow heaped around it, creating a cozy den. Sometimes, I'd go inside just to know her experience. Almost dark except for the small open doorway, silent and smelling fresh of clean straw. I thought she'd feel quite safe but she didn't share my opinion. Perhaps she preferred the open air and the smooth mat at the door instead of the prickly straw.

Some owners began buying more pure breeds and placing more importance on training. We, however, gave it no such significance. Only on days we felt inspired did we try training the dog but not knowing what to do, we confused the poor thing more than anything.

We all knew my Harold's view of dogs in the house. "The place for a dog," he reminded us, "is outside where it can be useful and won't track dirt in the house." His horror and disgust when visiting someone to be met at the door by the four-legged family member never changed and gave us kids something to giggle about. Anyway, Spike and later Lassie, politely refused our invitation when we urged them indoors in Harold's absence.

Today, I look at my dog, the cutest Shih Tzu in the world, curled up next to me in his own chair, and I can imagine Harold's reaction. This breed originated in China to stay indoors in the royal palace. Mine doesn't live in a palace but he's not a farm dog either, and I don't kid myself—a watchdog he is not. Some days I'm sure his one purpose in life is to nag me for walks, but the comedy of watching a floppy-eared Shih Tzu try to be dignified gives me daily entertainment.

In the sixties, people thought a toy or other small breed an anomaly in a farmhouse. Later, small dogs began appearing more often as a pet and companion.

Today under some circumstances, if a farmer shows the need for a dog, veterinary and dog food costs may be claimed as a farm expense on an income tax return. Canadian Revenue Agency must grant permission before claiming this expense. The dog must be a breed which lives and works outside.

Regardless of their pedigree or service, we love our dogs and many farms and families couldn't function without one.

26.
❀ Gardens for food and more ❀

From the time I was about six years old, I've been gardening. I liked to follow my mother down her rows of vegetables, asking questions. She gave me a job pulling weeds, showing me first what constituted a weed and what precious vegetable I must leave to grow.

"You can help me with your strong little fingers," she said (the first rule in motivating a child to work—tell them they're capable). "You know what a dandelion looks like (I had picked many bouquets to happily give her) so wherever you see them, pull them out if you can (another rule in motivating a child to work—tell them it's OK if they can't). See these ones with leaves almost like a dandelion? That's sow thistle, so pull those out, too."

Now on a mission, I set to work, not realizing my mother had not only gained a helper but also, a silent one. Harold used to say, "How can a little girl ask so many questions?" Louise gave me a job.

Her garden never reached the pristine, beautiful condition of those pictured in Better Homes and Gardens but to her, it was an essential piece of real estate. Her goal was pragmatic—healthy produce from garden to table, not a picture-perfect showpiece. No one stood out there admiring my mother's garden but it regularly birthed large and hearty food for a growing family and most importantly, at very little cost. Her garden on the farm covered half an acre—her pride and joy.

I think it was that same year when she gave me a postage-stamp-sized piece of dirt for my very own garden. She helped me stake out three or four short rows and handed me some seeds. I had already "helped" her plant her garden, so once my rows were staked with pieces of baler twine, I knew what to do. She then returned to her own work, having once again achieved some quiet time for herself, but at a cost—I no longer wanted to weed her garden because I was much too busy with my own. Come to think of it, maybe her motivation for giving me my garden was to reduce my help in weeding hers. Dare I say my parents actually were smarter than I?

People have gardened since the beginning of time, primarily to produce healthy food. Only in recent times has someone voiced other benefits like therapy for the soul, character-building, and family bonding. There is truly something thrilling about poking lifeless, hard seeds in the ground, sprinkling on water, and watching delicate life spring out of the soil. After a summer of building self-discipline to weed it whether you felt like it or not, (a good chance to work out your frustrations over the other parts of life) you get the huge satisfaction of bringing in your produce and actually eating it. Fresh from your own backyard, the flavour pops in your mouth at the first bite, all the more delicious after you've sweated over it all summer.

Gardens were a part of everyday life for anyone with a patch of ground until we fell in love with technology and industry accompanied by the idea of a life of leisure, and gardens disappeared from many farms and city plots. In recent decades though, our awareness of unsafe food and soaring prices has made us think again of sticking a few seeds in the dirt and watching them grow. In the past few years, gardening has exploded all over the world because people at home needed something to do, along with concern over the price increase and uncertain transport.

For my mother, gardening season began in late winter with the arrival of seed catalogues in the mailbox. She poured over them at the living room table with pen and paper, making lists and adding totals until her order was settled and mailed away, her eyes bedazzled by the beautiful photos of lush, boisterous plants. Today, we still have seed catalogues, but now seed racks sprout up every spring almost anywhere with the regularity of gophers from their holes. Every seed farm has its website, too.

Other creative ways of obtaining seeds are Seed Exchanges (the seeds are free) through some local libraries or a Seedy Saturday sponsored by either a farmers' market or community group. Personally, I think sharing seeds with friends and neighbours is the most satisfying way to grow friendships as well as gardens. One year, I got a small package of poppy seeds inside an Easter card, a lovely surprise.

Gardening teaches us about life. The first attempt isn't always successful, and in most cases, often a disappointment but perseverance brings rewards. Gardening is a learning process.

My city garden plot didn't reward me with the big harvest I got on the farm due to trees giving shade and the tree roots siphoning up most of the water. I turned to garden boxes as an alternative. They have their limitations but I still enjoy working in them and eating the delicious harvest, even if it's a small one.

Working together on a project creates stronger relationships. Families working together on a common purpose creates lasting bonds.

Every year, the condition of the soil improves in a new garden. The biggest weeds give up the fight a little more than the previous year, and the fall harvest grows bigger and more plentiful. Ah, how a sweet success encourages the hopeful!

Some years, the weather won't cooperate. A drought or a wet year will discourage any farmer and gardener. We learned that even when things don't go well, there are still some vegetables that will grow in our garden. That's why it's good to plant a variety. The deer liked the peas one year. Take note of what works and what doesn't. Adjusted your plans. Keep experimenting.

It takes perseverance, a plan and hard work to garden, but that's what anyone needs for success in any part of life. Gardening teaches that. Every year we learn something about the land and our own capabilities. We discover what we can grow and the particular varieties we like to eat.

If you're starting out in your gardening journey, the best advice I can give you is don't start too big. Be realistic about how much ground you can till and how much weeding you'll want to do in summer. Also, plant what you like to eat and learn how to grow it. Seeds are small—know how big the vegetable will become and don't be too liberal in sprinkling them in ground. Weed in the mornings if you can, before it gets hot and fewer mosquitoes are out. Water at night when it's cool so you don't lose most of your water to evaporation. If your children show interest, encourage them with small jobs, maybe their own garden, and don't explode if they pull up the odd young vegetable. They're learning too. Enjoy yourself. Make it fun. Marvel at nature. Let your soul heal.

And yes, ask questions. Always ask questions.

27.
❈ A Farm Wife's Prayer ❈

> Dear God, I am thankful for many things:
> Healthy children, snug and warm in bed,
> My husband gently snoring by my side,
> Our house around us, sure and fast,
> Keeping out the wintry blast,
> Our larder, fuel bin filled thus far.
> The knowledge that on the morrow
> I shall rise with strength anew
> And courage to face what the day may bring.
> For these things, I thank Thee, Oh Lord.
> —Louise Hathaway

I found these lines on a piece of scrap paper in one of my mother's books. She had developed the habit of cutting a used envelope apart and used both sides for notepaper: a grocery list on one side, this poem on the other, and as a bookmark in the book where I found it.

"Eight peaches, cheesecloth, Hollywood bread, bread." The simple list on one side and the prayer on the other, combined with a third duty as a bookmark, all symbolized her life: simple needs, backed by prayer and employing everything to its fullest extent.

Louise practiced recycling before the word appeared in our language. Old envelopes served many uses: grocery lists, scratch paper for calculations, or notes left on the counter for us to find after school. "There's a casserole in the fridge for supper. At 5:00, put it in the oven, 350 degrees. I have a staff meeting after school and will be late getting home." She kept a stash of her notepaper stuffed in a green, shell-shaped nut dish in the kitchen awaiting their second, third or fourth use.

This poem reminded me of a blistering hot summer day when I must have been about eight years old. After several sweltering days, the constant heat wore on everyone. I tried playing with my dolls in the shade of trees but gave up. I thought of a wonderful new idea and decided to talk to my mother about it.

Inside the house, the kitchen felt hotter than outside. The windows on the main level were painted shut. No one removed the storm windows with their three little open circles covered with a swinging wooden cover. The windows on the main level were never opened.

Warm air washed over me at the door carrying the sweet, buttery aroma of peaches. Louise stood at the stove canning the golden fruit while perspiration ran in rivulets down her face.

"Mom, it's so hot. Can we go to the lake?"

She glanced my way for less than a second. "No," she murmured. "There's too much to do." She turned away to the sink with a lifter full of steaming jars.

I returned to the trees and my dolls. I had to try. I knew her answer before I asked the question. My parents worked every day except Sunday and even then, at busy times.

The hard work yielded up a reward of satisfaction in knowing they had done their best to provide for their family. When the wintry blast wailed around the house in January, they remained snug and content, knowing they needn't worry. Hard work, careful planning, severe self-discipline, scrutiny of every penny, reusing everything two or three times—even a scrap of paper—to its utmost kept them going through all seasons. A summer holiday from teaching gave my mother time to can fruit and vegetables, sew new clothes, raise a garden, and squirrel away the harvest of vegetables in the cold room.

This poem is even more poignant in the context of the trials and tragedies hurled at my parents. Some days, life beat on them until they had no power to rise with 'strength anew or courage to face another day'. Those were terrible days, but in a moment when she sat down to write a poem, Louise allowed herself enjoyment of a good day when she felt brimming over with contentment and thankfulness.

We all need those times. We can work hard, but let's give ourselves time to stop, look back and enjoy the rewards of labour well done.

28.
❁ Our Rodeo in the Bush ❁

Almost anyone with livestock works in close proximity to nature, and sometimes nature takes an upper hand in farm management. My father experienced this phenomenon one summer when he took a few cows to the Kettles' quarter.

Harold bought Alex Kettles' quarter when Alex retired. His entire farm covered just one quarter, running a straight grain operation, meaning he didn't raise livestock although a big, ancient barn told a story of animals once living there. We always called this land the Kettles' quarter. It had a slough on one side, surrounded by grass and trees, so Harold decided to fence that area and put cows with their calves on it for a few months every summer to give the pasture a rest.

A week later, Harold announced at the supper table he'd finished the fence and we began planning which cows to move and how we'd do it. The two milk cows of course had to stay home and the other cows still awaiting the birth of their calves. Wild Cow would stay home since she might stampede during the move. The goers numbered five mothers with their calves. The land lay 3.5 km (a little over two miles) from our farm on gravel road.

The next evening, we started off. Harold drove the old truck ahead while one of us sat on the tailgate, holding a pail of grain and calling, "Come on!" The kids at the rear kept stragglers in line. We wore our rubber boots, of course, as we did every day for farm work. With holes in our pants, the girls wearing headscarves encircling sunburned faces, carrying sticks to extend our bony arms for herding. Yes indeed, pretty slick cowboys.

To begin our trek, we travelled the lane to the gravel road, then made a U-turn north. Once we passed our barn, the cows stopped calling to the ones at home and focused forward, settling into a steady pace. That made our job a simple one—keep up, pick flowers and joke with each other. On we ambled, the Great Hathaway Cattle Drive of the sixties—five cows and their calves, moseying up the long slope stretching to the horizon. We scanned the blue bowl above our heads to find the hawk we heard screaming. Was it calling us? We spread our wings and tried to answer it. The gravel crunched beneath our black, rubberized feet. A pretty pebble, a tiny buttercup, or a feather all found its way into a pocket.

As we ascended the rise, we looked back to the elevators of Marwayne standing guard above the trees in the valley. A meadowlark sang, Harold's favorite bird. Not a breath of wind stirred and we felt the sun burnishing our rosy cheeks. A car passed us, slowing down to lean into the ditch. We stared at the occupants and they stared back. We waved whether or not we knew them. It's what you do on the prairies.

We arrived at Kettles' quarter, Harold turned in the gate, and the cows followed. We rewarded them with grain poured in a row on the ground. The calves started sucking. We watched them for a while, but it seemed they'd be just fine, so we closed the gate and went home. Harold planned to check on them every day. Every time he went up, he took grain, poured it on the ground and called them. "Come on!" They always came out of the bush or slough, glad for their regular ration.

It became the usual routine of most years. One year, however, nature put her hand in and gave things a twist, just to keep things interesting. That's when the rodeo started. Harold drove up to check on them one evening and before he stopped the truck, he saw the wire gate lying on the ground. He assumed a prankster had opened the gate, but when he parked and looked closer, he saw the cows had pushed it down. Cattle tracks led him across the road where they had broken into Dan Ure's land. This quarter was a mass of unbroken bush. Harold walked the quarter until he found them, too spooked to herd back where they belonged. Their panicked behavior alarmed him. Something must have terrified them. These cows were our pets—family members. Under normal circumstances, they didn't take off at a dead run when they saw him. He went home and called neighbours, asking if they knew of anything unusual that could have scared them.

One of these neighbours told him a bear had been in the area, so he speculated this bear had spooked our cows, causing them to break down the fence in their escape. It's very rare to see a bear in this part of the province.

For the next several days, we went up every evening after supper at their regular feeding time. Louise, Harold and my sisters tramped through the bush on Dan Ure's quarter looking for them, hoping to herd them back where they belonged. A tangle of trees, fallen logs and short shrubs made up most of this quarter. They'd become so spooked, if my parents and sisters glimpsed them through the trees, they'd gallop off again on another mad dash to another part of the bush.

My brother and I were too young for any fun. We had to wait in the car with our homework and colouring books. When it got too dark to see, we'd just sit and wait, listening for voices, our signal they'd returned and we could go home. Sometimes we heard coyotes, not something we feared but in fact, it helped to break the monotony. Once we saw two or three half-grown calves race by and we expected to see our family members come after them. No one came, so we knew they had escaped them one more time.

I remember one night it took everyone so long to give up and return to the car, I decided (not telling my brother) the bear must have eaten them. I started planning how I'd take care of myself and my brother for the rest of our lives. The relief of having them back will always stick with me, but they were laughing and joking about someone falling over a log, so I couldn't tell them about my worries.

In the end, Dan told Harold he could leave them there until they calmed down and Harold agreed, not seeing another alternative.

Two weeks later, Harold made a new plan. He would go by himself with grain in the back of the wagon, the same wagon he fed them hay from all winter, hoping they'd remember it and think of good feed for a change from slough grass. If they followed, he'd bring them home rather than put them back on the Kettles' quarter.

We all waited at home, sitting upright in front of the TV, wide-eyed but not watching it. We wondered if he'd return at last successful or empty-handed once again. What a relief to see the tractor and wagon progressing down the road past our place headed for our lane, followed by every cow and calf, not a single animal lost. We celebrated by whooping, "They're home! They're home!" Past our house Harold led the parade, triumphant in the driver's seat, giving us a wave at our noses pressed against the windows, followed by the prodigal herd.

We did our best by our cattle. Things didn't always work the way we planned when nature intervened. We took cows to the Kettles' quarter every summer for several years, but never again did nature take a hand in Harold's farming, giving us a rodeo in the bush.

29.
❀ This is Snow Fun ❀

I'm a mouse living under the snow. I crawl through my tunnel and curl up in my little den. Holding my knees, I look up through the snow at the sunlight, diffused and pale blue, shining through my roof. I hear the wind whispering outside, the cows calling and ringing their bells. Some birds twitter. I wonder if anyone knows I'm here. Soon, the cold chases me out, back in the real world again.

Being seven or eight years old, one of my favourite ways of winter play took the form of tunneling in the snow. As winter blew in, my brother and I watched the drifts grow deeper in our favourite spots. We became connoisseurs of the snowdrift. We knew how deep it should become and that we needed a few days of wind to harden a nice crust on top to make a sturdy roof. Depending on the shape of the drift, we dug into the side or the top. To start, we'd poke a hole with our boot and then dig in with our mittened hands. Most often, James made his own burrow. Sometimes we'd each branch off a shared doorway. It all kept us busy most of an afternoon if it wasn't too cold. We'd carve out a couple of rooms, pretending to be animals or mountain men, or new immigrants, all eking out survival in the harsh prairie. We'd talk to each other through the snow if the wind didn't make too much noise.

Dressing for outdoor play required as much ritual as digging tunnels. We wore underwear under jeans which were under snow pants. Louise gave us each a pair of Harold's wool socks and we pulled them on over our own socks, tucked in our jeans, almost up to our knees. We wore leather mukluks, which our mother thought kept our feet warmer than boots, but I'm not sure about that. My feet always got cold first. Two pairs of mittens, one knitted pair inside leather ones also lined with sheepskin kept our fingers toasty and a scarf covered the lower half of our faces with a hood or toque pulled snug. Our mother tried to dress us warm enough to keep us outside as long as possible, but eventually, we got too cold and needed to come in.

We never ran out of something to do outside. Harold's portion of flat prairie didn't give us good sledding hills, but we made do at the dugout, sliding down one end after Harold tested the ice and judged it thick enough to hold us. It gave us a fair run from the top of the bank to the middle of the ice.

Sleds changed in style over the years. We found some worked better than others. Two aluminum flying saucers appeared under our Christmas tree one year that flew over the snow like swallows in spring and lasted throughout our childhood. Our own inventions had various levels of performance. A sturdy cardboard box glided on the snow better than some purchased sleds and it didn't matter when, after lots of good fun, it crumpled or ripped to pieces.

"There's lots more where that came from!" We boasted but then glanced sideways, hoping one would soon appear.

We went skating on the dugout too after someone cleared a path in the snow. Most often that job fell to us and just clearing it filled an afternoon. For something different, we made a circle or figure eight, leaving snow in the middle, at least until another day. We weren't a hockey family but maneuvering turns, skating backwards or other figures or games like tag kept us busy most of an afternoon. The booming of the ice always sent us scrambling for the bank, but we never broke through. Harold laughed when we told him at supper, saying it was just settling, much too thick to break. I still felt safer when I bolted to the side when that happened, just in case.

Games like fox-and-goose were good fun, and we sometimes got creative, making something we called a pile of spaghetti instead of the usual pie-shaped trail. Hide-and-seek in the dark after supper offered fresh appeal, especially if new hiding places sprouted up in the form of snow drifts.

Sometimes, neighbours with a slough or lake on their land hosted a skating party. Square bales or planks on pails served as benches around a fire invited us to gather and warm up. The fire most often functioned as the solitary light but sometimes someone got creative with another light source: a trouble light or string of patio lights. Someone played music from their vehicle or the latest form of portable player. Of course, food and hot chocolate always attended the party too.

In spring, the snow gave us new fun when little streams trickled through the barnyard. James and I loved patrolling them, using a stick to push little stones or pieces of straw out of the way to keep it running. If we got it flowing well enough, we'd use a little twig as a boat and follow it on its way. We played in these little streams for as long as the snow kept making more water. The barnyard sloped to the gully, so plenty of rivulets trickled through to the bottom of the yard. It never occurred to us that while having fun, we helped Harold to drain the yard of soupy mud.

Many a day saw me called to supper and I'd have to drag my boots through grass to wear off a thick layer of mud. Often, I'd need to stand them up-side-down on an air vent in the porch to dry. I often waded too far into the gully to the point that water overflowed my boots. I'd wring my socks out in the porch sink and hang them to dry. No harm done—I'd do it all again the next day.

With every change of season, new fun outside emerged for the taking.

30.
❈ Our Sojourn for a Christmas Tree ❈

Aunt Mattie's After Dinner Mints

We'd lean back, stuffed like turkeys at the end of a family meal. A pretty dish of After Dinner Mints then circulated the table, an offering brought by our Aunt Mattie. We groaned with the pressure on our waistbands but couldn't pass up the dainty treats, so pretty they couldn't possibly have any calories, could they?

> 1 cup white sugar
> 4 tablespoons water
> Pinch salt

> Stir together. Cook until you see bubbles on the bottom of the pan. Then add:
> 4 heaping tablespoons icing sugar
> ¼ teaspoon peppermint
> One or two drops of green or red food colouring (optional)

> Beat until creamy. Drop onto wax paper from a spoon. Work fast before it all hardens in the pan. As they cool, they will turn into delicate circles of sweetness.

∽

Bringing home the Christmas tree percolates into a happy tradition for most families, anticipated as much as any other seasonal fun.

Most families purchase trees from temporary vendors or department stores, but bringing it home involves special customs unique to each family. Others prefer a do-it-yourself option involving a happy drive in the country where they visit a U-cut business with groomed trails to access rows of cultivated trees. Some prefer a roughing it in the bush style—an old-fashioned drive to crown land for an escape among nature to chop down their own tree.

This ancient custom began in Germanic territories before Canada's inception, but like all customs, the practice has changed over time. Crown land, managed by each province's forestry service, requires a permit at a nominal cost except in BC where they are free. Wherever you apply for your permit, you'll find them happy to recommend the best areas to visit and will give special tips for a successful excursion.

At the Hathaway home, our usual tradition involved packing up hot chocolate and Christmas goodies and stuffing all four kids plus Harold onto the one bench seat of his old '55 International pickup for the long drive to Whitney Lake. Lucky for us, we didn't have to worry about seatbelts, something the old blue truck never had anyway. We rode along, wedged together like sardines in a can, snacking and listening to the radio crackle out Burl Ives crooning "Holly Jolly Christmas" and Andy Williams, "The Christmas Song."

Once we arrived, we tumbled out and stretched stiff muscles. Harold reached into the truck box and brought out his ax, rope, and a sled. Of course, he always had his trusty jackknife in his pocket, just in case.

We marched off into the woods in high spirits. "Oh, Christmas tree! Oh, Christmas tree! We've come to find and cut down thee!"

Whoever felt so boisterous soon fell silent. The tranquility of the forest settled over us all. We sensed we were disturbing the peace of nature's home. A blue jay, always the harbinger of alarm, screeched out its warning, flying off into the trees. A chickadee hopped above our heads, chirping its cheerful song, ignoring the blue jay's caution. We stopped to identify rabbit and mouse tracks. The trees stood high and silent, like sentinels guarding sacred ground.

As we moved deeper into the bush, we soon found ourselves in a knee-deep slog through soft snow.

"We need snowshoes, Dad."

"Snowshoes! What's that! I've already got two big feet to get me there."

"Well, how 'bout skis, then?"

"Skis! He-e-e-eavens! I might as well slide down on my bum right now without using skis to help me!"

We giggled. We panted.

"This one looks good."

"I like that one over there."

"The snow's too deep over there and I'm getting tired. Let's take this one."

Harold agreed. "Yeah, this one is the cat's pajamas."

"Have you ever seen a cat wearing pajamas, Dad?"

"No, and I've never seen a little girl ask so many questions, either. Back up now while I chop this tree down. Don't want to accidentally hit you."

He tied it on the sled for the tramp back to the truck. Depending on the depth of snow, we could be more or less picky. Hip-deep snow meant we chose one of the first trees we waded to or we'd soon become too exhausted to return to the truck.

The sun headed for home and so must we. By the time we carried our trophy in the house, our faces glowing with pride and adventure, Louise had supper ready.

Today, people would scoff and call our prize a Charlie Brown tree, but on those branches, hung our memories of the sojourn to find it, so we loved it. Harold carried down from the attic the dilapidated box of old tinsel, homemade decorations, and other sentimental ornaments. Then he'd lift out the string of lights, sit down with a box of new bulbs and start checking for burnt out ones. While he worked, we looked over the decorations and picked out our favourites, setting them aside to wait until Harold put the lights on the tree. Marilyn put a record on the record player and we decked the tree to the Harry Simeone Chorale singing "The Little Drummer Boy" and "Do You See What I See?"

An annual downside for Harold every Christmas occurred in the theft of trees from his shelter belt on the east field along Highway 45. Every year, he tramped down the field to count how many had disappeared. Each summer he tried to replace them but gave up, finally admitting defeat. It's sad that shelter belt theft still continues today. I doubt there's any pride in the home where those trees stood. The value of windbreaks by conserving water and providing shelter to domestic or wild animals is considerable, and all at a cost to the farmer.

In later years, the Hathaways' custom of retrieving a Christmas tree evolved into Harold bringing the box holding the artificial tree up from the basement. The simplicity of it suited them in their senior years, but while trimming it, they'd reminisced about the days of bringing home a fresh, fragrant tree from the forest.

31.
❀ A Most Successful Holiday ❀

After cars became commonplace, people began dreaming about driving across the country. Besides making dreams come true, the Trans-Canada Highway strengthened the transport and construction industries. It connects all the provinces, building a sense of national unity. It does not cross Labrador or the territories, nor enter Halifax or Toronto.

Every three years at Christmas, we travelled to Vancouver to visit family. My dad's parents lived there and his sister, Connie, with her husband, Harry, and family. Louise's sister, Varina, and husband, Wes, also raised their three children there. Until 1962, we took the train. I didn't know why we started driving. I thought little about it until I found my mother's diary of that first trip by car in 1962 through Rogers Pass.

The railway connected Vancouver with the rest of Canada since 1885. In a mad dash to catch BC into Canada before the United States got them, Prime Minister John A. MacDonald promised the once isolated town a railway if they signed up. The BC delegates sent to Ottawa in 1871 planned to petition for a wagon road, but when they arrived and heard the offer of a railway, well… they asked for a pen.

None of the politicians involved had any inkling how a railway could be built over the Rocky Mountains. The project triggered years of scandal, huge financial output, human life lost, and engineering feats the likes of which no one imagined including two spiral tunnels, but MacDonald's government at last fulfilled its promise to BC.

Construction of the Big Bend Highway, a job stimulus project in the Depression years, offered the first road through the mountains. No one bothered to pave it and its immense loop north and then south again made for a prolonged and treacherous drive to Vancouver. Logging trucks used it until the Mica Dam required its flooding over.

The Trans-Canada Highway united Canada better than any other means, making travel easier and people explored their country with interest. As it snaked west, plans for a route through Rogers Pass became urgent. This section posed the biggest challenge of the entire project, extending the original construction timeline. Even though sections in the east still lacked paving and Newfoundland needed any part of their segment, by September 3, 1962 Prime Minister John Diefenbaker opened the highway in a ceremony held at a point of significance—Roger's Pass.

Harold and Louise followed the news on CBC TV. Christmas couldn't come soon enough for them, eager to try out this new road now famous for conquering the rugged pass named after the explorer, Major A. B. Rogers.

I liked the train, but Harold and Louise understood the historical significance of Rogers Pass and wanted to save money on their trips to visit family, a fact highlighted in Louise's diary of their first trip.

Owing to its unproven state, they took no chances and packed more emergency supplies than normal travel items:

> We completed the preparations for a family of six. We packed one change of clothes for everyone, two sleeping bags and air mattresses in case of crowded accommodation. In case of emergency, I squeezed in a few tins of food, juice, tea, coffee, cookies, chocolate, thermoses, robes and pillows. To pass dull stretches of road, I tucked into our little car, field glasses, several road maps, notebooks and pencils.

Others didn't share our parents' adventurous spirit. We stopped in Calgary to stay overnight at Bob and Betty Miller's home, and Bob sat at Harold's side all evening, trying to persuade him not to go.

"Have Christmas with us," he said, "and go to Vancouver in the summer."

Harold looked sideways at him, smiled and put him off with as much tact as he could imagine. Bob's concern made my parents nervous enough to phone the train station, but being Christmas, more cautious travellers already filled the trains.

As a last resort the next morning, Bob stopped Harold as he passed out their door, holding out his axe. "At the very least, take this."

Harold shrugged, but took the axe to appease his friend. Once in the car, Harold scoffed at Bob's anxiety and Louise agreed with him, but her meticulous diary notes reveal her excitement and apprehension over a trip of historic significance:

> It appeared Providence smiled on us as we turned onto this famous Trans-Canada route. The delightful weather and the chalk-white foothills' scenery inspired us.
>
> The park warden at the park gates told us Rogers Pass remained in good condition, so after paying the fifty-cent toll, we continued on our way. We passed a power plant and an inviting pointer directing the tourist to Lake Minnewanka. Highway Number 1A took us into the town of Banff, a quiet town during the winter except for the activity caused by visiting skiers.
>
> We left Banff and went back to Number One, passing within four miles of Lake Louise. Memories of hikes in this area twenty years ago remind me there are many signs declaring this to be the Great Divide—the Great Divide from which rivers flow east to Hudson Bay, and west to the Pacific Ocean.
>
> The children tired of so many trees so to break the monotony they opened their Christmas gifts from our good neighbours, the Andrew Fergusons.
>
> Near the Sedan Lift, a sign stated "Vancouver 545 Miles." We crossed the border into British Columbia at 12:20 p.m. and where before there was just a light skiff of snow on the shoulder, the highway now lay glazed with snow until we approached the interior of British Columbia.
>
> The Kicking Horse River section has a rugged grandeur of its own. No sign on the highway marks the Kicking Horse Pass. The river runs far below in valley and chasm, hurrying west to the sea. On the other side is the mountainside to which the highway clings like a narrow ribbon. We felt no fear as the railing on the road assured us of safety. Cascades of mountain streams, now frozen, appear in shades of blues and greens, resembling stalactites. We used car lights in this section as the

sun's rays do not reach the road's shaded parts.

Mount Revelstoke National Park is the last park we passed through, so we handed in the fee stub at the exit gate. Revelstoke, a town of good size, also seems to be low in a valley surrounded by hills or mountains. The road from Revelstoke stood bare of snow.

Spence's Creek has all the marks of a lumber town. Two people fishing in the Nicola River assured us there are some inhabitants—we saw very few people on our trip through the mountains.

Boston's Bar, halfway through the Fraser Canyon, is near Hell's Gate Canyon. This is one of the most rugged spots of this mountainous country. The motorist passes between a sheer drop on one side and the chance of a rockslide on the other.

The horizon opens out as we approach the Fraser Valley with its green grass, large dairy barns and homes very close together. The sunset was beautiful as we drove in to Chilliwack and on to Langley, our first stop to visit our relations, the Harry Lang's, with whom we enjoyed Christmas Day.

Our children loved their visit with their grandparents, my husband's parents, who live in Vancouver on Sherbrooke Street. Grandma's cooking tasted so good and Grandpa's stories were interesting to all of us. Grandma, now eighty, goes alone to the big stores in downtown Vancouver once a week so she will not lose her bearing when she is older. Grandpa, two years her junior, walks the ten blocks to Fraser Street every day to shop and socialize.

After visiting my sister and her family in their lovely home on 41st Avenue, we turned our car eastward on December 30 to return to the prairies. Except for a stop in Drumheller, we followed the same route as we took going west.

When I sat down at home to assess our trip, I decided it had been a most successful holiday. Our on-the-road expenses amounted to one hundred and one dollars, ninety-six cents, of which we spent forty-two dollars and sixty-eight cents on gas and oil for the Rambler. We hope to travel by car over the same route in the summertime.

The Yellowhead Pass

The Hathaways made several trips to the coast and I can't be sure when Louise wrote this poem. She includes the history of the

Yellowhead Pass as well as explain its importance and describe its beauty. The act of writing a poem about a highway reveals her love of travel.

The low elevation of the Yellowhead Pass made for easier movement through some otherwise very rough terrain, first by First Nations peoples, then Hudson Bay employees used it and both rail lines (CPR and CNR). A road for heavy vehicles first built by interred Japanese Canadians during WWII opened in 1944, but they destroyed much of it during the pipeline installation. A rebuilding project began in 1952, but in 1970, a paved highway opened for cars.

This highway crosses the mountains much farther north than Rogers Pass. Both are part of the Trans Canada, making it a unique feature of a double highway bearing the same name. They named it after Pierre Bostonais, an Iroquois-Metis trapper and explorer who crossed the mountains on this pass, remembered for helping develop the area. His blonde hair earned him the nickname Tete Jaune, *yellow head* in French.

The Yellowhead Highway

Tête Jaune,
The name they gave you
Keeps in mind
A Company youth.
A youth with yellow hair,
Who, as he worked, discovered you.
You, the low wide valley
Through the Rockies.

Discovered many years ago,
You lay unwanted,
Little used by man
Until the cars made this
An age for tourists.
Now you're needed, now you're used
By countless thousands to traverse the Rockies.

We laud you, and we bless you,
You of the wide green valley,
You of the distant snow-capped peaks,
Among them, Robson, the giant of them all.

You of the green, pure rushing waters
Along whose banks and far beyond
Grow pines, firs and poplars,
Flanked below by greenery in abundance,
Among which beasts have found shade.

So now, to man, you give unstintingly
All the beauty and grandeur,
Given you to give,
By the Master first, and then…
Tete Jaune.
—Louise Hathaway

32.
❈ Apology ❈

On a Christmas holiday to visit family in Vancouver, we stayed with Aunt Connie and Uncle Harry. Harold's parents, Edward and Alice, lived across the street, so for the length of our visit, we saw them every day.

We had just finished supper in Aunt Connie's pretty, sunny dining room with its windows spanning three sides. We had shoe-horned ourselves in around the table—our grandparents, Alice and Edward included—sharing a delicious meal and memories of the old days when Aunt Connie and Harold grew up on the Clear Range farm.

Now stuffed like turkeys, we lingered at the table, reluctant to leave the convivial gathering and fun-loving conversation. Finally, Aunt Connie stood and took the first dishes to the sink, breaking the spell. Everyone pushed their chairs back and wandered into the living room. Uncle Harry got out his slide projector and started setting it up while Louise and Aunt Connie washed dishes, talking about kids and present days. I stayed at the table looking at a lovely book of garden flowers I discovered on a small shelf just behind my chair.

Aunt Connie finished washing dishes and went to the bathroom. Louise lingered, leaning against the counter watching me. "Found something interesting?" I looked up and she smiled. I nodded.

Edward came in and put a hand on Louise's shoulder.

"It's so nice to see you, Louise. I'm so glad you've come," he said.

"It's always nice to see you too," she replied and smiled.

They exchanged a brief hug and separated, still talking about the drive out and the roads home. In mid-sentence, his face melted. He put a hand on the back of a chair for support and gasped out silent sobs. "I'm so glad… you've come…" He leaned over and rested his forehead on his hand, gasping.

I stared, shocked to see him cry, the man who always wore a broad smile and often teased us kids. It seemed some palpable weight kept him bent over.

He stayed that way as if he couldn't straighten up. Louise paused, looking at him, then reached out and laid a hand on his shoulder, patting his back. The clock ticked. Voices floated in from the living room.

Aunt Connie came out of the bathroom and, without glancing into the kitchen, crossed the hall to join the others in the living room. Louise hesitated, but followed her. Edward straightened up, breathed a sigh, turned and followed the women. He never looked in my direction and I'm sure he didn't know I sat watching in the sunroom. I waited, staring at the place where he had stood, then followed.

We looked at slides of trips taken and other family events, laughing and joking as if no little drama had ensued in the quiet kitchen.

He died the next year. Following his wishes for cremation to get the prairie frost out of his bones, they sprinkled his ashes over English Bay as a salute to the country of his birth and happier childhood memories.

Today, I think of that day in Aunt Connie's kitchen and wonder if indeed he felt weighed down. I wonder if, while reminiscing over cherished memories on the farm, other memories surfaced he didn't want to recall: his romantic dream of an easy life on the farm dashed by back-breaking work, failed crops, never ending poverty, and the knowledge that his son- and daughter-in-law lost the farm because of his poor management.

Thinking of that day, I wonder if it was his apology to Louise for the trouble he caused her and Harold. Despite his proud demeanor, perhaps guilt followed him to Vancouver, knowing he left his son- and daughter-in-law to struggle while regaining their footing on the farm. I wonder if he ever tried to apologize to Harold, or if Harold's contempt and Edward's pride stood in the way. Perhaps he felt more guilt towards my mother, an innocent party in this drama—given a burden she should not have had to bear.

Perhaps he expected my parents never to speak to him again after they lost the Clear Range farm. Forever after, did he fear losing contact with his son and family? After all, he once dealt out unforgiveness himself to his brother. As a young man, he argued with Donald over the fence line between their homesteads. He left home in anger, never speaking to Donald again. No reconciliation ever passed between them and perhaps he also expected the same treatment from his son. What relief he must have felt to receive that first letter from Harold in 1947 with news of their move to the new farm, informing them of their new postal address so they could resume correspondence.

I wonder if Harold wanted to cut ties with his father and Louise convinced him to change his mind, stressing that despite Edward's pride and secrets, he should remember Alice's love for her family. Harold remained courteous to his father, but behind his back, didn't have a kind word to say about him. Forgiveness is a hard wall to climb.

Did Louise perceive all this that day in Aunt Connie's kitchen, forgiving Edward by patting his shoulder, or did the actual forgiveness come earlier and I witnessed a renewed expression of it? Perhaps other times and other words shared made all of it clear between them.

I felt as if I had entered in the middle of a movie. So much happened in both their lives I will never know, but this tender moment between father- and daughter-in-law revealed to me another side of my grandfather I hadn't known and my mother understood.

If truly an apology, it appeared heart-felt, deep and drenched in tears and I hope it healed a part of both their lives, clearing the way for peace and healing ahead.

33.
❀ If You Can't Move ❀

Today, DIY is the new title of an old concept. In the 1940s, *do it yourself* was the usual method of building almost anything. Many homes or animal shelters sprang into existence by the work of an inexperienced weekend carpenter. Nowhere did this happen more than at the home of Harold and Louise Hathaway.

Their purchase of the Marwayne farm in 1947 included a tiny, one-bedroom house with no basement, a two-car garage, a barn and chicken house. They moved there around the time of their second wedding anniversary with one-year-old Betty Anne. In the tiny bedroom, they squeezed the crib between the bed and dresser. A smaller, six-month crib fit on the other side like pieces of a puzzle. They'd have to make do since the purchase of the farm and crop failures strained their budget to the limit. They lived that way until 1951 when a third child's future arrival made a major renovation essential.

With money scraped together, they managed an addition to the present house. They had a basement dug in a square shape just east of the present location, big enough for an addition on the back, making the house twice its former size. The original house had two rooms: a kitchen and a bedroom. The new home boasted a dining room (once the old bedroom), a living room, a new bedroom and a tiny, windowless children's bedroom in the centre of the house.

The bathroom, of course, sat twenty feet behind the house in a cluster of trees, housed in its own shack—the outhouse (or biffy). Furnished with two holes on a bench seat over a deep cavern in the ground, it came equipped with an Eaton's catalogue to serve as both reading and wiping material. If we were already outside anyway, we used the biffy until we got running water in the house and Harold dismantled it and filled in the hole. In the house, a chamber pot under the bed relieved the needs of anyone needing to get up in the night, or in bad weather at any time. Some of these *thunder mugs*, as they were sometimes nicknamed, had a lid to contain the rising stench. A roll of toilet paper kept them company. They had other lovingly endowed nicknames like pisspot, potty or jerry.

In the renovation, a pail toilet reposed in the basement, a step closer to progress for the Hathaways. Plywood walls and a door enclosed this throne. Few went to the basement except to use this toilet or retrieve a jar of fruit from the cold room, so the toilet's door usually stood open. It allowed fresh air to waft in if browner air wafted out.

And waft it did. The five-gallon pail under the seat filled with amazing speed from the offerings of, eventually, a family of six, making it no place anyone wanted to stay longer than necessary. Harold emptied it when full, and we kids screeched and hid our heads under couch cushions if he did it when we were there to see and smell him carry it from the basement door to the kitchen door.

The open toilet door not only allowed fresh air but also a casual conversation. It's where Louise taught me to tie my shoes. We were getting ready to head out somewhere and she told us kids to get in the car while she went downstairs. Obeying orders, I put my shoes on and, with laces flapping, went downstairs to ask her to tie them. She gave me a look, and I knew this visit with her on that spot would be my last.

"Sit down," she said, "and I'll teach you how to tie your own shoes." Bending over, she untied one of her own and demonstrated while I followed her lead. I never asked for help again. Never dared ask.

That was in 1958 when I was six. My arrival in 1952 began a second cycle of first one, and then two cribs placed in our parents' bedroom after James' birth the next year. Betty Anne and Marilyn's beds filled the tiny children's bedroom. The writing on the wall wasn't just the kids' crayon scribble—it announced a message as bold as black felt marker.

As all kids insist on doing, we kept growing, and soon the family outgrew the house again. This time, they built upwards, adding a second floor. Harold hired two men from town to help him. Wilbur joined in, having built or renovated many homes in his history of raising his own family. None of these men were journeymen carpenters, but they brought more experience than Harold possessed and provided the extra muscle needed for heavy lifting.

A staircase rose up in the space where the children's bedroom once stood and, for the interim, their beds shuffled about wherever they could sleep in safety. Louise told me about the trials of living in the house during renovations. The dust! The noise! But most important, the risk to safety. Besides the futility of keeping the place clean while children played on the floor and breathed in the dusty air, their wellbeing remained top of mind.

"One day, I lifted the baby out of the crib," she recalled, "when a man working upstairs came crashing through the ceiling, landing in the crib from which I had just lifted the child moments before."

The new second floor served well for a few years as a cavernous space. The children, now numbering four, slept in three beds. We had our own chamber pot under one of the beds but we'd been told it was our job to empty it in the morning if we used it, so we tried not to as much as possible. Two dressers and a toy cupboard gave the barest necessities but we had lots of room to play!

In 1956, "the big bedroom" took up the north half of the entire floor space. At first made for a specific babysitter, it later became the private domain of the oldest child still at home.

By 1958, Louise and Harold felt more than ready to install running water. We kids rejoiced to learn of the demise of the pail toilet and its stench in the basement. The conversation during a bedtime routine went like this when Louise broke the news to us:

> "You mean, when we go to the bathroom, we just push on the lever to flush the toilet?"
>
> "That's right. That's how it will work."
>
> "And the water will carry everything away? There'll be no more awful smell?"
>
> "That's right."
>
> "Ho! I can hardly wait! No more going down to that stinky, ol' toilet!"
>
> "Will we still have to go down to the basement to use the toilet?"
>
> "No, we're having a bathroom made in the middle of the house below the stairs."

"Hurray! A real bathroom! Will it have a bathtub?"

"Yes, and a sink too, so you won't have to wash your hands or brush your teeth in the kitchen."

"Oh! That's going to be so-o-o nice!"

∽

Harold contained his excitement, but he no doubt felt just as enthusiasm. For him, it meant no more hauling and warming water for the ritual Saturday night bath. At that time, a hand pump stood in the kitchen over a large sink. Pails of water filled a large receptacle on the side of the wood stove called a "water reservoir." When hot, he lifted the metal bathtub from its hook on the wall, placed it on the floor by the stove and filled it with a mixture of steaming water from the stove plus cold from the hand pump.

Everyone bathed in the same water, starting with the youngest. The two youngest being small, bathed together in the metal tub, placed near the stove on the kitchen floor. Small children could bathe while someone just three feet away washed dishes. The kitchen had two doors, but for bath time, they were closed, retaining warm air from the stove for a more luxurious experience. By the time Louise and Harold got their turn, the water felt neither warm nor was it clean. More hot water from the stove helped a little. They had just as much anticipation for hot, clean water right from the tap as the kids felt for the flush toilet.

By now, Louise had sampled renovating and developed a taste for it. Ever a restless soul, she sometimes talked of moving, wondering if life could be easier somewhere else. Harold resisted, saying they were just fine where they were and moving would only cost more money they didn't have. Louise satisfied her unquiet spirit by changing the house, easing her conscience by paying for it with her teaching income:

1962: The purchase of a new car turned her thoughts to a new garage. The shambling door on the old garage closed with a powerful arm, most often remained open. Harold repaired machinery there and often parked the car outside. He drew a line at the idea of a new garage but agreed to a carport on the north side of the house. He poured the cement pad in the summer of '62 and finished the roof the next year, fitting the work between farming demands.

1963: Time for a new bathroom and kitchen. This work required more carpentry skill than Harold possessed, and they called the local contractor Len Espetveidt. Her request for a Lazy Susan in each corner confounded him. Being an innovation only seen in home magazines, ready-made parts weren't available yet and Len made them from scratch. His first attempt failed Louise's scrutiny, but the second model passed inspection. The new bathroom filled the bottom bar of the L-shaped kitchen, making it smaller and the table squeezed into the middle of the room.

1964: The dawn of energy conservation sparked the public's imagination, including my mother's. She wanted her laundry room on the main floor and a new, bigger porch at the kitchen door addressed both issues. A new porch stopped the cold air at the door, helping insulate the house on the west side where the wind blew its hardest. They cleared away the old, dilapidated porch, adding an insulated one with a water closet, a sink for Harold, and a laundry room. Then, stucco covering the entire house made it warmer, or so the theory went.

Once finished, a couple of mice scuttling through the kitchen, sending Louise into high dudgeon. She hadn't spent all that money on the house to turn it into a barn! She couldn't sleep at night, afraid a mouse might run across the bed as she lay helpless within. In the morning we'd skip downstairs like puppies after a long, refreshing slumber and turn into the kitchen with Corn Flakes on our minds only to stop short at the sight of Louise scowling into her coffee mug wearing a darker face than her morning brew. She hadn't slept all night.

Harold charged into the battle by setting a trap line. Marching through the house like Ivanhoe on a mission to save desperate villagers, he carried new traps from Tannas's Hardware, setting them in the back of cupboards, the basement, the bathroom, under their bed... He caught two mice in traps (in the kitchen) over a couple of weeks. After a length of time with no more prisoners taken, Harold declared victory and peace descended once again, at least in the house—possibly not in my mother's mind.

Sometime close to this year, a new, high-efficiency gas furnace replaced the old coal burner. No more deliveries of coal poured down a chute into the coal bin in the basement through a window and no more need for Harold to make two or three trips a day to stoke the fire in the burner downstairs. The metal register on the dining room floor where I used to stand to thaw out chilly feet and legs disappeared and the hole boarded over, requiring new linoleum once again. Parting with that nostalgic life, however, gave way to warm rooms upstairs. Warm air circulated into each room through new furnace ducts. We no longer had to leave the stair door open to allow warm air upstairs. Central heating had arrived.

1971: By now, the house looked nothing like its original form in 1947. It didn't need another addition since all the kids had left home, but Louise wanted one more thing added. A sunroom on the south side would be "so nice to sit in," she said. The sunroom became one of those ideas imagined but never used. After its installation, she found it became as hot as an oven. Anyway, everyone worked. No one had time to sit in it.

She imagined other ideas too, but by then, the kids had finished school and money went to post-secondary education. With effort, she controlled her active mind. In times of boredom or restlessness she talked of a change, causing Harold to groan, "I'm going to put this house on a turntable and every time you think you need a change, I'm going to spin it around and you'll have your change!" They'd both laugh. They lived a quiet life without renovations for a few years until Louise couldn't stand it any longer. Something just had to be done. That's when she decided it was time to build a new house.

1981: They ordered a new house built on the exact spot where the original, one-bedroom shanty stood back in 1947, but any similarity ended there. The new home stood massive compared to the original shack, even bigger than the farmhouse we kids grew up in. This project almost overcame my parents, now approaching their senior years. Once they chose a floor plan and hired contractors (from the Co-op, of course) the major effort of making so many decisions plus sorting their belongings for the move, carrying box after box to the new house and cleaning the old before its sale, wore them both out and they agreed never to do it again. Another farmer bought the old house, who moved it near Elk Point. Louise remained settled for a good eleven years.

1992: Harold never thought he'd leave the farm, but there came a time when retirement seemed right. Bowling, a Co-op meeting or a doctor appointment kept them on the road to Lloydminster almost every day. They were both retired, so what held them back? The farm sold and Louise, at long last, got the move she craved. They bought a home in Lloydminster where they lived a quiet life… for the most part anyway.

Old habits die hard. Louise couldn't give up renovating altogether. She added a sunroom on the back, changed the kitchen, and installed a new bathroom in the basement. The familiar sound of hammers and saws was tonic to her ears, but it felt like small potatoes compared to the fun she had on the farm.

34.
❀ Tragedy ❀

I remember October 17, 1973 as if it happened yesterday. I'm in Photography class on that bright, warm, fall day. This class filled part of my Biological Sciences requirements at Kelsey[8] Institute, Saskatoon. Each student received a camera on loan and given their assignment to take pictures over the course, developing them in the darkroom, working in small groups. There is no exam; their developed photos determine their final mark. On October 17th, with the time nearing noon, my group is almost finished developing. The red light outside the door is on, showing developing in progress so no one must open the door. Inside, another red light gives us illumination to work.

The voice of another classmate comes through the door. "There's a phone call for Sheri at the office from her dad. He's waiting on the line until she gets there."

About six of us are in the darkroom. No one speaks while we look at each other. I'm finished my photos but John still has his projects sitting in solution. Two students head for the door with me, but John darts in front of me.

"Can you wait until the time is up on my photos?" he asks. "It's my assignment for this week. It's got ten minutes left."

I hesitate. For Harold to call me in the middle of the day at school means there is an emergency, but he would understand if someone's mark is at risk. Still, ten minutes feels like an hour.

"OK." I don't want to ruin John's chance at a good mark. Our group gets time once a week for developing. He'd have to do it again next week and hand it in late, losing marks.

I call through the door, "I'll be there as soon as I can, maybe… ten minutes."

My mind churns while I stand staring at the door with my books and fresh photos on my arm. 'Mom must be in hospital,' I reason to myself. 'If Aunt Mattie is in hospital or worse, Mom would call. After I talk to Harold, I'll call the bus depot and find out when the next bus leaves. I'll have to miss a few days or more of classes, but I'll borrow someone's notes and catch up.'

Andrew approaches me, putting his hand on the knob, and looks at me with concern in his eyes. He and I look at each other. 'What could have happened?' We share the same thought. He moves back to John and asks in a low voice, "How much longer?"

"About two minutes," mumbles John. His voice sounds strained, embarrassed.

The bell on the timer rings. Other students crowd behind me. Andrew opens the door for me and I head for the office, now seeming so far away. I want to run, but my feet weigh like blocks of cement and my arms loaded with books make me sluggish. 'Just keep walking,' I tell myself—down the hall, down the stairs, and another hall.

I swing around the corner into the office. Mrs. Sidney, the secretary, is standing at the file cabinets. She turns to me and nods at the receiver laying on her desk. I sit down on the chair placed for people to sit and talk to her and put my books on my knee. "Hello?"

The other end is silent.

"Hello? Dad, are you there?"

Then Harold's voice, shaking. "Is this Sheri?"

"Yes, Dad. What's happened?"

"James is dead."

I hesitate. Then, "What?"

Harold starts to cry. Even in my shock, I remember thinking how strange it is to hear him cry.

"He didn't come down for breakfast this morning, so I went up… I couldn't wake him." He's crying too much to say more.

"I'm coming home." I stand up, still holding the phone to my ear. "When I find out when the next bus leaves, I'll let you know when I'll be there."

Harold is crying too much to respond.

"I'll call you later, Dad." I hang up.

"What's happened?" Mrs. Sidney asks.

"My brother's dead. I have to go home."

"I'll phone the bus depot," she says. "You get your coat. I'll tell you the time of the bus."

Two instructors come into the tiny office. They fill the doorway and ask what happened. I tell them and we stand, looking at each other. 'Why?' is the question on all our faces.

"Had he been sick?" someone asks.

"No," I said.

"Was he depressed?"

"I don't know."

Silence.

While talking to them, the secretary calls the bus depot. "The bus leaves for Lloydminster at 2:15," she says, hanging up. She is my mother's age but shorter, heavier, with grey hair. "Go home and pack. You've got lots of time."

"Thank you," I say and turn to go.

"And take care of yourself. You won't be doing yourself or your parents any favours if you walk in front of a car and end up in hospital." She looks into my face to make sure I am listening.

I look at her. "OK."

I open my locker and look inside, trying to think what to take. I stand at the open locker door and start crying. Sandy is sitting on a bench in the hall. She isn't part of my group in the darkroom and asks, "Is everything all right, Sheri?"

How do I say the words I have to say? "Sandy, tell Debbie my brother is dead and I'm going home, OK?" I look at her, not sure how she'll take the news.

"OK." Her face has no expression. Her casual walk down the hall makes me stop and watch her. I might have said I'm going for lunch.

Debbie and I share a one-bedroom apartment about three blocks from Kelsey. We're both enrolled in second year Biological Sciences, known as Bio Sci to the students.

At the apartment, I call home to tell Harold when I'll be there. He's calmer this time. "All right. Aunt Mattie will meet you and bring you home."

'How strange,' I think. This will be the first time Harold won't be meeting me at the bus depot and the first time for Aunt Mattie. I'm disappointed. I want to see my dad so much. The irony doesn't escape me that Aunt Mattie meets me when I thought just that morning in the dark room it might be her that had died.

While packing my suitcase, Debbie comes into the apartment. I look around the bedroom door to where she's standing in the living room.

"You're home early," I say.

"Mrs. Sidney told me to come and keep you company." She giggles with embarrassment. "She thought you might kill yourself."

"Oh."

She looks away and I return to packing.

I don't remember the bus trip. Aunt Mattie is waiting, looking sad. She takes charge. I reach to take my suitcase from the driver, but she holds out her hand and takes it, carrying it to her little white Chevrolet. Once on the road, she says. "I'm sorry for your loss."

"Thank you."

We don't say anymore for the entire half-hour trip.

She stops the car outside the kitchen door and Harold comes out. I'd never seen him looking like that before. He walks like an old man with slow steps. He holds out his arms to me even before I get out of the car, crying. We stand on the step, holding each other and crying. Aunt Mattie stays in the car while Harold and I cry. We drop our arms; Aunt Mattie gets out and we all go in the house. Louise is crying.

Aunt Mattie stays for supper but goes home in the evening.

Bit by bit, the story comes out. Louise doesn't say much, but Harold can't stop telling it, over and over. When he can't wake James, he goes downstairs and tells Louise, "I can't wake James. He feels cold."

Louise goes up, but they both realize what it means. They call the hospital but are told to call the police. The RCMP office doesn't open until 9:00 a.m. and 911 isn't in effect yet. They sit in the kitchen waiting for two hours.

When the ambulance takes the body away, Louise tells Harold he has to phone my sisters and me. She goes up and changes the sheets on the bed. She must have thought, 'this is the second time we say goodbye to a son,' reflecting on the time she packed up the baby things she set out to welcome Richard in 1947.

Until I arrive, they spend the day phoning people and crying. Betty Anne and her husband, Allister, are flying from Newfoundland and Aunt Bunny and Uncle Wes will pick up Marilyn on their way through Edmonton the next day. We cry most of the time as we do anything.

In the evening, I say goodnight to Louise. I'd been thinking of this moment all evening.

She turns to me. "There are clean sheets in the guest room." James died in that room the night before, removed just that very morning. He'd been staying with them for a few weeks until he found his own place. He'd quit his job in Edmonton and got a new job driving a dairy truck to the farms around Lloydminster.

"OK," I say.

She looks at me. "You don't have to sleep in that bed if you don't want to. The two single beds have clean sheets on them, too."

"No, I want to sleep in the guest room." I knew if I didn't sleep in that bed tonight, I wouldn't be able to look at it or go near it again. I had to do this.

I go upstairs and stand looking at the bed, picturing James lying there the way Louise described him, with his arms crossed over his chest. I change and lie down, thinking about James.

I surprise myself by falling asleep. I wake up with the sun shining in the window and lay there thinking, 'I did it. Now I can sleep anywhere in the house, but I had to do this last night.' I hear the familiar noises of someone in the kitchen and go downstairs.

Louise looks at me. "How did you sleep?"

"Good," I said.

She turns back to making toast.

"I had to sleep there last night, or I'd never be able to face it again."

She turns to me and nods.

All morning, Harold sits silent or crying in his chair in the kitchen, but in the afternoons, he goes out to the shop. Uncle Wes and Aunt Bunny arrive with Marilyn. They burst in the door, laughing loud. Uncle Wes is joking, making everyone laugh. Louise and I laugh too. I feel guilty but also great relief to laugh, like stretching muscles after sitting a long time. I think to myself, 'the world has gone crazy'.

Betty Anne and Allister arrive soon after, joining in the hilarity. They play along but by stages bring sobriety back into the room, giving sanity its space again. I'm relieved they are there. I need some sensibility, some quietness back again; room to grieve.

The next morning, we mill around in the kitchen after breakfast, cleaning things away and Harold goes out to feed the cows. I stand at the kitchen window and watch him. He moves as if wearing cement blocks on his feet. I wonder if he'll ever walk with that old familiar spring in his step again. Will he ever smile again, ever laugh and joke the way he always did? Now he just cries or sits in silence.

While he is out, Walter Kvill drives in the yard. When Louise and Harold first moved to this farm, Walter, then a widower, was the first to welcome them to the neighbourhood. Now, he is the first neighbour to share this sorrow. He is crying. He doesn't knock and comes in without speaking. We all stand in silence in the kitchen, crying. He goes to each of us, giving each a hug. He doesn't speak, just cries in silence. Then he walks out. He doesn't go to see Harold in the shop. That would be too much for both of them. They worked together whenever one of them needed help, intertwining their friendship. Another time, they'll meet and grasp hands in silent meaning.

The days pass somehow. The funeral home calls a few times. Louise asks me to help her pick out a suit for James to be buried in. A few flower arrangements arrive. People bring casseroles and visit. The United Church choir comes and fills the living room. It's good to have someone from outside the family there, someone to serve coffee to, to talk to… We sit around the living room not saying very much, talking about the weather, asking about someone's garden. Silent minutes seem to freeze everyone. Someone makes the comment this is a very sudden shock. Louise is cavalier. Sitting on the couch between two people, she says, "We don't seem to have much luck with boys. We lost our first boy as a baby." No one says anything.

Debbie phones one day and says the class has taken up a collection to pay for a bouquet. She wants to know the best place to order them in Lloydminster. Hearing her voice takes me back to my very dissimilar life in Saskatoon. I cry, making Debbie feel bad. "Ah, Hatch[9]," she says. She had started with a cheerful, matter-of-fact tone, probably not wanting to make the call at all. The only times we shared were the happy ones. I feel embarrassed and feel bad for making it more difficult for her, but I can't stop crying.

Knowing my whole class shares in my grief gives me a new perspective. I wonder who first thought of doing this for me. An instructor? Mike? Sonja? Mrs. Sidney? The time is too busy to think much about it. Flowers crowd together in the house and the bouquet from Bio Sci gets lost in the multitude. The days fill with visitors and funeral plans, leaving no time to make sure I see it.

People bring food, tears and sympathy. Along with each visitor, we cry most of every day, except for Louise. She remains calm, playing the perfect hostess.

Meals are difficult. The family gathers at the table where a re-warmed casserole sits on a hot mat. I look at the food thinking at any other time, we'd all enjoy it, but now, I can't taste it, don't want to look at it. We eat in small, slow motions, silent most of the time. Harold can't eat at all, just sits and cries.

It's time for the funeral that we've all been dreading. After the sanctuary fills up, the funeral attendants escort people to the hall in the back of the church. People fill every space. The limousines pick us up and we steel ourselves for a difficult service. In the front bench, my sisters and I sit together beside Uncle Mac, Aunty Madge, and our cousins. Behind us, Louise, Harold, Aunt Mattie, Aunt Bunny and Uncle Wes sit. A crowd stands outside on the grass around the front door. All doors remain open to help people outside hear the service. I hold it together through the service until Betty Anne grasps my hand. I look at her. She is crying, looking at the choir. Following her gaze, I see Elsie Midgley looking at me with pity, crying as she sings and I lose it. I can't keep it together and I cry through the service.

It finally ends and we walk out through the packed church, through the crowd standing outside on the grass. So many people. They part so we can walk out to the funeral cars. It's a relief to escape in the limousine. We sit in silence, sniffing.

"That was hard," Betty Anne says.

The drive to the cemetery gives me time to calm down. At the gravesite, we stand in silence around the grave until it is over. Marguerite Buckingham approaches Louise and touches her arm. Louise turns and falls into Marguerite's arms, bursting into tears. She hadn't allowed herself to cry since that first day and now the dam broke, all her grief gushing out, crying in loud, grief-stricken moans. Everyone cries, if they aren't already.

At last she releases Marguerite and we go home. I don't know if the church women serve lunch at the church, but I'm sure they did. The house fills with people again. My sisters and I go upstairs and Louise follows. We sit in the big bedroom and talk, Marilyn and I on the couch, Louise and Betty Anne on the bed until we're ready to face people again.

We hear Harold talking. "I don't know where they've gone but they're here somewhere."

Louise says, "We better go down and help Harold talk to people."

Every day, someone comes to visit. Now that the funeral is over, we can talk to them without crying, but still do when it is just the family at home. Visitors help to bring a bright spot into the house.

A few days later, the RCMP phones, wanting to come over to talk about James's death. Arriving in suits, a middle-aged man and his junior officer tell us James died of strychnine poisoning. They ask if Harold keeps gopher poison and ask to see it. They talk to Harold in the garage a long time. When they leave, I assume we won't see them again. At first Betty Anne tells me they checked Harold's gopher poison, and it hadn't been disturbed for years. Later I hear someone used it recently. To this day, I don't know the truth.

Aunt Bunny, Uncle Wes, Marilyn, Betty Anne and Allister all go home and I go back to Saskatoon. Louise goes back to teaching and I ask her why she's going back so soon. "It's better than sitting around the empty house," she says. Harold has no desire for work, but he has to feed the cows.

My friends and I carry on as if nothing had happened. Everyone at school treats me as they always did, and I need that. I need space to collect myself. I need to escape the constant despair, the glassy stillness, and reminders of James being gone.

The RCMP calls me at our apartment one evening. They say they're the ones from Lloydminster investigating James's death and ask they can come over with some questions. When they arrive, they look at Debbie and ask if they can talk to me alone and she says she'll go for a walk.

The senior officer does all the talking. He first tells me they still have more questions about James's death, so that's why they came to Saskatoon.

"Do you mind if we ask you some questions?"

"No."

"Was James gay?"

"What?"

"As you know, James died of a strychnine overdose."

"Yes."

"Well, strychnine is what gay people use to give themselves a sexual high. Did you know that?"

"No." To myself I'm thinking, 'I thought we were going to talk about how James died, not how he lived.'

"So, that's why we think James was gay and he accidentally overdosed."

I look away so I can think, remembering talks with James and letters he wrote to me about dating, talking about his girlfriend sometimes, his habits and way of thinking. I turn back to the two men. "James wasn't gay."

The older man lowers his head and looks at me while a flat smile stretches across his face. I look straight back at him. After a short silence, he asks, "Can you think of any reason why he might have wanted to kill himself?"

"No," I say.

"Do you know anyone who might have wanted to do him harm?"

"No."

He tells me they've been to visit my parents again. I wonder how that went. "Be sure to let us know if you think of anything."

"I will"

Soon after they leave Debbie comes back. "I'm sorry you had to go through that," she says. "You don't have to tell me anything. I sat outside the door on the step so I heard everything. I'm just sorry."

I don't mind that she heard. I'm glad she cared enough to stick around.

There is talk of James committing suicide. For years I say that's what happened, not knowing what else to think, but the idea never sat well with me. He never left a note, told no one he felt stressed, and didn't appear unhappy. He had just broken up with his girlfriend and Louise wasn't happy with him for moving back home. In the seventies, no one lived with their parents as adults. He had reunited with old school buddies and went out with them on weekends. He seemed happier than his days of working in Edmonton.

It is a sad commentary on societal thinking and laws of the seventies that the police travelled from Lloydminster to Saskatoon for the sole reason of asking me if James was gay. The gay rights movement was just beginning then. I don't know what the police could have done if I agreed he was gay. He was gone.

It's my theory he heard about strychnine and tried it, but as the police say, he didn't intend to give himself an overdose. He was experimenting as many young people do and, sad to say, always will, and he went too far. He was twenty years old.

Over the next weeks, we all try to carry on normal life. Some have a harder time than others. I go home every weekend for several weeks. All the bus rides blur together except for one in particular. The bus is full and I sit with a quiet woman about forty. No one speaks on the bus except two senior ladies sitting about three rows ahead. One of them boards the bus at North Battleford, finds an old acquaintance, and sets to work updating her on news from Lloydminster area.

"Do you know so-and-so?" she asked her friend.

"No, I don't think I do."

"Well, he's dead. He died last week," and then I heard, "And do you know James Hathaway?"

"No."

"Well, he's from Marwayne. His parents are Harold and Louise Hathaway. He died last October 17th. He was just a young person, you know. No one knows how he died, but he's dead, too."

I sit stony faced for the three-hour trip, but I decide never to talk about anyone in a public place.

~

At the end of a weekend visit home, I carry my suitcase downstairs and set it by the door for Harold to take to the car. Marking school work at the dining room table, Louise says to me, "You don't need to come home next weekend. Don't feel you have to come home every weekend. We'll be fine."

I hesitate but agree. I'm getting pretty exhausted and feel relieved, but also some guilt over missing a weekend.

That first weekend spent in Saskatoon feels odd. I don't know what to do with myself.

It's a few days after that weekend when Harold calls. "I'm calling to tell you Louise is in hospital. She didn't want me to tell you, but I think you should know. She's had a nervous breakdown. Don't let on you know."

"How is she?"

"She'll be in hospital for a week or so. I'll let you know when she comes home."

"How are you?"

He pauses and I wonder if he's going to cry. "As good as can be expected."

"Dad, how did it happen?"

"I came in the house and she was crying and couldn't stop—I didn't know what to do."

I can imagine. "Should I come home?"

"No, just carry on," he says. "She didn't want you to know, and she'd feel bad if you come home on account of her."

Later, after she comes home, I phone and I ask how she's feeling.

"I'm fine. I just went to the hospital for a rest. I'm fine now," she says.

"Dad said you didn't want me to know, but I always want to know if you're not well," I say.

"No, I know, but I was just tired and needed a rest. I'm fine now."

"Do you want me to come home?"

"No, soon it will be Christmas and Marilyn will be here. I'll be fine."

Marilyn and I come home for the holidays and Aunt Mattie comes down for Christmas Day. We spend a quiet Christmas, just the family. Harold still walks slow, acting like he no longer has a reason to live. We just try to make it through Christmas Day and each day following. Nobody goes anywhere and no friends come over. It feels good to just be at home, quiet.

Two days before New Year's Eve, the police call again. They want to talk to Marilyn and ask if they can come over. They'll be over around eleven o'clock.

Just before they are due to arrive, Harold stands from having mid-morning coffee in the kitchen and heads for the door.

Louise looks up. "The police will be here soon. Aren't you staying in case they want to talk to you?"

"No."

"You really should stay, I think."

"I'm not staying." He went out to the shop. His behavior makes me wonder how the police treated him on previous visits.

The same two men as before come in and talk to Marilyn in the living room. I'm doing laundry in the porch and Louise is making lunch in the kitchen. They talk to Marilyn a few minutes and on their way out, they stop at the laundry room door.

"I see you're doing laundry," the older man says.

"Yes."

"Are you home for a few days?"

"Yes."

"Are you going to be here for New Year's Eve?"

"Yes."

"Do you already have plans for New Year's Eve 'cause I know of a good party I'd like to take you to."

I gasp. "I'm already going out with someone."

He throws his head back. His laughter hits the ceiling and fills the tiny room. "I knew it! I knew you'd have a date!" He laughs as he walks out the door. I looked at the younger man, wondering if he also asks young girls out on a date that he'd just met on the job. His senior officer was old enough to be my father. As the young officer passed me, he looked away.

Louise leans over the corner of the stove to put her head into the porch. She speaks in a loud voice, too loud to be talking to me, pronouncing each word with care. "Sheri, who are you going out with on New Year's Eve?"

The door clicks as the younger officer shuts it behind him.

"I'm not going out with anyone, Louise. I just said that to get rid of him."

She turns back into the kitchen. I put my hands on the washer and cry.

Harold comes in after the police leave. As he walks through the porch, he looks into the laundry room. I wipe my eyes and look at him. With his hand on the kitchen doorknob, he stands looking at me. He looks concerned but helpless to know what to do, while I wish I could do something for him. He opens the door and goes into the kitchen.

I wonder how those officers treated him on past visits. If he cried in front of them, did they laugh at him? If he didn't know what it meant for someone to be gay, did they humiliate him? Did they suggest he was negligent by not knowing what his son was up to or even suggest he may be responsible for James's death? All are possible.

A few weeks later, at the end of a class day in Saskatoon, I'm standing at my locker in the empty hall, getting homework ready. All other students are gone, but I'm later than usual to go home. Mrs. Sidney walks past the end of the hall, looks down its length and sees me. She stops.

"You're still here?" she asks.

"Yes, but I'm just on my way home."

She pauses, then says, "You've changed over this year."

I look up, surprised.

"You used to be more carefree, and now you work so hard, stay so late each day."

I look into my locker to think. Had I changed? "Usually I go home earlier," I say, "but I just had something to finish."

"Well, take care of yourself and have a good evening," she says. She usually never speaks to the students, always busy in the office.

"Thanks, I will," I say. I watch her go through the double doors, grateful for someone's thoughtful words.

If I had changed, my father changed more. For the rest of his life, he could not bear to hear James's name spoken, too painful a reminder of that awful day. The day James died changed my father into a sad, sentimental, slow man, unsure of himself and always on the verge of tears. The mention or even the thought of his mother, the sight of a beautiful prairie sunset, a particular hymn he loved, brought him to tears, now flowing so easily when before we never saw him cry.

In any crisis he used to know what to do—how to fight a fire, how to work hard and save money to pay taxes, talk to a doctor for a medical problem, hold pillows over the windows in a hail storm… but the day James died he hadn't seen it coming and been helpless to prevent it. Holding pillows over the windows wouldn't cut it that time. All his life he worked to keep his home and family safe, fighting back any evil, but that night, it came in anyway and took his son while he slept. His smile didn't return again for a year or more, but even then, something was missing, a sadness behind his eyes.

When his grandchildren arrived for a visit, we saw a twinkle of that old joy return. He'd put on a clown act for them, making a fuss over whatever they played at or saying funny words like "hidey didey" when they arrived and wave both hands and one foot when they left. "There's four kids to wave to," he'd say. "And I don't have four hands. Wish I could lift the other leg to wave that one too. Next time, I guess I'll have to lie on the ground." Without them, he may never have had a reason for joy.

35.
❈ The Program ❈

The Hathaways loved a program. We conscripted all the family and many guests—some to sing, some to act in a skit, someone to read a poem, the audience invited for a singalong, tell a joke or offer good wishes to the guests of honour.

I hated the Hathaway program as much as I dreaded every school and Sunday School Christmas concert. For Louise and Harold's 25th anniversary, I gave them a party but no program. Guests came, they visited, they ate food; they left. Simple!

When talk circulated in family letters or phone calls about our parents' 50th anniversary, I knew what was coming. I wanted to stop this train before it got going.

"Do we have to have a program this time?" I asked Betty Anne on the phone when the topic turned to a celebration. "Wouldn't people rather just eat and visit?"

She ignored me and got right down to business.

"We're having a program in the Anglican church on July 8th. Allister and I will do a skit, I'm giving a history of Mom and Dad's lives together, then there'll be audience singing of old songs and we'll give people a chance to stand and tell a story about their memories shared with either Mom or Dad. You're singing a song. I have one picked out for you and I'll accompany you on the piano. The church women are serving lunch."

I sighed. I could hear Harold in my head. "Just the usual song and dance!"

On a weekend home to visited Louise and Harold, Louise and I sat at her dining room table with our tea and she brought out a slip of paper and pen. "Let's plan the food for the party."

I looked at her. "Don't you think we should wait until Betty Anne gets here?" I said.

"No, you and I can do this." She scanned her notes.

I leaned closer. "I think she's going to have plans when she gets here."

She looked at me. "We can do this much. Betty Anne is planning the program."

A day or two later, Betty Anne arrived and the song and dance got underway. Amid the chaos, we sat down for tea and Louise brought out her list of food.

"Here is the list of food Sheri and I made up," she said.

Betty Anne took the list out of Louise's hand. "Let's see." She took the pen. "We're not having this," she crossed off an item, "and we're not having this," she crossed it off, "and we're not having this." She began writing at the bottom. "We're having open-faced buns, squares and fruit."

I tried to catch Louise's eye to wink at her but she wouldn't look at me.

On the appointed day, we got on with it—the usual song and dance. We had the skit, the audience sharing of stories, and the sing-along. At last, the time came for my rendition. During the planning, Betty Anne had told me to introduce it and I prepared a few words on a page that I clipped to my music. I sat on stage, awaiting my cue. Betty Anne finished leading the singalong, producing beaming faces all around, everyone having had a good time singing old favourites. As I stood to begin my part, Betty Anne stood from the piano bench and moved in front of me. She was on a roll and couldn't stop herself. I sat down again.

"Sheri's going to sing now. This is our anniversary card to Mom and Dad. It's the anniversary greeting from us, her children to them on this, their fiftieth year together, and you will sit and listen. You won't sing this time. You will just sit and listen while Sheri sings and I want everybody to pay attention...."

In case someone didn't yet understand, she repeated herself. The audience sat completely mollified, their smiles lowered into sober, silent stares; everyone put in their place and told what to do while sitting in it. Satisfied, Betty Anne moved to the piano bench, turned and waved at me. "Go to the microphone."

I sighed, unclipped my introduction from the music, laid it aside, and stood up. The words begged to be said. They jumped up and down waving their hands shouting, "Pick us—say us!"

I adjusted the microphone and took a deep breath. "Now you know why I was so quiet growing up," I said. "By the time I came along, there was nothing left to say."

While I waited for the laughter to subside, I glanced over at Louise and Harold. I hadn't seen Harold laugh like that for years. He leaned over, melting, weak with helplessness. His mouth stretched across his face and his jaw sagged open. His head fell onto his right shoulder, his body leaned to the right, shaking. He gasped for breath. Louise looked straight ahead, wearing that tight-lipped smile she wore when controlling herself. She reached over and grasped Harold's left arm, holding him in his chair. Someone might think he'd been drinking, but he never drank alcohol.

It did my heart good to see him laugh like that again. The years bombarded him with many attacks, and he weathered it all the best way he knew how—he just kept going. He had no counselling, no medication, just support from friends and family. Life changed him from the tough egg he'd grown into as a young man to a soft-shelled variety that cried easily, sentimental, forgetful and often confused. To his dying day, he couldn't bear to hear James' name spoken since it brought him too much pain. I think he thought about him every day, anyway.

Laughter endured as his only balm. It healed some wounds or at least covered them over to make them a little less painful. That ointment didn't come often enough in his later years. He and Louise left the farm he loved and moved into Lloydminster, but soon after, dementia began taking his life away in the slow, creeping way it does.

On another day, Louise and Betty Anne, reminisced about old friends in their living room. Louise tried to remember something about the family they discussed.

"Harold, who bought the Castel farm?"

His face brightened, and his shoulders straightened. Dementia crept in on his self-esteem in stages, but on that day, he enjoyed a lucid day. His eyes lit up at being acknowledged, asked to contribute.

"Vern Lowrie." He spoke the name clear and solid, sure of himself.

Louise paused. "I don't think that's right. I'm going to look in a book." She left the table in search of her Marwayne history book.

Harold's eyes dulled and his shoulders sagged. Sitting beside him with our tea, I looked at him.

"It doesn't pay to know anything," he said. So much self-confidence seeped away from him and no one, not even his wife gave him credit for much anymore.

Louise came back to her chair. "It was Vern Lowrie that bought the Castel place," she said, missing the irony. Harold looked at her but said nothing.

It felt good to see him laugh that day, surrounded by friends. It was worth it to have a program just for that.

36.
❀ Life with Louise ❀

In this book, I've covered almost every aspect of Prairie life during my parents' generation. There is just one more topic left to tackle, perhaps the most difficult and personal for me, and that is the subject of mental illness and how society dealt with it. I will relate some personal experiences. For some readers, they will seem absurd. Others may find them familiar in some way.

We children had a cardboard box of dress-up clothes that we girls enjoyed playing with, but not James. A particular mask resided in that box that terrified him. It was a witch's mask, made of soft rubber. It looked very realistic to a four-year-old. When he saw someone wearing it, he screamed at the top of his lungs and ran away. Even if he saw it laying on the floor, he'd scream and hide until someone put it away in the box. Once my sister swooped it off the floor and rushed it at him, making him cry.

When we were little, he and I had our midday nap in our parents' bed, usually with our mother joining us for a short time. When he and I woke up, we'd sit up and begin talking and looking at the children's books kept there to read to us. One day, as we looked at the picture books and talked about the stories, suddenly James looked up at the doorway and screamed. Betty Anne stood in the doorway, removed the mask from her face, and laughed. Marilyn and Mom rushed up from behind her, also laughing. They'd been waiting in the hall. They looked at each other laughing, turned and left in a group, very pleased with themselves. He quieted once they left, but soon a masked face slowly eased in the doorway again and James screamed louder than before. I remember the disgust I felt, even at age five, when our mother removed the mask from her face and turned to Betty Anne and Marilyn for their approval, all laughing.

It was one thing for our sisters who were then only children to tease us, but I expected our mother to support us and teach kindness. I said to James, "It's only a mask."

"I know but I can't help it," he said.

They regularly teased James and me but James defended himself with outbursts of anger so eventually, they stopped. I was quiet and let them do it and it continued all my life. Even today, my sisters laugh and talk about me, even in my presence. It became a habit they've never seen a reason to stop. It's too much fun for them and our mother joined in, enjoying the inclusion in their clique.

Our mother was easily influenced by the power of suggestion, causing her to take on unexpected opinions or act in uncharacteristic ways. At other times, she could be a loving mother and worked hard to keep us all clothed and fed. She sewed most of our clothes for school. One year she made matching curtains and a rolling blind for my bedroom window, an unexpected and special gift. She could be very generous.

Dark days crept in without warning. I remember her standing in the kitchen making a meal and crying, and me trying in vain to comfort her. For some reason—perhaps a symptom of depression—she sometimes wanted people to think she was a victim and invented complete fabrications, usually about one of the family, or exaggerated certain true incidents. Our father was often the focus of these stories.

When I was about ten, she was angry at Dad for something and berated him for a long time in the kitchen while he stood, trying to defend himself. Nothing he said satisfied her and it seemed to me she would never stop. Thoroughly belittled by her words, he mumbled his defense, standing with arms hanging at his side. He turned to the annex beside the stove and started folding and inserting old newspapers. I was in the living room where I cold hear them and just see Dad through the kitchen door.

The annex was a small wood and coal-burning heater, not meant for cooking but just to add warmth to a cool kitchen. Perhaps he meant to start a small fire but probably just wanted to give his hands something to do. To make an opening, he used the portable handle, inserted it in one of the iron plates, and lifted it out. In his nervousness, the plate slipped off the handle and landed with a thud on the stovetop.

"Don't throw that plate!" she said.

"I didn't throw it, I dropped it," he mumbled.

"You threw it!" she said and continued.

It was a day I wondered if our parents would separate, and then what would happen to us children? Would we have to live with our mother without the buffer and dependability of our father? In my childish mind, I didn't understand that our parents would never separate because our mother needed our father for his strength and stability. He was the rock on which she depended. For Harold's part, he would never leave Louise because he loved her and meant his wedding vows when he said them on June 23, 1945. This incident surfaced again many years later when I would discuss this day with my mother.

After twenty years of an unhappy marriage, I knew I had to warn my parents there was a very real possibility that my husband and I might separate. I stopped in at their Lloydminster home one day, not sure how I would say what I had come to say. Dad stayed at the table for coffee but soon disappeared to tinker in the garage. I checked my watch. My kids were soon due home on the school bus. I had to go. I blurted out the words to Mom. "I don't think my marriage will last much longer. I wanted you to know. This probably isn't a surprise. I can't stay longer today to talk more. The kids will soon be home."

I had tried to warn her of problems before. This time, she didn't say much and after a quiet moment, I reached for my purse and jacket. As I headed for the door, she stopped me. She related her version of the incident about the stove plate. By this time, the story had changed in her imagination.

"One day Dad and I were talking in the kitchen on the farm and he got mad. He picked up a stove plate from the annex and threw it across the room!" With wide eyes, she waited for me to react, expecting me to feel sorry for her, believing her situation was so much worse than mine.

It's true Dad had a temper at times as we all do, but he would never do such a destructive thing and anyway, I had witnessed that event and knew she changed it to put herself as a victim. Those plates were made of cast iron and if he had thrown it, it would have made a hole in the wall or done other severe damage. I felt sorry for my father that day, wondering how many other people she'd told that story over the years. Anyone who knew him would know it to be impossible for him to act in this way, but to have someone whom he loved and made a commitment of marriage tell such stories about him must have been devastating if indeed he ever knew.

At about age eleven, I decided I would grow my hair long. In a matter of months, it reached my shoulders with bangs resting above my eyebrows. I had long hair for years before Mom seemed to notice. I was about fifteen when she started commenting, "Your hair is in your eyes. Get it out of your eyes!"

I'd been trimming my own bangs and, admittedly they had grown somewhat long. I'd planned to trim them the next time I washed my hair—on Saturday, of course—the routine day we all bathed and washed our hair in preparation for church on Sunday and the week ahead. Wednesdays were for baths only, not washing hair. The chronic shortage of water on the farm ruled over our water use. On weekdays, I took a glass of water to my room every night, dipped my comb, and wet my hair so I could wrap it around brush rollers. I sometimes got tired of curling my hair and sleeping on the rollers every night, but I liked my hair long with a soft curl at the ends.

After a few days of constant nagging, I knew someone must have said something about my hair to Mom. I only hoped she would soon turn her attention to something else. I trimmed my bangs and kept the long hair in a ponytail but it made no difference.

One day she appeared in my bedroom doorway and smiled. "I wondered if you'd like to get a perm," she said. "It will keep your hair curly every day without having to put it in rollers at night. It will have body and hold its curl all day."

I felt thrilled to have my mother support me at last. I readily agreed and she made the appointment for the upcoming Saturday.

When we were small, our mother cut everyone's hair, snipping the girls' hair just below our ears in a style called a pageboy. When I grew my hair long, I trimmed it myself or Marilyn trimmed it. The offer of a professional style was an unbelievable luxury. I imagined myself flopping into bed without the usual chore of putting in curlers and still arriving at school with lovely curls the next day. I counted the hours until my appointment.

On Saturday after lunch, I said goodbye to my mother and walked into town. I greeted the stylist and chatted to her while I settled in the chair and she put a cape around my shoulders.

"So you're getting a perm today," she said, resting her hands on the back of my chair and talking to my reflection in the mirror.

"Yes," I said, smiling back at her.

"OK," she said, "Let's get started."

She gathered my hair straight up over my head, put an elastic around it, reached for a pair of scissors, and cut it off just below the elastic. My heart stopped and I froze. The short hair fell down over my head. She dropped the hank of hair into the garbage and turned back to me. Looking at my face in the mirror, she said, "Didn't you know you were getting your hair cut?"

"Yes," I said, trying to breath.

She looked at my reflection a moment, concerned and uncertain. "From the look on your face, it doesn't seem like you did." She hesitated. "Are you all right?"

"Yes," I said.

We were both very quiet after that. She went to work, trimming, adding curlers, and then the perm solution. I continued watching in the mirror while I struggled to control my emotions. By the time I came out of the dryer and she combed my hair, I felt numb.

"You're all done," she said quietly. "Just stay a minute while I phone your mom."

I wanted to leave but I waited, staring at the stranger in the mirror while she dialed the number. "Hello, Louise, I'm calling to tell you Sheri's hair is all done. I don't think she knew she was getting it cut today but it is done now anyway. Yes, you can pay me on Monday. Goodbye."

She took the cape off my shoulders and brushed the stray hair away. "Now, I hope you like it." She glanced at me in the mirror. "I'm sorry if you didn't know you were getting it cut."

I eased out of the chair. "Thank you," I said.

"You take care, OK, Honey?"

"Yes. Goodbye."

When I walked in the kitchen door, Mom looked up from getting supper. "Do you like it?" I didn't reply. She looked at me and raised her chin. She had won.

I started getting raw vegetables ready, standing at the counter. She called the family to come for supper. My siblings stood staring at me in silence.

"Don't you like Sheri's new hairstyle?" Louise asked them. "Sheri, turn around so they can see your face." I turned around, feeling foolish. "Doesn't it look nice?" Louise turned to Betty Anne and smirked. Betty Anne looked confused, reading the anger and hurt on my face. I turned back to my task at the counter.

Betty Anne said, "Well, Sheri, it does look nice." I kept working and said nothing.

We heard Dad's footsteps in the porch and the screen door close. "Harold, come in here and see Sheri's new hairstyle."

Dad came to the kitchen door.

"Sheri, turn around so Dad can see you from the front."

I whirled around and glared at him. His face changed from cheerful to sober when he read my face and he hesitated. "Yeah, well… that looks nice, Sheri." He didn't sound very sure.

I'd had enough. I bolted through the kitchen. Marilyn and James parted to let me pass. As I headed upstairs, I heard Dad ask, "Didn't she know she was getting it cut?" There was no reply.

When I'd finished crying into my pillow, I stood up and looked at the foreigner in the mirror. "No one will ever do that to you again," I promised her.

I went downstairs and ate supper with a silent family. Within a year, my hair was long again and no one complained.

Years later, the topic of that haircut came up in conversation while my mother visited me in my own kitchen over coffee. "I thought that when you saw it, you'd like short hair," she said.

"It's more important to have a parent a kid can trust more than long or short hair," I said.

Her eyebrows raised. She seemed thoughtful but said nothing.

As my sixteenth birthday approached, I wondered if anything special would be done for me. Neil Sedaka's hit song "Happy Birthday, Sweet Sixteen" released in 1961 and by 1968, North America had a well-established specialness attached to the idea of a girl turning sixteen. I didn't dare ask for any kind of special celebration.

"Your sixteenth birthday is coming up," Mom said one day.

"Yes."

"How shall we celebrate?"

"I don't know," I said, hopeful.

"Shall we take you for supper to the Prince Charles?"

The Prince Charles Hotel was an old building in downtown

Lloydminster. It wasn't a special place but I was happy to be going out anywhere for supper instead of the usual meal and cake at home.

"OK," I said, very pleased and surprised. She said the family would go on the first Saturday before my birthday, making it a day for buying groceries at the Co-op and other errands.

Two days before the big day, as I passed through the dining room, Mom turned from her sewing on the table and said with a downcast look and sad voice, "We're not going to the Prince Charles for your birthday. Dad says it's too expensive."

I didn't believe her. If our mother made plans of any kind, Dad never interfered. I went outside and stood watching him work on the new carport, trying to form the words I wanted to ask.

"Hey! How's it going?" he asked cheerfully. "What's new?"

I hesitated and he stopped to look at me, waiting. "So, we're not going to the Prince Charles for my birthday?"

His brow furrowed. "What's this now?"

"Mom said you told her we can't go to the Prince Charles for my birthday. She said you decided it was too expensive."

The furrows cleared from his brow. "Leave this with me," he said. "I'll take care of it."

I didn't ask about it again. I knew I could trust him.

On the Saturday after my birthday, we drove into Lloydminster as planned. Everyone got their errands done. At suppertime, Dad didn't drive to the Prince Charles. He turned the car up to the new restaurant in town. It was considered the best restaurant in town, much more expensive than the aging Prince Charles. I felt very grateful to my dad that day. I never thanked him but I should have, somehow, quietly, without my mother knowing or hearing. He wouldn't have wanted a fuss made over a conflict between him and Mom. I never understood why she built up my hopes to dash them and put the blame on Dad. It must have been around that time when I made the conscious decision to be a different kind of mother for my own children if I had any. My children would know they could depend on me.

In the summer of 1985, Mom and Betty Anne planned a celebration for our parents' 40th wedding anniversary to take place in the United Church hall. Letters of invitation flew to family members living farther away. An ad in the local paper invited all local friends. In no time, the entire region knew about the coming event. One day, a friend of Dad's met him on main street and congratulated him on his upcoming anniversary. Then he asked, "What's it been like being married to Louise for forty years?"

Dad hesitated. His friend would know he was lying if he said his marriage had been wonderful and he would look like a fool. He wanted to remain faithful to Louise while also admitting the truth. As ever, he fell back on his habit of using old expressions, trying to make a joke.

"Thin. Ice." He wasn't smiling.

It was the only time I heard him say anything derogatory about Mom. My siblings and I also felt like we walked on thin ice every day. She very easily slid into depression and we learned to be careful what we said or did to keep her in good spirits if it was in our power to do so.

While our lives carried on at home, Mom taught school and was a good teacher. Several of her former students have told me she was their favorite teacher. She loved her students and worked hard to see them succeed. On holidays, she took pictures or collected mementos for use in a lesson when school resumed. She kept some students' school work as a keepsake, even preserving them into her retirement. At some point, she paid the fee for one of her student's post-academic training, seeing that the girl had potential but knew her own parents couldn't afford the cost of the course she wanted to take.

She enjoyed close friendships with other teachers, keeping track of birthdays and sending cards. She often invited them and their spouses to our house for a meal. In the summer holidays, she painted landscapes and gave some away to friends.

She enjoyed attending teachers' conferences. I think they reminded her of her younger years at Normal School and all the fun she had with friends, but she loved learning, too. When the government stipulated that all teachers must hold a degree, she dove into correspondence courses with enthusiasm and welcomed the chance for a trip to the city for summer intersession courses at the university.

She volunteered for several events in town: the history book committee, the agricultural fair, church functions, and others. She was well-liked and respected throughout the community.

After living away for several years, marrying, and starting a family, my husband and I decided to move to Marwayne. When I told my sister of our plans, she said, "I never wanted to live close to Mom and Dad. I never wanted to have to deal with Mom's drama." I knew what she meant but I told myself everything would work out somehow and I didn't worry. Over the next years, the wisdom of her statement made itself clear.

In spite of keeping busy, Mom had a restless mind and a love of gossip. One day after an AWANA meeting (a church group for children) where I volunteered as a leader, a dear friend said to me, "Sheri, I feel I should tell you your mother is telling people she's raising your kids for you. She says you drop them off at her house every day and spend the whole day shopping."

I appreciated my friend's courage and honesty. I knew this was something my mother could do. My first thought was, 'Why does she have to do this now, just when I'm dealing with my marriage breakup and a move to the city for the kids and myself?' Then I realized my marriage problems might be the very reason she did it, jealous of the attention in gossip I knew I must be getting, however unwanted that was for me. Her ever-competitive nature made her want some of that attention, to garner sympathy as the real victim and create a sensation.

The truth was that I rarely left the kids with her. I had tried to talk to her about my marriage problems but she either laughed, telling me I had made my bed and now I had to sleep in it, or that she didn't want to get involved so I stopped trying. Once the breakup was known to the public, she might have felt hurt that she hadn't been kept apprised.

My second thought was, 'Who would ever believe such a story?' Instantly, I remembered an incident from the previous week when an elderly lady said to me, "I hope you appreciate all that your mother is doing for you. After all, she's raising your kids for you."

At the time, I laughed at her. I wondered what kind of crazy idea this small, grey-haired woman had thought up. "My mother isn't raising my kids for me," I laughed, but I noticed others standing nearby exchanging glances. Now I understood better what that incident truly meant.

I wondered if I should confront my mother about her fabrication, but I decided it wasn't worth it. I was already spread too thin planning a move to the city and a future life for the kids and myself. I didn't have room in my emotional storehouse to deal with one more stressful situation. Also, the damage was already done. There'd be no way to stop the gossip or bring back those stories now already in others' ears. The kids and I would start a new life in a new place where no one knew us and no one told lies about us. I looked forward to a fresh start for us all.

A couple of years after moving away, I met a woman from Marwayne on the sidewalk in downtown Saskatoon. After our initial greeting, she said, "You must really miss your mother. After all, she did everything for you."

I tried to visit my parents as often as I could but with a busy life of four children at home, it was hard to get away. I always felt my visits weren't often enough and yet, when I did visit, I felt like I was in the way. After Dad died, I decided to visit Mom every long weekend, sometimes with the kids, other times if they visited their dad, I went alone. Every time I phoned her to say I was coming for a visit, she'd say, "You don't need to come." I went anyway.

During one visit while I sat in her living room talking with her, she got up and called a friend. After some conversation, she said, "I have to go because Sheri's here and, you know, I have to make lunch." I went into the kitchen and started making sandwiches.

"What are you doing?" she asked.

"I'm making sandwiches for lunch."

"I'll do that."

"Mom, I can make sandwiches."

She took the knife out of my hand. "No. I'll do it."

Once when I phoned to say I was coming she again said, "Don't come. You don't need to come so often." Two days later, she phoned me. "Please do not come to see me this weekend."

"Why?"

She hesitated. "You don't need to come so often. You have your life and I have mine. I'm just fine. You stay home."

I gave up. "All right, I won't come. Two days later on the Saturday I had planned to be visiting her, Betty Anne phoned.

"Mom says you told her you were coming to visit her and never showed up."

"She told me not to come. She phoned especially to tell me to stay home so I thought she had plans of some kind. She always tells me not to come when I call to say I'll be visiting her. I decided this time, I'd do what she wanted."

At the same time, Mom's concern for my children and me compelled her to buy a house in Saskatoon for us to live in. I don't know what I would have done without her help. We lived in that house for six years and I appreciate it, but it was a tenuous situation with Louise as proprietor. Sometimes she wanted me to pay rent but the amount kept changing. Other times, she told me not to pay her anything. At one point, she decided to pass ownership of the house over to me and had all the papers drawn up and finalized. A week after receiving my copy of the paperwork, she changed her mind, went back to the lawyer, and had it all reversed. When I accepted a teaching position in Alberta, she sold that house and divided the money among my sisters and me. It is impossible to explain her indiscretions while at the same time, her sudden acts of generosity that exceeded anyone's expectations.

One weekend, Mom and her best friend, Marguerite, decided to travel to Saskatoon together. Mom would visit me and my children and Marguerite would call on her son and family. Marguerite had supper with us before going on to her son's house and after the meal, she said to me, "I'd like to go for a walk and I wondered if you'd like to join me."

As we circled the block in the dim evening light, we first talked of ordinary things. Then she said, "I'm worried about your mom." She told me she could see changes in Louise, once the poised and considerate teacher and community volunteer who now seemed to be losing her desire to be polite, sometimes saying hurtful things to people.

I agreed that I had noticed that tendency as well. The family was accustomed to Mom saying inappropriate and upsetting things to us at home, but she had always confined it there, remaining polite to others outside the family. Now she seemed to be losing the filter that stopped her from saying unkind words to almost anyone.

Whenever I visited her, I tried to take her out for a meal, but I dreaded the possibility of meeting a former student or acquaintance, afraid of what she might say to them, or to me within their hearing. I once said to her, "You can't say insulting things to people, or about them while they're standing right in front of us. They can hear you."

"Oh, that doesn't matter," she said.

"Yes, it does matter, Mom," I said. "You hurt their feelings. It's unkind."

She looked at me, smiled, and looked away.

A year or two after James died, while Marilyn and I visited our parents, suddenly in the middle of our conversation, Louise blurted,

"I'm going to adopt a little boy!"

We both stared. She smiled with her eyes sparkling. The idea faded, not to be heard again for several years, but it resurfaced occasionally. Did she want to prove to herself that she could raise a boy successfully to adulthood? Did she think she had to prove something to herself and others in her circle of friends? She always said it with delight and excitement as if she were talking about adopting a puppy. I think the effect of losing Richard and James devastated her more than anyone realized, already tragic.

The ridiculousness of the idea struck us because we all knew our mother to be dedicated to teaching and friends and in fact, had looked forward to her children moving out so she could concentrate fully on her career. I believe her fantasy of raising my children also stemmed from losing her own sons. She wanted another chance to raise children, particularly boys, and prove to herself and others that she wouldn't lose them. I believe she blamed herself for their deaths far more than anyone realized.

Years later when she visited me in my kitchen, Mom and I talked about my kids' personalities, which then turned the conversation to me and my siblings as children. The kettle whistled and I stood up to make tea while she sat quietly thinking.

"When you kids were little, I couldn't wait for you to grow up and move out so I could get on with my career."

"I know," I said.

Her eyes widened. "You do?"

"Of course," I said. "We all knew."

What she felt when hearing this, I don't know. She didn't say anything more on the subject. Open affection was not the norm in those days of hard work and survival, and we understood that our parents cared about us, but the clarity with which she made us feel we should leave home as soon as possible made it unnecessary to say so in words.

After Dad passed away, again in the middle of a conversation, she blurted out, "I'm going to adopt a little boy!"

I looked at her. She was eighty-five years old.

"Don't you think I can do it?" she asked, raising her chin.

I hesitated. "A child is cute and fun to have around but they have needs, and sometimes need care in the middle of the night. They grow up, develop their own ideas and opinions, want to do things their caring adult never thought of, and require lots of energy and patience. They don't stay little and cute forever."

I was at risk of sending her into a spiral of depression and I said no more. She was probably lonely after losing Dad and returned to her old plan of raising a boy.

It's a fortuitous twist of destiny that, as much as she wanted to nurse, she never got her wish. She was happiest as a teacher and I believe she never would have enjoyed nursing if she'd had the opportunity. She didn't want to take care of Dad in his later years when he developed dementia and should have had extra care. She refused to go to the doctor with him or monitor his medications (at one point, he overdosed himself) and often made fun of his memory loss. She refused the idea of having a home care aide come in to care for Dad. She didn't trust a stranger in the house.

This has been a difficult chapter to write. I didn't include it in my first draft. Hymns and poems describe a faithful and adoring mother. Hallmark cards fill their shelves with products dedicated to Mother's Day, a mother's birthday, or sympathy in the loss of a mother. Many speak fondly of their mother and the wonderful they received from her. I wanted that friendship with my mother. As an adult, I set out to see that friendship grow while I lived at Marwayne. It took many years to realize it would never happen.

The irony is, I think she knew she hadn't been the mother she should have been. One year for Mother's Day, I gave her a card that expressed a mother's faithful and adoring love in flowery words. She read the verse and said, "Well, thank you, Sheri. Of course, none of it is true… anyway, thank you for the gesture."

All the stories in this book are true and most are happy, but in between those pleasant memories are the times when family life slid sideways. We all did what we could to keep our lives on an even keel, to dissuade Mom away from unreasonable ideas, keep her happy, and maintain peace.

Some of the stories in this book are based on my mother's telling but I have been careful to confirm their verity through the use of historical documents—birth and death certificates, land titles, or verification from others. Time colors all memories, but my mother learned the use of tall tales to manipulate actuality toward her own ends.

There came a time in my life when I found myself reliving over and over, those times when my mother had lied to me or about me. I realized I was going to have to forgive my mother or I'd turn into a miserable, bitter old woman. Even though she had passed away by then, I had to do this for myself—for my own peace of mind, my mental and physical health.

Forgiveness is hard work. Every time I found myself reliving a lie or hurtful words, I'd say, "I forgive her," and try to mean it. After months of this exercise, I realized I wasn't getting anywhere and in a moment of desperation, prayed to God, "I have to forgive her but I can't do this alone. Please help me do this." It was the end of the day and I went to bed.

In the morning, I woke up and instantly felt different. I felt light, and yes—corny as it sounds, I felt free—free of the nagging bitterness that had dogged me for months. I knew then that this is what Jesus meant when he promised a life of freedom. I didn't understand how it could work through the night while I slept but I thanked God for what seemed to me, a miracle.

I still need to renew my forgiveness when memories return to haunt me. I haven't had a miraculous healing again like I did that night years ago, but I still need to confirm my forgiveness, to replenish it, if you will. Forgiveness is a hard wall to climb. I sometimes slip and have to climb it again, but I'm able to see sunshine now when previously a cloud blocked my vision. Yes, she did and said things to me and others she shouldn't have, but I can look at those times now with acceptance and a feeling of victory over the hurt.

Most people have secrets and Louise had her share. Whatever made her behave the way she did, she never revealed that influence. Perhaps she never knew what it was, herself. Life is hard. We all have struggles to overcome. Life is a mystery. So much more is known today about mental illness. If she had consented to testing, what would that diagnosis reveal? How would her life, and her family's life, be different?

In 1974, Margaret Trudeau revealed in an interview that she'd been hospitalized to receive psychiatric treatment because of "the serious emotional stress" of her public life. Her brave act began the slow change in the stigma society placed on mental illness. My father scoffed when he heard it in the news. Her husband, Pierre Trudeau, was never Dad's favorite politician and he joked about Pierre causing all the trouble for Margaret, but my mother took it seriously and thoughtfully. I looked at her on that day as she seemed to turn something over in her mind. I wondered what she was thinking.

In my parents' lifetime, treatment for mental illness was never done or even considered, except for a severe case like the times she had a nervous breakdown. On days when depression or confusion stalked her, we all tried to cope in the best way we could. In those days, the emphasis was on strength and survival, finding humor in hardship, remaining constant through adversity, looking for beauty, and showing love without saying the words, "I love you."

Lilacs grew at kitchen doors—strong, resilient, lifting beauty out of sorrow.

Appendix: 1945 Shower & Wedding Gifts

Louise had re-written this list on a piece of light cardboard by the time I found it. I don't know the form of its first version. She used the Sharpie she relied on in old age for its bold black ink, making it easier for her failing eyesight to read. It might have been first recorded in a decorated memory book of the type often used in the forties and fifties, but being a teacher who liked to employ old notebooks for diaries and used envelopes for shopping lists, it's possible this too, found its first home in a humble notebook. The fact she rewrote the list proves how precious the memories remained for her, hearkened back by these unpretentious items.

Some gifts reveal the value of money—a simple one or two dollars for a gift in some cases —others show a different value scale from today. The more unusual gifts of those days help reveal a picture of life in the forties.

Shower gifts:
Cup and saucer (heather)—Aunt Janet Loury
2 cups and saucers—Mrs. Alice Hathaway
2 cups and saucers—Connie Hathaway
China tea pot—Mrs. Anderson (in Surrey)
Guest towel and face cloth—Marjorie Gilbert
Bowl covers—Mrs. Mabel Rogers
A pair of edged pillowcases—Mrs. Matthews and Irma
Linen tea towel—Mrs. Hazel Nielsen
Pot holder and paring knife—Mrs. Stan Lowry
$15.00—Mother and Dad
Cookbook—Mrs. Lila Whitehead

Wedding gifts:
Rose bed throw—Aunt Janet Loury
Green bed throw and sheets—Mr. and Mrs. E. Hathaway
A pair of white blankets—Connie a nd Harry Lang
32-piece breakfast set—Varina and Wes
Silex coffee maker—Alyse Nelson

Silver Pyrex Casserole—Phyllis and Bob Ingram
Rectangular Pyrex cake bake, twin set of silhouette pictures—Lila and Cecil Whitehead
Cup and saucer (rosettes) and $2.00—Elizabeth and Bob Miller
$1.00—Mr. and Mrs. J. Chisholm
2 tea towels—Ruby Hilts
2 Irish linen guest towels—Ruth Freebury
$55.00 for a 6-place silverware service—Mother and Dad
Pillow cases—Jean and Sam Sutherland
Bath towel—Irene McCourt
Cushion cover & tea towel—Mrs. Drake
$6.00—Minnie & Jack Briley and Mrs. Kidd
Picture—Mr. & Mrs. Wm McDonald
2 pictures—Mr. & Mrs. Gene Wheeler
Pyrex casserole—Mrs. Jack Hansen
Water glass set—Betty Carson
Syrup jar—Mrs. Carson
Cake plate—Vivienne Doull
Pillow cases to embroider—Mrs. Doull and boys
Pyrex bread pan—Ella Doull
Pyrex cake pan—Mrs. Holmes
Angel skin pillowcases—Irene Wilson
Buffet set & pot holder—Clara McLean
$5.00 U.S.—Aunt Jessie Johnson
Blue bed throw—McLeans and Wobesers
Pyrex pie plate—Mrs. Tullson
$5.00—Mr. & Mrs. A. J. McLeod, Evesham, Saskatchewan
$1.00—Mrs. Sarah Whitehead, Macklin, Saskatchewan
Cup and saucer—Mrs. E.B. Walker
2 tea towels—Edna Reid, Evesham, Saskatchewan
Mexican linen tablecloth—Mac
Flowered tablecloth—Mrs. Wirachowsky
Satin tablecloth—Florence McLeod
Embroidered runner—Mrs. Paterson
Stand-up picture—Kathleen Allen
1 pair bath towels—Margaret Innocent
$2.00—Mrs. Mae Hawkins
Cushion—Elsie MacLeod
$24.00, given at the house: Mrs. Yeadle, Mrs. H. Graham, Mrs. Tyner, Mary Castel, Lily Hayes, Mr. & Mrs. Jim Pierce,

Mr. & Mrs. Dan Campbell, Mr. & Mrs. Pierce and Maud, Mr. & Mrs. A. Castel, Mr. & Mrs. Lloyd Osbeldeston, Mr. & Mrs. G. Boyce, Mr. & Mrs. C. Boyce, Mrs. Lowrie, Mr. & Mrs. Banks, Mr. & Mrs. Harold Boyce. We used this money for a 6-piece dinner set in Creampetal.

∼

I remember my curiosity about the silhouette pictures as a child and asked my mother if they represented someone she knew. She smiled and said, "No, just a set of nice pictures some friends gave us for a wedding present. It was the style back then to give pictures at a wedding."

"Why?"

She shrugged. "It was what people thought made an nice gift for a couple just starting out, maybe not having anything to put on the walls."

Later I understood the concept of fashions changing, coming in, going out, something else beginning… like society itself breathing.

The Creampetal china reigned in the Hathaway home as the usual dishes used every time for company. It went out of production in the sixties, and when Louise saw an ad in the paper for all the Creampetal china going up for sale by the Home Economics department of Vermilion College, she bought it all. It's now shared among family members, a memento of her life.

Endnotes

Herold's First Love

[1] *When exhausted or unwell, "I've been through the wringer":* This is referring to the wringer part of wringer washing machines. The wet clothes were fed through two rollers that squeezed out excess water. The clothes came out very flat, almost stiff, said to be "wrung out".

Louise

[2] *Bessborough and Lady B to arrive tomorrow on CN," she wrote on March 20th:* Sir Vere Ponsonby, 9th Earl of Bessborough and 14th Governor General of Canada gave consent for the new CNR hotel in Saskatoon to be formally named the Bessborough Hotel. Completed in 1932, it didn't open until 1935 due to the difficult financial hardship of the Great Depression.

[3] *Without exception, the farmers of the area had recently walked away from established farms in the dust bowl of sourthern Saskatchewan*: Elizabeth McLachlan, "Louise's Story", *With Unshakable Persistence, Rural Teachers of the Depression Era*, (Edmonton: Newest Press, 1999), 75.

[4] *Fortunately, her new family was congenial, for in such cramped quarters privacy was nonexistent:* (McLachlan 1999), 76.

Reserved in War

[5] *Former owners of the Clear Range Farm confirmed* by Alberta Genealogical Society, a homestead search. Erastus H. Switzer, PAA ref. Acc. 1970.313 film 2782, file 1424328. Cornelius George Wheeler, PAA ref. Acc. 1970.313 film 2834, file 1695022. https://www.abgenealogy.ca/ab-homestead-index-page

Walking the Clear Range Farm

[6] *A government stamp on the return address:* Which government, whether county, provincial, or federal, or the amount of the taxes owed remains uncertain.

Getting There

[7] ***Jim Adamson's description of his Percheron's destructive power:*** (J. Adamson 1980)

Tragedy

[8] ***Kelsey Institute:*** Now named Saskatchewan Polytechnic

[9] Debbie called me Hathaway at first, then Hatchaway, and later shortened it to Hatch. Soon everyone in our class called me Hatch. I didn't mind as we often gave each other nicknames. Twenty years later I met a classmate in the mall and the first thing she said to me was "Hi, Hatch!" making my daughter look at me with surprise and curiosity, and later ask for an explanation. My past had caught up with the present.

Bibliography

Louise

n.d. About CGIT. Accessed October 14, 2020. http://cgit.ca.

2020. Collins Dictionary. Accessed October 15, 2020. https://www.collinsdictionary.com/dictionary/english/hectograph.

Cooley, Donald G. 1978. *Better Homes and Gardens Family Medical Guide.* New York: Better Homes and Gardens Books.

Forgotten Echoes Historical Society. 1982. *Forgotten Echoes: a history of Blackfoot and surrounding area.* Blackfoot, Alberta: Forgotten Echoes Historical Society.

n.d. History. Accessed October 14, 2020. https://heritagesask.ca/pub/virtual-projects/The%20Biz%20at%20the%20Bezz%20(Sheradan%20Done)%20Photos.pdf

King King, Paul Varughese, Gaston De Serres, Graham Tipples, John Waters. 2004. The Journal of Infectious Diseases. May 1. Accessed May 22, 2020. https://academic.oup.com/jid/article/189/Supplement_1/S236/823023

2010. "Making Medicare: The history of healthcare in Canada." Canadian Museum of History. April 21. Accessed July 29, 2023. https://www.historymuseum.ca/cmc/exhibitions/hist/medicare/medic01e.html

McLachlan, Elizabeth. 1999. "Louise's Story." *With Unshakeable Persistence*, 74-81. Edmonton: NeWest Press.

2019. "Rock and River Outdoor Pursuits." Accessed May 15, 2020. https://www.rockandriver.co.uk

Ronaghan, Allen, ed. 1973. *Earnest-Minded Men.* Kitscoty, Alberta: Modern Press.

2013. Saskatchewan One-Room School Project. Julia Adamson. May 26. Accessed October 14, 2020. http://sites.rootsweb.com/~cansk/school/Saskatoon%20Normal%20School.html

Sheryl Ubelacker, The Canadian Press. 2015. CTV News.ca. February 23. Accessed May 22, 2020. https://www.ctvnews.ca/health/canadian-doctor-recalls-measles-pre-vaccine-toll-1.2249491

2023. "Go Into Your Dance." IMDb. Accessed July 29, 2023. https://www.imdb.com/title/tt0026418/

U.S. Department of Health & Human Services. 2019. Centers for Disease Control and Prevention. April 19. Accessed May 22,

2020. https://www.cdc.gov/vaccines/pubs/pinkbook/meas.html
2019. World Health Organization. December 5. Accessed May 22, 2020. https://www.who.int/news-room/fact-sheets/detail/measles

Reserved in War
2020. "Alberta Homestead Index." Alberta Genealogical Society. Accessed March 15, 2020. https://www.abgenealogy.ca/alberta-homestead-index
2016. "Charles Booth's London Poverty Maps and Police Notebooks." LSE London School of Economics and Political Science. Accessed March 15, 2020. https://booth.lse.ac.uk
Foster, Franklin Lloyd, and Alan Grant Griffith. 2001. *Bordering on Greatness*. Lloydminster, Alberta: Foster Learning Inc.
Hamilton. 1942. "Justifies His Stand." Globe and Mail, January 27.
Hathaway, Alice, interview by Harold Hathaway. 1971. "Wes, Bunny & Mother" (February 27).
Hathaway, Louise. 1967. "The Hathaway Story." *Pioneering the Parklands*, edited by Marwayne Farm Women's Union of Alberta. Winnipeg, Manitoba: Inter-Collegiate Press.
Kishlansky, Mark A. 2020. Britannica. September 13. Accessed March 15, 2020. https://www.britannica.com/place/United-Kingdom
n.d. "Exemptions from military service in WW1." My Learning. Accessed July 29, 2023. https://www.mylearning.org/stories/scheduled-occupations-during-the-first-world-war/770?
n.d. The Cabinet Papers Financing the War and Taxation. Accessed March 15, 2020. https://www.nationalarchives.gov.uk/cabinetpapers/themes/finance-labour-control.htm
2020. "Victorian Crime." The History Press. Accessed March 15, 2020. https://www.thehistorypress.co.uk/the-victorians/victorian-crime/
2020. "World War Two — Conscription Definition." History on the Net. September 19. Accessed September 19, 2020. https://www.historyonthenet.com/world-war-two-conscription-definition

On Holiday in War

Liptak, Andrew J. 2014. Postal History Corner. February 17, 2014. Accessed June 29, 2019. http://postalhistorycorner.blogspot.com/2014/02/canadian-domestic-letter-rates-from.html

Smithsonian National Air and Space Museum. n.d. The Evolution of the Commercial Flying Experience. Accessed July 29, 2023. https://airandspace.si.edu/explore/stories/evolution-commercial-flying-experience

Walking the Clear Range Farm

Copies of land titles for the Clear Range Farm obtained from Alberta Land Titles: https://www.alberta.ca/find-land-titles-documents-plans.aspx#jumplinks-2

Hardstaff, Wallace. 1980. "The Hardstaff Family." *Echoes of Marwayne Area*, by Marwayne Historical Society, 631 - 632. Lloydminster, Alberta: Meridian Printing.

Hathaway, Louise. 1967. "The Hathaway Story." *Pioneering the Parklands*. Winnipeg, Manitoba: Intercollegiate Press.

2020. Inguinal hernia. Accessed July 15, 2019. https://www.mayoclinic.org/diseases-conditions/inguinal-hernia/symptoms-causes/syc-20351547

Province of Saskatchewan, Royal Commission on Agriculture and Rural Life. 1957. Report 11: Farm Electrification. Regina: Queen's Printer.

2020. "The Edmonton Journal." Newspapers.com. Accessed May 15, 2019. www.newspapers.com

Wright, Glenn T. 2006. "The Veteran's Land Act." The Canadian Encyclopedia. February 6. Accessed August 15, 2019. www.thecanadianencyclopedia.ca/en/article/veterans-land-act

Richard

Elof Carlson, State University of New York at Stony Brook. n.d. "Scientific Origins of Eugenics." Image Archive of American Eugenics Movement. Accessed October 31, 2020. http://www.eugenicsarchive.org/html/eugenics/essay2text.html

Edmonton Journal. 1947. "Marwayne area lashed by storm." July 11: 17.

Hathaway, Louise. 2008. "Myself - Lavinia Louise McLean." *The McLean - Hathaway Story*, 39. Lloydminster: Meridian Printing.

2019. How Did C-Sections Begin, and Why are they so Common? January 22. Accessed July 15, 2019. https://www.birthinjuryguide.org/2018/05/how-c-sections-begin/

n.d. Making Medicare The history of healthcare in Canada, 1914 - 2007. historymuseum.ca. Accessed October 15, 2020. https://www.historymuseum.ca/cmc/exhibitions/hist/medicare/medic-2h02e.html

A Big Change in Harvesting

Barrons, Charles. 2018. Farming the Old Way. January 8. Accessed January 13, 2020. https://images.squarespace-cdn.com/content/v1/53052d10e4b0b111f005ebe2/1515453503257-PILK4C69V9DHXHSZM4NMke17ZwdGBToddI8pDm48kHsbJAAYrxlgFWdQHEJBRX4UqsxRUqqbr1mOJYKfIPR7LoDQ9mXPOjoJoqy81S2I8N_N4V1vUb5AoIIIbLZhVYy7Mythp_T-mtop-vrsUOmeInPi9iDjx9w8K4ZfjXt2d

Carroll, John. 1999. *The World Encyclopedia of Tractors and Farm Machinery*. London, England: Lorenz Books.

2017. First Commercial Combine Harvester Developed in 1885. June 23. Accessed January 13, 2020. https://blog.aghires.com/first-commercial-combine-harvester-developed-1885/

Ganzel, Bill. 2007. Harvesting Wheat. Accessed January 13, 2020. https://livinghistoryfarm.org/farming-in-the-1950s/machines/harvesting-wheat/

2018. "History of the Combine Harvester ." Tractor Transport. Accessed July 29, 2023. https://www.tractortransport.com/blog/history-of-the-combine-harvester/

Herber, Sandra. n.d. Grain Elevators of the Canadian Prairies. Accessed January 20, 2020. https://www.sandraherber.com/grain-elevators-of-the-canadian-prairies

John Deere. n.d. *The Operation, Care and Repair of Farm Machinery*. Moline, Illinois: John Deere.

Reinhardt, Claudia. n.d. Farming in the 1920s. Accessed January 19, 2020. https://livinghistoryfarm.org/farming-in-the-1920s/

Ross, Jane. 2015. Grain Elevators. April 24. Accessed January 20, 2020. https://www.thecanadianencyclopedia.ca/en/article/grain-elevators

Connecting Neighbours
Boyce, Irene. 1979. "Telephone Service North of Lloydminster." *Echoes of Marwayne Area,* by Marwayne Historical Society, 328. Lloydminster: Meridian Printing.
Lorenz, Glen. 1979. "Bridging the Communication Gap." E*choes of Marwayne Area*, by Marwayne Historical Society, 328. Lloydminster: Meridian Printing Ltd.
1979. "The Marwayne Mutual Telephone Association." *Echoes of Marwayne Area*, by The Marwayne Historical Society, 469-470. Lloydminster: Meridian Printing.

Throwing Rocks at the House
1953. "Edmonton Journal." Newspapers.com. July 4. Accessed July 15, 2020. https://www.newspapers.com/image/469666837/?terms=hail%2BMarwayne
1949. "Edmonton Journal." Newspapers.com. July 13. Accessed July 15, 2020. https://www.newspapers.com/e/?clipping_21983&fcfToken=eyJhbGciOiJIUzI1NiIsInR5cCI6IkpXVCJ9.2OTU5MDQ1MCwiaWF0IjoxNTg1Nzc0ODY1LCJleHAiOjE1ODU4NjEyNjV9.yL--A-5Rovu-CcbU-Qn1GXUvcbFDzKm6fqSg0qRob7E
1949. "Edmonton Journal." Newspapers.com. August 9. Accessed July 15, 2020. https://www.newspapers.com/e/?clipping_=33958977&fcfToken=eyJhbGciOiJIUzI1NiIsInR5cCI6IkpXVCJ9.eyJmcmVlLXZpZXctaWQiOjQ2OTU5NDEwMCwiaWF0IjoxNTg1Nzc2MjQ5LCJleHAiOjE1ODU4NjI2NDl9.0O9c3pl-RYUkyaALqE4kU6EkXb1gP_S-0fFVSLEhfjY
1947. "Edmonton Journal." Newspapers.com. July 16. Accessed July 15, 2020. https://www.newspapers.com/e/?clipping_7&fcfToken=eyJhbGciOiJIUzI1NiIsInR5cCI6IkpXVCJ9.3MDQ3NDk4OSwiaWF0IjoxNTg1Nzc3MzU0LCJleHAiOjE1ODU4NjM3NTR9.MrZoclDfLsbe7AFISn1sZ5ewSzlgi59Tcf8qtCRT6rg
1947. "Edmonton Journal." Newspapers.com. July 11. Accessed July 15, 2020. https://www.newspapers.com/e/?clipping_29&fcfToken=eyJhbGciOiJIUzI1NiIsInR5cCI6IkpXVCJ9.3MDQ3NDkxMiwiaWF0IjoxNTg1Nzc3NTczLCJleHAiOjE1ODU4NjM5NzN9.gEpoKXFLSfuM3UDKsDAXIZkdLInVUDN4YV8HSL8lw8M
1949. "Edmonton Journal." Newspapers.com. July 15. Accessed July 15, 2020. https://www.newspapers.com/image/?clipping_

fcfToken=eyJhbGciOiJIUzI1NiIsInR5cCI6IkpXVCJ9.
WF0IjoxNTg1Nzc5MDE2LCJleHAiOjE1ODU4NjU0MTZ9.
pVfldaS3mflp4ao4btsu6nJUXZ5Xilz2IErzlxVEuRA

1953. "Edmonton Journal." Newspapers.com. July 23. Accessed July 15, 2020. https://www.newspapers.com/e/?clipping_3&fcfToken=eyJhbGciOiJIUzI1NiIsInR5cCI6IkpXVCJ9.2OTU5MDc2NiwiaWF0IjoxNTg1Nzc5MDE2LCJleHAiOjE1ODU4NjU0MTZ9.pVfldaS3mflp4ao4btsu6nJUXZ5Xilz2IErzlxVEuRA

1949. "Edmonton Journal." Newspapers.com. August 8. Accessed July 15, 2020. https://www.newspapers.com/e/?clipping_958900&fcfToken=eyJhbGciOiJIUzI1NiIsInR5cCI6IkpXVCJ9.2OTU5MzkyNCwiaWF0IjoxNTg1NzgwNTAzLCJleHAiOjE1ODU4NjY5MDN9.AJnCOGDKYp3hHJm5atprhQWKR3IOK7pGG4ci9WcaOQ

Empowered by Electricity

Adamson, Jim. 1980. "Jim Adamson". Vol. 1, *Echoes of Marwayne Area,* by Marwayne Historical Society, edited by Marwayne Historical Society, 814. Marwayne, Alberta: Marwayne Historical Society.

ATCO Electric. 2018. Rural Electrification Associations. June 25. Accessed July 18, 2018. https://electric.atco.com/en-ca/about/service-area/rural-electrification-associations.html

Champ, Joan. 2001. Rural Electrification in Saskatchewan in the 1950s.pdf, Saskatoon: Western Development Museum. https://www.yumpu.com/en/document/view/13235763/rural-electrification-in-saskatchewan-during-the-1950s-western-

Marwayne Historical Society. 1979. *Echoes of Marwayne Area.* Lloydminster: Meridian Printing Ltd.

Novecoscky, Abbot Peter. 1994. "St. Peter's Abbey Newsletter." *St. Peter's Abbey.ca*. Accessed February 7, 2022. https://stpetersabbey.ca/wp/wp-content/uploads/2021/03/Vol16No2_Spring-Summer1994-min.pdf

Milton

2021. Adoptive Families Association of BC. Accessed July 23, 2021. https://www.bcadoption.com/resources/articles/history-lessons

2007. BC Protestant Orphans' Home. Accessed July 23, 2021. http://web.uvic.ca/vv/student/orphans/poh.html
2021. History of Child Welfare in Ontario & Guelph/Wellington. Family and Children's Services. Accessed July 23, 2021. https://www.fcsgw.org/history-of-child-welfare-in-ontario-guelph-wellington/

Getting There

Adamson, Jim. 1979. "Jim Adamson." *Echoes of Marwayne Area*, by The Marwayne Historical Society, 91. Lloydminster: Meridian Printing.
2016. A History of Seat Belts. September 16. Accessed July 15, 2020. https://www.defensivedriving.com/blog/a-history-of-seat-belts/
Boyer et al. 1993. "Mass Society, Mass Culture." *The Enduring Vision*, by Boyer et al., 810-816. Toronto: C.C. Heath and Company.
Britannica, the editors of Encyclopaedia. 2020. Model T Automobile. *Encyclopaedia Britannica*. February 27. Accessed July 15, 2020. https://www.britannica.com/technology/Model-T
2020. Chilton Answers: What's the difference between the Model T and the Model A? Accessed July 15, 2020. https://haynes.com/en-us/tips-tutorials/chilton-answers-what-s-difference-between-ford-model-t-and-model
2021. Canadian Fuels Association. Accessed April 8, 2021. https://www.canadianfuels.ca/perspectives-2017/the-great-canadian-road-trip/
n.d. Discussion Forums>Tractor talk>Deutz Tractor Identified - Need more info. Accessed 15 2020 July. https://www.yesterdaystractors.com/cgi-bin/viewit.cgi?bd=ttalk&th=384965
Edmonton Journal. 1959. "65 would be the highest limit in any province." March 28.
Hathaway, Louise. 1979. "Harold & Louise (McLean) Hathaway Story." *Echoes of Marwayne Area*, by The Marwayne Historical Society, 423 - 425. Lloydminster: Meridian Printing.
Mclean's. 1930. "Speed Limits Being Raised." October 1.
2019. Seat Belt Legislation in Canada. October 4. Accessed August 12, 2020. https://en.wikipedia.org/wiki/Seat_belt_legislation_in_Canada

n.d. The Great Depression: Depression Humour. Accessed July 15, 2020. http://www.canadahistoryproject.ca/1930s/1930s-08-depression-humour.html

Holusha, John. 1987. New York Times. March 10. Accessed July 29, 2023. https://www.nytimes.com/1987/03/10/business/chrysler-is-buying-american-motors-cost-is-1.5-billion.html

Aunt Mattie

Edmonton Journal. 1962. "UCW is Organized on Presbytery Level." Newspapers.com. Newspapers.com. January 30. Accessed October 23, 2020. https://www.newspapers.com/clip/33819613/edmonton-journal-ucw-organized-30-jan/

McLean, Mattie Terry Harris, interview by Wes Saunders. 1996. Mattie Harris McLean (January 17).

McLean, Mattie Terry Harris. 1990. *Memorabilia of a Century.* Lloydminster, Alberta: Meridian Printing.

UCW, Women of the. 2018. "UCW Handbook." United Church of Canada. March. Accessed October 23, 2020. https://www.united-church.ca/sites/default/files/handbook_ucw.pdf

It's a Farm Dog's Life

n.d. History of Pet Food. Accessed October 22, 2020. https://www.petfoodinstitute.org/pet-food-matters/nutrition-2/history-of-pet-food/

Intuit TurboTax. "Is it Deductible? My Pet." Last modified January 29, 2016. Accessed February 17, 2018. https://turbotax.intuit.ca/tips/is-it-deductible-my-pet-3856

Modern Farmer. "The Most Famous Dog: Lassie." Accessed March 20, 2016. http://modernfarmer.com/2014/06/famous-farm-dog-lassie/

Neatorama. "Kibble Me This: The History of Dog Food." Accessed February 17, 2018. http://www.neatorama.com/2013/05/20/Kibble-Me-This-The-History-of-Dog-Food/

n.d. "Pedegree.com." Dynasty Dog: Royal History of the Shih Tzu. Accessed February 17, 2018. https://www.pedigree.com/dog-care-articles/dynasty-dogs-royal-history-shih-tzu

A Most Successful Holiday

2021. Canadian Fuels Association. Accessed April 8, 2021. https://www.canadianfuels.ca/perspectives-2017/the-great-canadian-road-trip/

http://www.geog.uvic.ca/dept2/faculty/smithd/477/2010/2010_05_paper.pdf

Cooper, Alex. 2012. "Revelstoke Review." 50 Years in the making: the opening of the trans-Canada. July 18. Accessed April 7, 2021. https://www.revelstokereview.com/life/50-years-in-the-making-the-opening-of-the-trans-canada/

Dewar, Jennifer Cleveland and Brittany. 2010. "Connecting Canada: a History of the Railway through Rogers Pass from 1865 to 1916." Dokumen. December 10. Accessed April 7, 2021. https://dokumen.tips/documents/connecting-canada-a-history-of-the-railway-through-rogers-history-of-the-railway.html?page=1

2017. "Parks Canada." Kicking Horse Pass National Historic Site. 09 13. Accessed April 8, 2021. https://www.pc.gc.ca/en/pn-np/bc/yoho/culture/kickinghorse/visit/spirale-spiral

Reynolds, Ted. 1962. CBC Digital Archives. September 8. Accessed April 9, 2021. https://www.cbc.ca/player/play/1564883587

Waugh, Jeff. 2009. Yamnuska Mountain Adventures. April 12. Accessed April 9, 2021. http://www.jaspernationalpark.com/yellowhd.html

About the Author

Sheri Hathaway is a mother, grandmother, writer, and watercolor artist living in Saskatoon. Her articles have appeared in Folklore, the Western Producer, and Saskatoon Home among others.

Other books by Sheri:

Available now in e-book or paperback on Amazon
2 Women 2 Generations 26 Poems

Novels by Sheri coming soon:
King Saul's Servant
The Housecleaner's Dogs

If you enjoyed this book, your short review on Amazon, Goodreads, or your favorite social media is a great help and so appreciated.

Visit Sheri at sherihathaway.com to see what else she is doing.

Manufactured by Amazon.ca
Acheson, AB